THE LIVING LIGHT DIALOGUE

Volume 11

THE LIVING LIGHT DIALOGUE

Volume 11

Through the mediumship of
Richard P. Goodwin

Living Light Books

The Living Light Dialogue Volume 11

Copyright © 2019 Serenity Association

Through the mediumship of Richard P. Goodwin.

All rights reserved. Printed in the United States of America. No portion of this book may be reproduced—electronically, mechanically, or via internet transmission—without advance, express written permission of the publisher except in the case of brief quotations embodied in critical articles and reviews. No derivative work—games supplemental material, video—may be created without advance, express written permission of the publisher. For information address Living Light Books, P.O. Box 4187, San Rafael, CA 94913-4187.

Cover design copyright © 2019 by Serenity Association

Cover photograph by Serenity Association, 2019; copyright © 2019 by Serenity Association.

www.livinglight.org

Library of Congress Control Number 2007929762

FIRST EDITION

This volume of teachings is dedicated to the spirit friends who brought to Earth the Living Light Philosophy. With eternal gratitude, we pray that we may demonstrate these principles and continue to bring to publication these teachings.

CONTENTS

Acknowledgement ix
Preface xi
Introduction xv
CQA 25 3
CQA 26 11
CQA 27 20
CQA 28 30
CQA 29 42
CQA 30 53
CQA 31 66
CQA 32 78
CQA 33 89
CQA 34 102
CQA 35 113
CQA 36 123
CQA 37 138
CQA 38 155
CQA 39 168
CQA 40 180
CQA 41 188
CQA 42 199
CQA 43 210
CQA 44 226
CQA 45 236
CQA 46 249
CQA 47 258
CQA 48 269
CQA 49 280
CQA 50 295

CQA 51. 308
CQA 52. 320
CQA 53. 328
CQA 54. 338
CQA 55. 350
CQA 56. 368
CQA 57. 381
Appendix. 400

ACKNOWLEDGMENT

Grateful acknowledgement is made to the many friends and associates for invaluable aid in compiling this book, for their helpful suggestions, for their loyal interest and encouragement.

Special acknowledgement is due to those who painstakingly and selflessly transcribed and proofread the text.

PREFACE

It was through the mediumship of the Serenity Association founder, Mr. Richard P. Goodwin, that a philosophy known as the Living Light was given in more than 700 classes over a twenty-five-year period.

To be specific, the philosophy was imparted through Mr. Goodwin by a magistrate who had lived on Earth some 8,000 years ago. The former magistrate is known to Living Light students as "the Wise One," and he narrated the journey of his soul on the other side of life, the experiences—especially the difficulties—he encountered in having to face himself, as well as the teachings he earned to help himself through the realms in which he traveled. It was his decision to share the teachings with souls on both sides of "the curtain."

Prior to the advent of the Wise One, Mr. Goodwin had prayed for a teacher from the realms of light. Mr. Goodwin, since age fourteen, had been the instrument through which spirit was able to communicate with those seeking help. But he saw that his mediumship brought only temporary solace, because the people he was trying to help soon became fascinated with the phenomena and ignored the help that spirit was imparting. He prayed for someone who would bring forth teachings that would benefit any soul seeking a path to a greater awareness of himself and of God.

His prayers were answered in 1964 when the Wise One came through for the first time. Mr. Goodwin, at first apprehensive about what this new teacher would impart, was taken into deep trance and not able to control what was being revealed through him. Upon hearing the recorded classes afterward, however, he became convinced of the goodness of the teacher and of the value of the simple, beautiful teachings. This, then, was the beginning of the Living Light Philosophy given to Earth through the mediumship of Richard P. Goodwin.

In carrying out the request of the Wise One and Mr. Goodwin, students of the Serenity Association transcribed from audiotape the classes that had been brought through. Because most are in the form of teacher-student interaction, the classes became known as The Living Light Dialogue; and the students were instructed to publish the classes as a multi-volume set of the Living Light Philosophy. Volume 1 was published in the autumn of 2007.

The present book, Volume 11, continues the Church Questions and Answers series of classes, which were delivered by Mr. Goodwin on the first Sunday of the month during the devotional services of the Serenity Spiritualist Church. Volume 11 includes the lectures from CQA 25 through CQA 57, covering the time period of April 4, 1982, through May 5, 1985.

The foundation of the classes—the foundation of the Living Light Philosophy itself—is the Law of Personal Responsibility which states, in part, that we are responsible for all our experiences, and that our experiences are the return of the laws that we have established with our thoughts, acts, and deeds. Through greater awareness of our thoughts and by exercising our divine right of choice, we may choose to establish laws of greater harmony and goodness.

The Living Light Dialogue teaches that we have come to Earth to learn the lessons that are necessary to free us from the dictates and limits of our own thoughts and judgments, which are the mental patterns that we follow through our own lack of awareness and are so very potent, forceful, and limiting. These teachings guide us in making the necessary changes in our thinking in order to free ourselves from those patterns and to express our soul consciousness.

The choice of guiding the direction of our life, as stated by the Wise One when he speaks of being with a person, place, or thing, is, in essence, of being in this world and not a part of this world. He further explains that no matter what experiences we encounter, no matter what we do or do not do, we—our spirit—may view the experience in objectivity from a soul level of consciousness where peace reigns supreme.

The teachings of this volume help us to restore harmony or balance in our life by flooding the consciousness with spiritual affirmations and prayers, a few of which can be found in the appendix. When reason is restored, by balancing our sense functions with our soul faculties, we will consciously experience peace. Without annihilating our ego or our sense functions, we will find a pathway of expression for our soul. Where there was once disturbance, now there is acceptance. Where there was disease, now there is poise. And where there was hopelessness and despair, now there is reason, divine neutrality; and peace shows the way.

If you make the effort to apply these laws, such as, "If man is a law unto himself, what are you doing with the law that you are?", and demonstrate the wisdom of patience, the truth of this philosophy will be your living demonstration.

As the teacher states in CC 130, "My journey of many centuries and much experience has brought me here to Earth to share with you these simple teachings that have come as the effect of a long, long, long journey. Let not your journey be so long in the realms of illusion. For it is not necessary for you. For in your evolution, you have earned an awakening. But it is up to you to do something that is constructive and worthwhile."

INTRODUCTION

[This introduction was written by Mr. Goodwin and originally appeared in *The Living Light*, which were the first teachings of the Living Light Philosophy published in book form. The entire text of *The Living Light* was republished in *The Living Light Dialogue*, Volume 1.]

> "Think, children. Think more often
> and think more deeply."

The teachings in this book were given as a progressive series of lessons to a group of four students who were sitting for spiritual unfoldment with me beginning in January of 1964. The communications were regular until October of that year, when nearly a seven-year silence ensued, and resumed in 1971 to the present. They were received in three ways by me as a channel. The main text was taped from a direct control of my voice in deep trance at special sittings of our group, during which I had no experience of the voice or what was being transmitted. A few scattered verses were given independently when I was privileged to see and hear our teacher clairvoyantly. I have also been a channel for this communicant when speaking from the podium at church and in answering difficult questions at our public seminars.

Nearly all we know about our teacher is contained in the lectures. He reports that he had tried for sixteen years to break through an interference barrier that the channel had to deep trance. When our conditions were in resonance with his patient wisdom, he came through ready to teach his understanding. I have seen him as an old man dressed in white with long flowing white hair. He has blue eyes, slightly smiling and deeply compassionate. I have always called him the Old Man. The students liked to call him the Wise One. He is surely one of those often called a Teacher of Light. I do not know his country, although he indicated at one time that he was from 6000 B.C., and a form of a judge in his time.

The text is often difficult, but it is complete, having been transcribed word for word from the original tapes recording the trance voice. It is presented with a minimum of punctuation to be freer for the individual interpretation of each reader. The lessons given before the long silence are phrased with many allegories often paradoxical. There are repetitions and renewals of theme, but it is explained that if an understanding is not perceived, compassion dictates that it be said again. Some of the topics have but a simple mention with little development but all are revealed, we are told, according to merit.

The Old Man is a fine teacher. He has in a hundred ways intertwined his allegory, progressive explanations, unfolding exercises, and timely references to reach a multitude of levels of individual understanding. A notable change is his more direct style of presentation beginning in 1971.

There is an endearing intimacy of person that can be felt through his lectures, a meaningful and loving encounter with a wise friend. Like an old man, he makes a mistake and conscientiously corrects himself a few paragraphs later. He listens often and carefully to our earnest discussions of his words. He consults with a group of experts on evolution and cites their learning in his lesson. His use of the direct address "children" or "my children" is not patronizing but infinitely loving and supportive.

A word must be said about the teachings. The Old Man makes clear that his lessons are not dogma, a creed or a narrow way, but simply his own understanding offered to us as a form of instruction to aid us in our own individual progression. When he speaks of Laws, he does not refer to man-made rules or moral traditions but to the cosmic and atomic way-things-are, the natural world of what-is, the universal laws of life, part of the original creative design and through which creation is fulfilled. These laws are beyond the possibility of being changed, suspended, transcended, or destroyed but they are ever a tool of mankind, not his master. First, through our awareness of the universal laws and then slowly through our developed understanding, the powers of creation are accessible to us. Not power over men's minds or circumstances, but power over whatever is selfish and imperfect in ourselves is the way up the eternal ladder of progression. When the Old Man cautions us concerning the Law of Responsibility or gives us a thinking exercise to explore the Law of Identity in a dynamic manner, he prepares us to take another step. And all move in accordance with the Law of What Can Be Borne.

Our teacher shows us how the two worlds are drawn together. In his realm, he describes, there is a great diversity of thought, many schools of understanding; but the Light is always known by the Light. Because of the interdependence of the two realms, listening to our discussions helped to clarify his teaching to others on his side of the curtain. His love and gratitude he humbly equates with ours.

The lessons to be perceived are not new, they are very old, but they are new to certain levels of our being. I would personally advise the reader, after reading this volume of discourses in full, to make a daily habit (or when there is a feeling or need) to sit quietly with the book. Open it at random and be guided to the Light by the passage that is there for the day. This technique is still used by the original students who were given the lessons and by many students after them who have studied in unfolding classes with me through these teachings.

Go beyond the words into feeling, into the immediate meanings for you. Touch into the inspiration that flows into the form of this book. It is from the Divine.

> RICHARD P. GOODWIN
> *San Geronimo, California*
> *June, 1972*

CHURCH QUESTIONS AND ANSWERS

Church Questions and Answers 25

As our chairman has already stated, this is your opportunity, once a month, to ask your questions of a general nature that we all may benefit. And so if you will be so kind as to raise your hands with your questions, I will reach as many people as time will permit.

Yes, the gentleman on the aisle, please.

Yes. Would you explain what you mean by the principle of music?

Thank you very much. The gentleman is asking what we mean in this, the Living Light Philosophy, by the statement "the principle of music." We understand that what we call in this world music is a harmonious balance between lower and higher frequencies; that our ears perceive these frequencies and we understand that to be sound. The principle of music, and what we mean by the principle of music, is that perfect harmony which is a balance between the frequencies that our ear registers.

Now many people have varying tastes of what they call music and that, of course, is dependent upon the frequencies that they are living in, in consciousness, and, therefore, are in rapport with. If, for example, our mind is filled with imbalanced thoughts, thoughts that are discordant, thoughts that excite the senses, thoughts that are not harmonious, nor bring to us a peaceful and enjoyable life, then it is, of course, understandable that we would be receptive to like-kind frequencies, known as sound or music. I hope that's helped with your question. Thank you.

The lady here, please.

Can you please speak to us on the nature spirits and how they relate to us and the weather?

Yes, thank you. Surely, all of us, I'm sure, will agree that nature just doesn't happen out of nothing, for we all realize and, of course, experience that something does not come out of nothing. What comes from nothing is what is nothing, and that's known as nothing or no thing. So everything comes from something. Because we may be ignorant at the moment of what that something is does not change that demonstrable law that something has to come out of something.

And so the lady has asked, perhaps a sharing of some understanding of what is termed the nature spirits. That term did not begin with the Serenity Association or the Living Light Philosophy, nor will it end there. Civilizations for untold eons of time have been familiar with what man calls the nature spirits: the spirits of fire, the spirits of earth, the spirits of air, the spirits of water, the spirits of all elements that compose what we know to be nature. They are intelligent beings. They are subject to the laws of creation, for it is the dual laws of creation in which they are given birth and, therefore, have form, differing in that respect of what we call and know as eternal life.

We understand that man, being spirit—spirit being formless and free, having a covering known as soul and a conscious awareness of that covering known as soul—experiences what he calls individuality: a self-awareness in consciousness dividing him from the whole or individual. When man, in his self-awareness, experiences this individuality, this difference, he knows limit, limitation, form, and must, as long as he insists on that type of self-awareness or awareness of limit, he must continue to experience limit and form.

Nature spirits, animated with Life Principle, which is formless, free Spirit, serve the purpose of which they are composed, whatever element that may be. Their life, their responsibility is dependent upon the work they do and have been designed, by the laws of nature, to do.

Man's thoughts are an inseparable part of the whole. Man's thought, being a dual principle, being creativity, being a part of creation, is in principle the same realm of consciousness in which nature spirits are formed, created, live, and die. Our bodies, being a part of nature, have form, life, and so-called death. And so do those nature spirits that keep our body, hopefully, in a fair degree of health and happiness.

Because of the laws of personal responsibility that apply to all form, when man's thoughts are discordant, out of balance, they have a direct effect upon the nature spirits who are responsible for the forms of nature. Some of the American Indian religions were most familiar and worked actively with what we term nature spirits.

Man has been given charge of all creation, that is, all of nature. But man, in his ignorance and denial of the demonstrable truth of personal responsibility, has disregarded his effect upon nature. And because of his ignorance and disregard, disrespect of that for which he is responsible, including each and every thought in his consciousness, because of that, man experiences in nature the so-called catastrophes, disasters, the discordant types of weather conditions. And that is the effect of discord in consciousness. We see it in our own personal lives. And because we deny it by blaming others for the discord, by blaming others for the transgression of the natural laws of abundant flow, by blaming outside for what is caused inside, we continue to live in the darkness of ignorance and despair. We seem to have no problem in our life in accepting responsibility for what we judge to be the good experiences in our life. We only seem to have difficulties in accepting responsibility for the disasters, the struggles, the pain, and the suffering that we have, at times, in our life.

Man will continue to experience the opposites in creation, the highs, the lows, the seeming goods and bads, the blacks, the whites, and all the other experiences that the laws of creation have to offer, for they are dual laws. They are perfect, balanced, opposing vibrations. As long as man identifies with the thought of I, and not the I—for when man stops identifying with the thought of I, he is freed from the form. And being freed from the form, he is freed from the duality of creation; being freed from the duality of creation, he becomes the I which he truly is. Therefore, knowing the truth is the first step in accepting the truth, for we know many things. And as knowledge knows much and wisdom knows better, man does not tarry in the realms of knowledge, but moves on far beyond knowledge. Because man cannot be free in knowledge, for it has an opposite, known as ignorance. Man can never be free identified with the laws of duality. I hope that's helped with your question.

Thank you.

You're welcome. Yes, the lady in the back, please.

Do we have space brothers on other planets in this solar system?

Thank you. In reference to your question, intelligent life, in the sense of the Life Principle intelligently expressing through form or creation, intelligent life is not limited to the planet Earth. The planet Earth, if you wish to view the planet in its state of evolution or growth, it's halfway. And that's all. It's not in its beginning stage. It's not in its ending. But it is halfway. So we can all be of good cheer in the knowledge that we're halfway there. We're not just starting.

Yes, we, through the Law of Responsibility, are directly linked to all intelligent life. Now some people do not consider some of the life forms on this, the planet Earth, as intelligent life. That is unfortunate for them. For that only reveals that they have been so busy in the form in which they are presently expressing, they have yet to consider that intelligent life is everywhere around and about them.

We are our brother's keeper is certainly a teaching of many ancient philosophies. And we can only keep what we are responsible for. Therefore, being our brother's keeper, we are indeed brothers. And yes, indeed, we are responsible for the intelligent life forms, not limited to other planets, not limited to other solar systems, not limited to any form, but responsible for all form. Because, in truth, when we face not what we think we are, when we face who we are and why we are, we will then realize beyond a shadow of any doubt that we are an inseparable part of a great whole, therefore, are responsible to the whole. Whether we deny our inseparable part or not in no way frees us from our responsibilities, for ignorance of the law is no escape from the law.

Many things in life we do not wish to view. We do not wish to view them for we have judged what they offer. And we have judged what they offer in keeping with what we have already experienced. How unfortunate that we live in the shadows of yesterday, for the mind cannot judge without past experience. And so the Bible teaches us to judge not that we be not judged, for he who judges lives in that which has been and, living in consciousness in that which has passed, does not see the Light that frees him, for he lives in the twilight zones of yesterday. I do hope that's helped with your question. Thank you.

The lady over here, please.

Is it possible for an evil influence to come to you from the outside or does it only generate from within?

Thank you very much. In reference to your question on evil experience, we understand the law is constantly demonstrable: like attracts like and becomes the Law of Attachment. If you wish to call it evil, then let it be in consciousness for you. But we must remember, it can only enter our universe by like kind, for that that is in one is in all in its potential. So whatever our experiences in life, whether we like them or we dislike them, let us not deny the Law of Personal Responsibility, the effect of which is called freedom. Let us look where the cause is. It is ever within. It is never without. It is supported by experiences that come in keeping with the Law of Attraction. But it is within. And if we will be honest with our self and accept that demonstrable truth, we have stepped on the path that will free us, for we are, in truth, a part of the whole. What any part is capable of experiencing, we are all capable of experiencing. What any part has in potential or expression, we all have in potential or expression.

Remember that we cannot tolerate in others what we refuse to educate within ourselves. So let us not be concerned with evil, for placing one's attention upon that that is not harmonious or balanced or good sends the divine, infinite, neutral, intelligent Energy, through our choice in consciousness, to that within us. Let us place our attention upon what we want to become. Let us remove our attention from what we want to overcome. Because by removing our attention from what we want to overcome, we understand the divine, neutral, intelligent Energy flows, through our conscious choice, in the direction we wish to send it. And because we and we alone direct that divine Power, we and we alone are responsible for it. But as we place our attention on what we want to overcome, we live in the shadows of the past, for what we want to overcome is what we judge *is*. And because we judge it *is*, we place our self in consciousness of what has been. But when we place our self in being, on what we want to become, we free our self from what we think we have been. I hope that's helped with your question.

Yes, the gentleman here, please.

Would you talk some more on selfless service and give some examples of the application of selfless service?

Thank you. That is a subject very dear to me, very close to my heart. It's called selfless service. So many of us think that we are doing selfless service. We think that and because we think it, we see that we are only doing self-service. Selfless service is service minus, or less, the thought of self. So if we think we're doing selfless service, it's one of the first indications that we are doing self-service. Because it takes the self to think that we are serving, and that is contrary to the demonstrable truth of selfless service. When we go to do what we understand to be service minus the self, we have no thought, no dictate, no judgment of what the job is we are called to do, how long it will take, how much it will cost, what we will get out of it, or what we won't get out of it, how tired we are, where we have to be, or what we have to do. Being freed from all bondage of self, we are now in the experience of selfless service.

You see, the law that we set into motion to serve selflessly will attract unto us, in keeping with that law, opportunity. And opportunity is like the hands of the clock: it meets every so often. And if we are freed from the thought of I when the hands of the clock meet, day in and day out, we will see opportunity. Opportunity to do what we truly desire to do. But if we are blinded by the constant thought of I, then opportunity will knock at our door and we will not recognize it, for we cannot hear it, let alone see it, for we are so busy, so active with the thought of I.

What does it behoove man, who is an inseparable part of a whole, knowing the demonstrable truth that what one experiences, all can experience—for it is the divine intelligent Power that is being used by others that is available to us, that we use it through our error and abuse it. The power intelligence is everywhere present; it's never absent or away. It's waiting for us to use, not to abuse.

It is sad that we abuse the goodness that is constantly flowing through our universe. For, you see, lack of use is abuse. We all have talent. It is available to us and we alone are the obstruction to it.

I have for many years of my life taught to many souls and revealed unto them their soul talent. Unfortunately, so few, so few accept that which is. They know deep inside of them, they have a natural feeling for it. But the limited experiences of the earth realm block their use of that which is natural to them. A soul talent is not something that some gift-giving god, some "Santa Claus" god—that I do not believe in, for it is contrary to demonstrable law—has given to someone and not to another.

How far from the truth that is. Whatever the talent is—and they are varied, of course, as man himself—whatever the soul talent is, that soul has spent centuries in evolution, in evolutionary incarnation upon incarnation perfecting that particular service to the universe. To enter Earth with all of that effort that has already been into a limited form of this planet and to abuse that which has taken centuries to acquire, to blatantly abuse it by the lack of using it, surely is the error of all errors. And because the law is not only just, kind, and compassionate, but the Law of the Universe is infallible and clearly states that lack of use is abuse. And that that we abuse shall be taken from us, not by some gift-giving god, but by the lack of use.

When we permit our minds, from their limited earthly experiences, to judge that we can't do this and we can't do that with the talent we know that we have, then we are placing before us one page of a gigantic book. And that's the only page we will read. That, surely, is a great sadness. For every servant is worthy of their hire. And when we let the shadows of the past go, we live in that that we have earned in this great eternity. For not only do the workers win but the wise workers live the best of all.

Thank you.

APRIL 4, 1982

Church Questions and Answers 26
[Eleventh Anniversary Service]

As our chairman has stated, this is your time for your questions concerning things of a general interest to all of us. And I want to take a moment in respect of the eleven years, today, exactly today, that marks the anniversary of this church and the miracle of life, called survival. For in keeping with our philosophy and our efforts, that's what we understand the miracle of life to be or what we understand survival is.

Now the reason for that rather interesting statement from our philosophy, the Living Light, is really quite clear. We all have, in keeping with the experiences we have merited in life, we all have various thoughts and judgments of the way things should be. It is the very nature of our mind to control all things that come within its sphere or zone of action. And so it is when we look around and about us and we see there are things that we believe, in keeping with our own limited experiences, are not the way we believe they should be, we make varying degrees of effort to change them. The result of our effort, of course, is revealed in the demonstration which is, of course, always [and] forever the revelation. So with what we cannot change in life we sooner or later adjust to or leave. And so in keeping with that demonstrable truth, the Serenity Church was founded eleven years ago today, based upon the philosophy that many will come and many will go. That those who remain will do one of two things: grow or go in consciousness. That may seem to be rather a harsh way to look at a spiritual purpose, but our minds see things rather soft or harsh in keeping with our own understanding.

And so it is in life that freedom, the effect of self-control—not the effect of controlling everything outside, for the only thing we can ever in all eternity control is that for which we are responsible. Now we do have, by divine grace, the wonderful opportunity, moment by moment, to control that for which we are responsible. Responsibility meaning the ability to respond. So we do have the ability to respond to our own thoughts, attitudes, motives, and activities. So as we respond intelligently to that for which we are responsible and in keeping with the demonstrable law that like attracts like and becomes the Law of Attachment, we need never again be concerned with controlling what is outside, for we know the truth that frees us: to control that which is inside. In keeping with the law that like attracts like and becomes the Law of Attachment, that that is around us shall be harmonious with us. That, my good friends, is the path of freedom. It is the path of peace. It is the demonstrable path of abundant good.

Let us, then, be interested in what we are doing in our house of clay, in the temple of God. Let us be interested in where we are in consciousness, for to awaken where we are in consciousness at any given moment reveals unto us that which is and that which is to be. Let us no longer be concerned with that which has gone, for it has served the purpose for which it entered our life. Let us never forget that all things that enter our life are in keeping with the law that like attracts like. If we do not like what enters our life, then let us change the level of consciousness that has attracted it to us. Let us no longer walk the path of the defeatist. Let us no longer walk the path of failure, constantly in the delusion that we can change anything outside our realm of responsibility.

Let us change what is in our consciousness, for there we have the ability to respond to it. For those things in our consciousness are the children we have given birth to. And because we are the mother and the father of the thoughts in our consciousness, we have the power, we have the control, we have the right to change them, to refine them, and, in so doing, bring them into a state of harmonious action in our life.

For life itself, as so many have often said, is only a mirror. It has no cause; it only has effect. It is the principle that sustains life that is neutral, that is divine, that is an acceptance of totality. Let us not forget that, my friends. Let us pause in our consciousness when a thought, a judgment, rises that will not let us have the peace that is our divine right. Let us pause for the seventy-two hours necessary for our soul to be freed through the eighty-one levels of consciousness. Let us be honest with our self and we will never again be disturbed by that which is beyond our control. For we know the law so clearly: that which disturbs us is that which controls us. Let us not so easily sell out to the disturbance that is ever amongst us. Let us rise in our consciousness and let us be what we know we truly are. Thank you.

Now it is time for any questions that you have. Yes, the gentlemen here, please.

You just mentioned something in your talk about a seventy-two-hour cycle.

Yes?

Could you elaborate on that?

We understand from effort and demonstration that it takes approximately seventy-two hours—whenever we have a thought that is disturbing to us, whenever we have a condition or attitude of mind that robs of us the peace which we are, if we will pause and release that disturbance, that thought, and that attitude, release it from our consciousness for a period of seventy-two hours, then we will have the demonstration: the revelation that it is only one level of your consciousness that disturbs you. It is not all levels of your consciousness. So whatever it is that you have to do and whatever it is you think disturbs you, remember to pause and release that for a period of seventy-two hours and you are giving yourself, the true you, the opportunity to be freed from that which controls you, which will reveal to you it is only one level of many levels of consciousness. I hope that's helped with your question.

The lady in back of you, please.

Could you speak to us on God being ever equal to our understanding?

In keeping with the teaching of this philosophy, God is ever equal to our understanding. We cannot experience that [which is] beyond the realm of consciousness of our own expanding understanding. We can theorize about many things, especially God and the purpose of life. But we cannot experience in our heart and in our being that which is beyond the equality of consciousness that we, at any moment, have grown to. Therefore, God is ever equal (God in our consciousness, the experience thereof) is ever equal to our understanding of that moment. Does that help with your question? Thank you.

This is why some people, they pray for God and pray for this and pray for so many things. And then the things and the ways do not come. And then their God, equal to their own limited understanding, their God becomes smaller as their understanding shrinks in the intolerance of the level of consciousness. Thank you.

Yes, the lady here, please.

Can you speak to us on the soul faculty to ignore, as opposed to lack of attention?

Well, we understand that energy follows attention, and that which we place our attention upon we have a tendency to become. The principle to ignore is not to direct energy, through the vehicle known as attention, to the level of consciousness within our self that we do not wish at any given moment to experience.

The lady in the back, please.

Would you please speak to us on the essence of the nature of male and female vibration that each of us expresses?

Yes, if you're speaking on the essence of a thing, we must understand the essence of a thing is the principle of a thing, therefore, is that which sustains the thing, is beyond the thing and is not the form, which is the personality. Therefore, we must first be in personality (or identified with) in order to understand form, whether it is positive or negative, male or female. Because we must become the thing to understand the thing, and in so doing we cannot perceive. We can, however, conceive. Then, surely, we will understand that the divine Neutral Principle, which sustains all creation, when we rise in consciousness beyond the duality of creation, which is the form or personality of form. We rise in that way in consciousness through the lack of identification with things which are dual. Now remember, identification—we ofttimes understand that we are over-identified with a particular thought in our mind. We are over-identified with a particular judgment. It is that over-identification that causes us to become the thing and we are then bound by the thing that we are identified with.

Now we understand that identification is the becoming of the I, the thought of the I. It is not the I, the principle of life, which is the problem that we experience in life. It is the thought of the principle or the I of life that is the problem. When we identify with anything, in consciousness what happens is we possess or own. When the mind possesses or owns in its consciousness, it becomes the thing it believes it possesses or it owns. So we understand in this philosophy to redirect simply means to no longer identify, no longer be possessed by that which we believe we are. For that which we believe we are, we are only in a dual world or mental world of consciousness. We are what we believe as long as we live, breathe in a realm of consciousness of a mental world which is controlled by the dual Law of Creation.

See, no one can have a thought that they do not experience its opposite. Therefore, the peace that passeth all understanding is beyond the realm of understanding. It is in the light of wisdom and does not have duality. Does that help with your question?

Yes, it does.

Thank you. The lady here, please.

As the media is bombarding us with the Falkland Island situation, could you give us some hints as to how we can cope with that?

First the question must rise in consciousness: Does it disturb us? If it disturbs us, then, of course, the law for us has been established; that it's on its way, if not already there in our consciousness, to control us. Now it disturbs us in keeping with our own understanding. We have a choice, of course, all of us. We can expand our understanding. We can grow in consciousness and, in so doing, see the cause, and therefore no longer be disturbed by the effect. Or we can refuse to grow in consciousness. We can refuse to make that effort within our self and be controlled by what we understand to be circumstances, disasters, injustices, and etc.

Now, God, to most of us, I'm sure we would agree, means good. When we feel good, we think of God, even though we may not think of God consciously. But when we think of God, we think of good. When we think of God, we don't think of bad. If we do, then we have a kink in our consciousness or, perhaps, a missing link. Who knows? We'd have to investigate, of course.

The Falkland Islands, like any other disturbance in a world of creation, is an effect. Our understanding of that effect is in keeping with our own experiences of our own past. We look around the world and we see, "It's so unjust that man kills man, that dog eats dog. It is so unjust. It is so unjust that people walk and crush the snails like rice krispies. It is so unjust." Well, what are we going to do? Does the plant feel that it isn't just for someone to walk by and step on a snail that's eating it up? I don't think the plant feels that that's injustice. I think that the plant, which is a consciousness being expressed through a limited form, I think the plant feels a feeling of relief, perhaps even gratitude. Perhaps even the thought of divine justice, that some giant came along and stepped on the snail that was having it for a lunch. *[Some in the congregation laugh.]*

So let us understand, perhaps, a little bit, about the human jungle of which we, of course, are one of the animal species. I don't think any of us would deny that. Ofttimes I don't think we like to admit it, but the demonstration is the revelation. Do we express the animal traits that we view or don't we? That is the question. I think we all agree, we eat, so-called, we justify it for the purpose of living. We justify that we eat up the living plants. We justify we eat up the animals and we eat up everything else. And we eat up people's emotions and thoughts and go on down the list.

So when we speak of injustice, let us stop and let us think. "Is there injustice within my consciousness? Do I feel any moment of guilt? Do I feel any moment of regret for what I have done?" If we do, then we must be honest and pause, and we must think. Now we can justify that we did it for survival. We did it because someone else did this and someone else did that. But this is what we're talking about in our understanding with the Falkland Islands.

So we can look at the Argentine side, and we can see how they think. We can look at the English side, we can see how they think. And we can go all over the world and see how everybody thinks. Who is the aggressor? Who is the oppressor? We are constantly, as long as we insist on living in a world of creation and becoming a world of creation—our purpose in evolution is to be in a world, never a part of the world. Our purpose in evolution is to be with a person, place, or thing, never a part of a person, place, or thing. The separation of truth from creation is known as freedom. So let us pause and not be controlled by being disturbed by things that we have not yet made the effort in our understanding to realize the causes thereof.

What can we do about that which is out there? We can do everything [about] that which is out there, whether it is the Falkland Islands or anything else, by doing everything about what's in here. For if we do something about what is in here, that which is around us will start to change in keeping with the changes that we alone are making.

Now we can say we're only one. I tell you, the flight of the butterfly affects the entire atmosphere of the planet Earth! That is a proven, scientific, demonstrable fact. Now if the flight of the butterfly affects, though microscopic, of course, affects the atmosphere of this entire planet, what do we think one thought of one human mind does in the universe? Many of the ancient Indian tribes of North America, not all, but many, realized the great responsibility that man has to his surroundings, to his environment, to nature, to everything that his thought comes in contact with. Well, think about that, my friends. There is no space, nor time, nor distance to a thought you entertain in consciousness. It doesn't take two years to reach Saturn. It doesn't even take two seconds! Stop and think of the great responsibility that we have not only to the planet Earth and all that is upon it, to the atmosphere that surrounds it, to the universes, to the planets in outer space. We have a great responsibility.

And because there are intelligences far advanced beyond our self that are well aware and affected by the thoughts men think, we have been watched for centuries, and for centuries shall we continue to be watched. As we watch the little pets that we put in our cages and we judge what they do and we find it interesting to see how they act, let us not forget, we are in a cage our self: the cage of our own consciousness. We are never alone. We are watched and monitored right around the clock, whether we like it or not. Then let's become aware and become honest with our self, and let's start cleaning up, as they say in today's language, our own act. And we will be so much better for it.

Thank you.

MAY 2, 1982

Church Questions and Answers 27

This is your opportunity, as our chairman has said—once a month—to ask the questions that are of interest to you and to all of us. So if you'll kindly raise your hand, we'll reach as many people as possible.

The lady here, please, in the aisle.

How is it possible to help a friend who is thinking negatively? Is it right to be insistent when the person wants to do his own wrong thinking?

That's a very good question. Is it right to be insistent when a person wants to do their own thing? Of course, that is dependent upon the Law of Personal Responsibility. Ofttimes in our lives we have children in our care and though they want to do their own thing and we know that it is not in their best interests, we have to insist and take corrective measures in keeping with the Law of Personal Responsibility. How does one help another who insists on living in what we understand to be a negative way and detrimental to oneself? Well, there is one thing that is demonstrably true in creation: there is a bottom to all things. Ofttimes we find the more help we give them to reach the bottom, so they can climb back up, the sooner are positive results. It is clearly stated that when we have had enough of anything in life, we will make the change in our thinking which will bring about the change in our experience.

And so, though it may seem questionable to some of us, we must understand: anyone who insists upon negative, detrimental experiences in their life is certainly getting something out of the experience. We do not do anything in life that we don't get something out of it. That is in keeping with the Law of Creation. Consequently, a person who insists upon living in those realms of consciousness, in those attitudes and patterns of mind, is getting something and that something is usually the energy that we are releasing to them in, unfortunately, our pity, which is absolutely in no way, shape, or form beneficial to them. With my own students I tell them enjoy the realm that they insist on living in. I know that someday they will become so weary of it they will cry for any change, and it certainly will be better. Does that help with your question?

Yes. Thank you.

Thank you. The gentleman here, please.

It's my understanding that personal responsibility is a primary tenet of this philosophy. Does this mean that all that we encounter is caused by us? And can we, therefore, draw no line between self and other?

Yes, in keeping with the Law of Personal Responsibility, all experiences in life we are personally responsible for. All experiences that we entertain in our own consciousness have been set into motion by a law. Whether or not we are aware of that law does not exempt us from that immutable law. We come to earth in keeping with the Law of Personal Responsibility. We merit different parents. We merit different parts of the country. We merit different countries. We merit different experiences in keeping with that law. The Law of Personal Responsibility is an infallible, immutable law applying to all form. Whether that form be human, animal, or plant, the law is infallible and impartial. Now when we awaken and accept that demonstrable truth, that is when we become, in that moment, the masters of our ship and the captains of our destiny. It is only in those moments of total acceptance that we experience the divine will, the will of God. And in those moments, and those moments only, are we freed.

Bondage is an experience, the effect of attachment. When we accept personal responsibility for all our thoughts, acts, and activity, we are demonstrating unto our self the truth that frees us. And in those moments there is no bondage, for there is no attachment. We can only attach to anything through the Law of Ignorance. Because, you see, my friends, when we accept the truth, we then know, in those moments of acceptance, that we are an inseparable part of a divine stream of consciousness; that the only difference we see is the difference created by what the Hindus call *maya*, what we call illusion. Illusion is what is known as the poles of opposites, the positive, the negative; the good or bad. It only exists in a mental world. There is no good or bad, there is no positive or negative, there is no duality, there is no opposite to the Divine Spirit which we are, which is the neutrality that sustains all life, for it is, itself, the essence of life.

So when we want our desire to be free—to be free we experience in degree. We experience the freedom from this bondage or attachment and we experience the freedom from that bondage or attachment. And so, step by step, degree by degree, we are freeing our self through the so-called struggle of what we know as creation. When we understand that the mind, our mind, is a vehicle, it is an instrument that we use—that it is not us—when we truly awaken to that truth, we will be in creation, in the realms of duality, never a part of them. But only in the moment of awakening can we use the mind for what it was truly designed. We are not the mind; we are the power, the intelligence which uses the mind. We are not the body; we are not the form. We are the formless, divine, infinite, eternal Spirit that is using it at this moment.

Some of us, through our own effort in awakening, are using these instruments, these vehicles intelligently with the light of reason. Some of us have forgotten that they are instruments designed for our use and we have permitted our self to believe in the illusion and the delusion that we are the form and not that which moves the form. Does that help with your question?

I suppose.

You're welcome. The gentleman over here, please.

I was wondering, I've been curious for a long time. How—does—are there people from space (the flying saucers), are they the overseers of the planet? And are they sent from God?

Well, in the final analysis, the things we like and don't like, there's only one source, there's only one sustenance to them. And, of course, man calls that Infinite Intelligence or God.

In reference to your question about space people: we call, usually, anything that we are not familiar with, "space," "spaced-out," or "space people." And so it is, of course, a very broad statement to make. I am sure that many people think that the Spiritualists believe in "space people." Because most people don't see their own spirit, how could they possibly see another? Let us remember we can only experience, seemingly without, what we are already experiencing within, for life is a mirror of illusion and that's all that it really is.

In reference to intelligent beings overseeing the planet: in keeping with the demonstrable Law of Life in all planets, yes, in that respect, it is true. There is always something, somewhere, someone, some intelligence overseeing something. We oversee the cat and dog. We do it dutifully or not. We oversee the plants and all the other things. And be rest assured, something, somewhere, is overseeing us. I hope that's helped with your question.

A lot.

The lady in the front, please.

We understand that flowers bring a healing vibration. And we also have been told that flowers are good for the nature spirits. Would you please explain that?

Well, in reference to flowers, the effect of a spiritual principle: now there are a lot of questions in reference to nature. We must understand, first, that without nature we would not be in this form and [have] this form to use. Because it is only through nature, the spirit of nature, the nature spirits, that any form exists on this planet or any planet.

Now when the mental world becomes discordant, out of balance, with the harmony of nature, then we have problems in nature. Balance is the law through which the Divine Intelligence flows unobstructed. And it is the unobstructed flow of the infinite, eternal Divine Intelligence that brings health, happiness, and abundant good, whether it is the plant, the tree, or the human. It is thoughts in a mental world that are contrary and contradictory that cause an imbalance in that mental world. It is the effect of that imbalance that is the obstruction to the divine flow. Flowers, like many plants, flowers are, in the evolutionary scale, higher evolved in the plant kingdom than other plants. It is that evolutionary process, that refining process that brings about more of a balance in the aura of the flower through which this Divine Intelligence may flow less obstructed and bring about harmony or health to the receiver. Now I hope that's helped with your question.

Thank you.

Yes, the gentleman on the aisle, please.

About personal responsibility, how does it interact between two individuals? Say I create my own universe. Am I the creator of your answer to me? Or are you the creator of my question to you?

Excellent question. In respect to two people and the Law of Personal Responsibility: you see, someone can say good morning to a person and the person they have said good morning to gets very emotionally upset. It is how we interpret, which is, of course, ever our choice, how a person speaks, how they act, how they think, what they do, why they do it. All of these things take place within our own consciousness. They take place within our own mind. Because a thought takes place within our mind and because it is our mind, we are never left without the possibility to do something about it.

Now the law clearly states that like attracts like and becomes the Law of Attachment. Now many married people, during the honeymoon phases, love to hear that statement that like attracts like and becomes the Law of Attachment. After a few months—sometimes weeks, sometimes years—they don't like to hear that demonstrable truth anymore. Which only reveals they've moved farther and farther away from the truth that will free them: personal responsibility. So if you are communicating with another person and they respond to your communication—or they do not respond—all your feelings, all your thoughts, and all your judgments are taking place within your own consciousness. And because it is taking place in your consciousness, you certainly can do something about it anytime you choose to change your thought. Does that help with your question?

Somewhat, yes.

Well, it takes a degree of self-control. And to the degree of self-control—the mastery of your own mind that you have accomplished—are we freed. Is there anymore to your question?

Yes. What about circumstances in which it would be termed an accident if one did not pay attention to the Law of Personal Responsibility? That accident which may involve two people, which person is responsible or do they share that responsibility?

In reference to accidents, they're only a lack of understanding the law through which the experience took place in the first place. Now we share the responsibility for all our thoughts, acts, and activities. If your thoughts, acts, and activities are involved with another individual, you have your share of the responsibility. Yes. Does that help with your question?

Yes, definitely.

You're welcome. The lady back there, please.

Could you please explain the principle of marriage?

Well, some people say marriages are made in heaven. I haven't found the heaven, yet, where they are made. That doesn't mean people don't have a very harmonious marriage if they accept the laws of personal responsibility. But, you see, when we go to discuss the principle of something, in the discussion, because we must use a dual vehicle known as the human mind in order to express it, we lose the very essence of the principle itself. Now I'm sure if you will accept personal responsibility in any marriage in which you are or are contemplating, then there will be no problem.

When we accept, "Well, I don't appreciate the experience that I am having and, more than that, I don't appreciate that I was ignorant to what I have done to experience this. But this is the moment that I have conscious power over. So in this moment, will I make the effort to do something about it?" Let us remember, friends, bondage exists in attachment. And whenever we think of that which has been, we are automatically attached. For that that has been has served its purpose and therefore no longer is. It is only through the Law of Attachment that it continues to exist within our eternal consciousness, which is the present moment. Thank you.

Yes, the lady here, please.

I wanted to know about stress and disease—the relationship between the two.

Because stress is a vibration of discord, and discord (that that does not flow in ease)—discord is dis-ease. That is what disease really is. When we have stress, that reveals that we have contradictory and conflicting desires; that we are, through our errors, unable at that moment to gain control over these contradictory and conflicting desires and, therefore, experience many things, one, known as stress, another as time-pressure, another as frustration, and on down the list. Now when we make the daily effort to become aware of these desires within our consciousness, we put them into proper perspective for us, we tell them when [and] what priorities they have for us, we begin to gain control over our mind, and our mind, we are no longer the victim of. We are the victim of anything we are attached to. That is why we say—and have said for many years—freedom is the effect, the effect of self-control. For in the controlling of the self we are freed from the bondage and attachment; we are freed from the experiencing of these contradictory and conflicting patterns of mind and, therefore, do not experience discord, disease, and lack, limitation and all that is restrictive.

Remember, limit exists only in the mental world. There is no limit, there is no restriction to that world known to man as spiritual consciousness. It only exists in a mental world. When we think of what we call self, we enter a mental world. This is why many people are able to accomplish many things beyond the demonstrable, so-called, powers of the human mind. It is because they give up, at least momentarily, that great illusion called self and, in giving that up, are no longer limited by a mental world that is restrictive and limited. Does that help with your question?

Thank you.

You're welcome. The gentleman here, please.

When we find we're attracting irresponsible people in our life, what can we do about it?

Oh, we can do a great deal about it. And I certainly would work on it immediately. In fact, I work on it every day. When we attract irresponsible, what we understand to be irresponsible people, flaky people, people who do not fulfill their commitments, people who are late and tardy, have no consideration, let alone respect, for themselves or others, it's time to work in the spirit of honesty and to pause. To ask oneself the demonstrable truth, "What inside of me is attracting these types of experiences?" For the law is very clear: we grow or go. If they stay around our universe, these irresponsible, flaky-type of people, then we can be rest assured we are making no effort to change the law that we are emanating. It's all inside our self. And it's a wonderful awakening to look around, especially if you have responsibilities as a teacher or a minister or anything, and look around and see what you're attracting. Because a lot of things you don't like and you've got to pause and think and take corrective measures inside yourself.

You see, my friends, we all have, in potential, everything that we experience. It lies there. We may not like people who demonstrate being late. We may not like people who demonstrate the disrespect and lack of consideration in not fulfilling a commitment, you see. We may not like that, but we must accept that the level within us does exist, in potential. We may not recall us ever demonstrating it. Our ego may not permit that, but be rest assured it is there. And it sneaks out at the right time under the right circumstances for us. So we can do a great deal about attracting irresponsible people.

Now sometimes a person will say, "Well, I'm in business and I'm attracting these irresponsible business people, but I've never been irresponsible in business." Well, the principle of the Law of Irresponsibility is not limited to business. It may be to a wife or a child or go on down the list. We have to look at the principle of it and take a look to see: in our entire life, have we ever, ever been irresponsible? And if so, we must go to work on that weakness that we may strengthen our self and not experience those type of people in our universe. Does that help with your question?

You see, that's the wonderful freedom of personal responsibility. Doesn't matter what the experience is. Good, bad, or indifferent. Doesn't matter how we judge it. It does matter that we become the captain of our ships and the masters of our destiny. That is not possible in any way, shape, or form without the constant acceptance of the demonstrable Law of Personal Responsibility.

If you go to the grocery store and the checker's real nasty to you, stop and think—that doesn't mean you become passive and mowed over like a blade of grass, every week, on the lawn. But it does mean that you look inside for the cause. Because to continue to look outside for the cause is to keep you in the bondage and the illusion of old creation. And there is certainly something much greater than this world.

This world is here to be used, to be enjoyed. We cannot use it properly, we cannot enjoy it fully until we understand the laws that govern it. For when we understand the law that governs anything, it is the first step in gaining control over it. And so, if we do not make the daily effort to understand the laws of the experiences that we encounter, then there is no way that we can ever gain control over them.

Thank you very much.

JULY 4, 1982

Church Questions and Answers 28

As our chairman has stated, this is your opportunity, once a month, to ask questions that you find of interest to you. So if you'll be so kind as to raise your hand, I will be happy to reach as many as possible.

The lady here, please.

How can we avoid directing energy to the self?

Yes, in reference to the question how can we avoid in directing energy to the self: when we understand what we mean by the word *self*, what it truly represents, then we will awaken the light of reason within our consciousness to see why and how it is so very detrimental.

The lady has asked the question, "How can we avoid directing energy to the self?" When we ask our self the question "Who am I and what am I?" what rises within our consciousness is all of the things in life, in creation, that we have already identified with. We must understand that we cannot—it is not possible to be, in reality, anything that we have not first identified with. Because we have already identified with many things and because the many things we have already identified with are not harmonious and, therefore, not beneficial, it does not behoove us to give energy, through the vehicle of thought, to self. Because when we ask our self who are we, it is ever dependent upon what level of consciousness responds to the question of the moment. Because the daily effort has not been yet made to gain control over the varying levels of consciousness in which our soul is constantly expressing, then to identify with what we call self is not only a most unreliable way to live life but it is a placing of our eternal being ever subject to the whims of the human mind.

Now our mind changes in keeping with the experiences of any moment that it registers and records in consciousness. It is a reactor. Whenever we permit the divine, neutral Energy to be directed through the vehicle of thought to what we call the self, we have lost being captain of our ship. We have, in those moments, lost being master of our destiny, for we are then only the victims of what is already recorded in consciousness and we react accordingly.

We teach in this philosophy a process of redirect: to take conscious control over the human mind and consciously choose where we wish to direct this neutral, infinite, intelligent Energy. Because the Energy, which we are receptive to, is not only infinite [and] neutral but intelligent, it will do what we send it to do. It has the intelligence to do what it is told to do.

So often in life we think and we desire and we want to accomplish many things. When we speak our word forth into the universe, knowing that it shall not come back to us void but accomplish that which we send it to do, that law is only applicable in the moment that we are free from the thought of self. For to speak forth our word and for us to expect it to return to us not void, but fulfilled, takes control over the human mind. For when we speak the word, there are many levels of consciousness that are reacting within us. Those levels are not all harmonious. And because they are not harmonious, because they are discordant, they utilize the Energy that we are receptive to in that moment; they dissipate the necessary intelligent Energy when the word is spoken, and therefore it returns unto us void. And we live so many of our days in frustration.

To avoid this Energy going into self-thought takes a conscious control moment by moment—an awareness of not only who we are but an awareness of what we are. As long as we permit our mind to tell us that we are the thought of the moment, as long as we permit our mind to tell us we are the feeling of yesterday, as long as we permit our mind to identify with what has been, without our conscious, direct control thereof, then we shall ever be the bondage that we are. We cannot make the change until we first see what is happening within our own consciousness.

The first step on being free from that bondage is an acceptance of the Law of Personal Responsibility. Without accepting the Law of Personal Responsibility, all other laws are null and void in our efforts to apply them. Because, you see, my friends, without accepting the Law of Personal Responsibility, we cannot be free from the self, the self-thought, which is dictating a repetition of experiences that have already been. Therefore, we live in the shadows of yesterday when we live in the thought of I. That which is the I is formless and free. It is not dependent upon form; therefore, it is not limited. The thought of I is the limit. The thought of I is the bondage.

We understand that we are Spirit, formless and free. Spirit is not form. Therefore, it is free. Anything that is form is limited and, therefore, is bondage. Now limit or form exists only in a mental realm of consciousness. It does not and cannot exist in a formless, free spirit which we are.

We enter limit, we enter form, we enter bondage with the thought of I. In that process we identify. We cannot identify nor can we experience creation without the thought of I. Therefore, we understand the thought of I is necessary in order to experience the dual law known as creation. The wise choice, then, of course, is to be in creation, to be with a person, place, or thing, but never a part of a person, place, or thing. And that takes conscious effort moment by moment by moment. When we are ready, willing, and able to make that conscious, moment-by-moment effort, we will live and never *be*, but we will live the truth that we are. We will no longer struggle, for we will no longer, through the Law of Identification, be attached to persons, places, or things. That is the home from whence we have come. It is the home to which we are returning in consciousness.

It does not mean, nor do I mean to imply, that when we pass through the so-called change or transition known as death do we return home to the formless, free Spirit that we are. Returning to the formless, free Spirit from whence we have wandered is a process that may happen at any moment of your conscious choice. I do hope that's helped with your question.

Thank you.

Thank you. Yes, the lady in the aisle, please.

Is it best, if you are seeking the truth, to follow a leader?

The question is, "Is it best, if you are seeking the truth, to follow a leader?" First of all, in the question, of course, as in all questions, are contained their answers. For the mind to question, "Is it best, if you are seeking the truth, to follow a leader?" is already telling the mind that number one: it has not found the truth; number two: it has made some effort to attempt to find the truth; and number three: it is yet waiting to be successful. Now all of those things are revealed within the question.

If we have forgotten how we wandered from the truth, then, of course, it behooves us, if we believe, from demonstration, that someone has found the truth, then, of course, it behooves us to make the effort to find and to follow those who we believe have found what we are seeking. For they will only be instruments through which we, slowly but surely, go on the path that frees us in our own consciousness.

Remember, no one can give us anything that we do not already have. All a person can give you is what they have already found. And in that giving be the demonstration of what you already have and are waiting to awaken to. So I do hope that has helped with your question.

Thank you.

Thank you. The gentleman on the aisle, please.

Yes. I wonder if you can give us something on good and bad luck and an individual's response to chance.

A most interesting question. The gentleman's asking for something on good and bad luck—is that correct?

Yes.

And the Law of Chance. To accept, first of all, to accept the word *luck*, what it implies and what it means, to accept the word *chance*, what it implies and what it means—let us pause to think—denies the Law of Personal Responsibility: that everything in life that we experience we alone have established the law for the experience. It implies (luck) that there is an intelligent power that is giving to some—by some unknown and mysterious law that we cannot control—is giving good to some and so-called bad to others. That, a man will pause to think, is not a power, nor a god, that anyone with any intelligence would be willing to serve. Therefore, this philosophy clearly teaches and demonstrates there is no luck; there are no chances. There are no accidents. There are no experiences in life that are beyond the law, though we may not at the moment of the experience understand the law that we have established. But we must also understand that ignorance of the law is no excuse, nor exemption from it.

There is no luck, my good friends. There is no such thing. It never did exist. It never will exist. It is a delusion created by our mind to deny the law when we are struggling through life.

It is difficult to accept the Law of Personal Responsibility. It is difficult to accept that we are the captain of our ship and the master of our destiny when things are not going what we think are our way. If we will, in those moments of so-called struggle, if we will in those moments of seeming difficulty, declare the truth—"This is but an effect of a law that I alone have established. I am ignorant at this moment of what that law is, for I have yet to make the effort to awaken myself to what my mind is doing to me. But I shall from this struggle and I shall from this grief accept the possibility of something better. And in that accepting I know I establish the law to make greater effort that I may have experiences that are beneficial to me, that are more harmonious and fulfilling to my desires." There is no other way.

The world has been filled for centuries with lucky gods and bad luck gods. It has been filled for centuries with what man today calls savior gods. But we must ask our self the question, "Is it our sincere desire to continue to be the victim and the slave of something somewhere that is beyond our conscious control?" When we awaken inside of our self, we will not only know beyond a shadow of any doubt that we are, and we are experiencing everything that our minds have dictated is necessary for us.

There is good in all things. And he who makes the effort to see the good in every experience that he encounters in life establishes the Law of Freedom from the bondage of those experiences. It takes more effort to see the good in a so-called bummer experience than it does to see the good in an experience that is in keeping with our judgments of the moment of experiencing the experience. That, of course, is understandable. That is how children act, or better stated, react. But we cannot be children forever. There comes a moment in which our debt to life is due. And when that moment comes we may face it with a joyful spirit, we may face it with an attitude of encouragement, or we may blame the president, the politicians, and everything else for the way that we feel as we are experiencing the chickens who have come home to roost. It's ever and forever up to us. Life is as beautiful, it is as good, it is as wealthy, it is as fulfilling as we alone choose to make it.

Now I admit it is most difficult for life to be that great when we insist on living in the shadows of something that has passed. For to live in the shadows of that which has been is to darken our view of that which is. It's like today. To me, all days are beautiful. Hot, cold, or whatever. Because it is up to us how beautiful they will be. Now if we want a day to be terrible, we make great effort to set every law into motion with everyone we meet to have a nasty attitude, grouchy, so that we can support the judgment that we alone have made. Many of us seem to have a deep, inner love to live that way, for we experience an energy flowing through others to us. We get attention, as little children burn houses down, sometimes, to get attention. As they squirm and jump around in their chairs to get attention.

Now remember that the form known as the human being—or even the animal form—requires sustenance to survive. It requires being receptive to energy that is flowing through the universe. When we, in our receiving of this divine, intelligent Energy, when we ground this Energy with self-thought, we sooner or later begin to experience a depletion in our vital body. We have what we commonly refer to as a lack of energy. Enthusiasm is something that everyone else has. We haven't experienced it, perhaps, for years. We are despondent. We're discouraged. We are filled with what is commonly referred to by mankind as self-pity: feeling sorry for our lot in life. Now it takes a great deal of energy to sustain that type of thinking, and it's grounded within our own aura. And therefore, the energy necessary for the full charge of our vital body for a spirit of enthusiasm is non-existent for us.

Yet our vital body demands that it have the sustenance and energy that is necessary. And so we spend much of our time telling other people how miserable life is, how rotten it is, how terrible the economy is, how it's destined to get worse, how business is about to collapse, and every so-called disaster that our human mind can possibly conceive from present and past experience. And in so doing we soon find that misery not only loves company, it is indispensable for its existence. Therefore, we must get as many people as we can find to listen to our tales of woe. As they listen to our tales of woe, we suddenly, as we view them looking worse, feeling worse, we suddenly feel a little bit better. There's some kind of a charge taking place within our consciousness as we see them sinking. Well, my good friends, we, in those moments—it's called dumping the package—we, in those moments, have suddenly become aware, by eliminating a portion of self-thought and that negative thinking, we've become aware of this energy that's flowing through us. Now if we can get enough people to be miserable—it's the way the human ego works, until it gets educated—if we can only get enough people to feel miserable, to be crawling like gophers in the ground, we have this false charge of energy.

It's like a person, you know, they make great effort and they lose a little weight and the first thing they do is start bragging. And nothing makes them feel better than to have every fat person they can find around them for close friends. Because, you see, it makes them feel so good. Now if they make great effort to get thin and the only people around them are thin people, well there's really no charge there at all, you see. You see, feeling good is a necessity in life; it is not a luxury. For feeling good is experiencing God. Now how you have chosen to feel good is where the problem seems to exist in life.

Now if you say, and you have established that law, "Well, the only way I feel good is going to Hawaii for three weeks every other month," and you find, with your budget, that you can't go to Hawaii for three weeks every other month, then you no longer feel good. And that's really sad, because feeling good is a necessity. But you don't have to put the stumbling blocks of what you have to do in life to feel good. When you permit your mind to dictate that you can only feel good by doing such and such a thing and that such and such a thing you have permitted to be beyond your conscious control, such as you don't have the money or this or that or whatever the problem is, then you've got a serious problem in life. And perhaps something happens out of the blue that you don't understand, you've made some effort you're not consciously aware of, and you get to go to wherever you want to go and you feel good. And you call that luck. Well, the only luck about it was the luck of ignorance of not being aware of the laws that we alone, in personal responsibility, have set into motion. I do hope that's helped with your question.

Yes, the gentleman here, please, on the aisle.

I was wondering if you would give your explanation of why the full moon has an apparent effect on so many people's emotional or magnetic body.

Oh, I'd be more than happy to share my understanding. Because so many people have so little control over their mind. It's really quite simple. Our body contains a very high percentage of fluid. The magnetic field of the planet, concerning the liquids, is controlled by the varying phases of the moon in its relationship to this particular planet. And we are forms, we are spirit in forms on this planet. It affects the fluids and the waters in our body. And without some conscious effort to control our emotions we're simply the victim of so-called circumstances. The victimization, of course, being the unwillingness [to apply] and the ignorance of the laws, which are totally impartial and apply to all form. That help with your question?

Yes, sir.

The lady in the back, please.

Could you share with us your understanding of the number three?

Well, I'm sure that we all understand that there is no manifestation of anything without the dual Law of Creation. It takes the negative and positive poles of life to bring into being the manifestation of anything. And it's a wonderful question because it has to deal, of course, also with the human mind. A person wants something to manifest in their life and they think about it consciously, and that is an electrical force that goes out into the universe. The only sadness is they do not consider the magnetic field that is necessary to set into motion in order for it to manifest into their life. And so as I explained earlier in our discussion on the thought of I, they set this law into motion with a conscious electrical thought, and the necessary harmonious thought from the magnetic field, known to man as the subconscious mind, is contrary to what the conscious thought is; and it returns unto them void. And so, as they say in today's vernacular, when we get our act together we won't have any problem about our life and the manifestation of the good that is our divine birthright.

Well, now a person may say, "Well, if good is our divine birthright, then how come I've missed divinity since I was born?" And, of course, that would be a very good question. We came to Earth contrary to what we like to think, [which is] pure innocent of all experience. We came to Earth and as we entered this planet we no longer identified with that which has been, because we entered what you understand to be as new mental bodies, new bodies, new vehicles of expression. Now it is possible for man to be aware, through the memory par excellence, of that which has been before he entered Earth. But what will it behoove man if he's not willing to make the effort to find out who he was a year ago, six months ago, or even a day or an hour ago?

So when we pause to think in all of our activities, we will not only see more clearly where we're headed but then we will not have to be so concerned about, "How am I going to do this and how am I going to do that?" When our mind asks our self the question, "Well, how am I going to do this?" then we are limited to what we've already done in life. And if it's something you want to do that you haven't already done and you ask yourself the question, you go through the computer of what you've already done, you immediately get a feeling of discouragement, doubt, and all the negatives because that's what you've asked.

You see, you want to bring—repetition is the law through which change or evolution is made possible; it is not the law itself, but it is the law through which it is made possible. When you want something new in your life—say you want new experiences. You want to have a better life than what you've already had. You've got to ask something besides self, because self can only offer what has already been. And you don't want what has already been; you've already made that decision! So how are you going to have something, something better?—[when] your mind says, "I'm tired of what has been. I want something better." How can you say, "I accept the possibility of something better" and you're saying that to a computer that's limited with what has already been? That doesn't even make sense. It's pure hypocrisy. It's absolute, pure hypocrisy.

To speak forth the word, to say at one time, "I will do such and such, and such and such" and then to let the days or week or so pass and totally reverse the decision you have made—can you imagine what kind of experiences you're going to have in life? Now how can you expect anyone to rely upon you, in any sense of the word, when you're not even capable of relying upon yourself? Now many people say, "Well, you know, I want to get up at a certain time. I want to be on time. I don't want to be a person that's, that's known as someone that doesn't have any type of respect, consideration, or character." And then turn around, the alarm goes off and go back to sleep. Well, what kind of self-control is something like that? Don't you see, my friends? Don't speak forth the truth, "I accept the possibility of something better or something greater," don't speak it to a computer that there's no way possible it can offer you something better. It can only offer you what has already been.

That's like a person who goes on a diet. Well, here the diet has done so much and they've lost so many pounds. And they say, "Great. I did a great job. I got a terrific charge of energy from all my friends. I told them how great I was doing." And then, of course, the old pattern [rises]; they get into self, they open up the trapdoor to what has been and all the fat comes back on again. Then, they go along; they get disgusted and discouraged with that. And they need that charge of energy of feeling good again. And they go back on to some other diet that's not in the computer yet, but the pattern is established in the computer of self. So it doesn't matter what diet you try. You're going to have the same experience year after year after year after year after year because you are living in a computer that already has registered the experiences and that's all that it can offer you.

So, my good friends, as I shared to my students long ago, accept the possibility of something greater. Please speak to something besides the self that can only offer you the stuff that you got tired of having already.

Thank you very much.

AUGUST 1, 1982

Church Questions and Answers 29

Spiritualism being, for over 134 years now, a religion of the moment. The interest of our congregation and the activities of current events, of course, are important to all of us. And so it is on the first of the month that your questions need not be restricted to what's going to happen to you hereafter, because what's happening to you and to me today is what will happen hereafter. Because we don't change when we change our suit, unless we change our thought, which changes our attitude. So I will, indeed, once again, be grateful to share with you the understanding given to me on any questions that you may have that are of interest to you today. For unless a religion applies to our day-to-day interest and activities, then one cannot possibly reap the benefit or harvest from that that is only interested in what tomorrow may bring [and] not interested in what today is. So if you have any questions, if you will be so kind as to raise your hand, I will be more than happy to reach as many people as time will permit.

Yes, the gentleman on the aisle, please.

Will you share with us your understanding of the soul faculties which correspond to physical and material abundance?

Yes, in reference to the soul faculties that are related to the abundant flow in one's life—is that your question?

It is.

Yes. We understand, particularly, the soul faculty of gratitude. You see, my friends, when we express gratitude for what we have, by opening that faculty we open the door to the acceptance of ever-increasing good to continue to flow. For example, if we believe that there is good in our life, by placing our attention, which is our energy, upon that which is, we establish the law for more to enter. Now the Bible tells us clearly what that law is, if we will pause to think. It says, "To those who have, yea, even more shall I give. And to those who have not, even that shall I take away." And so it shows us clearly that as we demonstrate gratitude for what we have, we establish the Law of Increase. Because we are not placing our attention, which is our energy, upon the obstruction, the way is clearly shown to us.

It is interesting, especially in these current times, that so many people, placing their attention upon what has been and comparing what is to what has been, seem to be having less as each day goes by. It is because the attention, which is our energy, is placed upon a shadow, and therefore is placed upon that which has died, which has gone, and only relives in our consciousness. Not placing the attention, the energy, upon what is, we lose what is and live in what has been.

Truth, we know, is individually perceived. We also know that the Power, the Peace, the God that is, is in the moment of our awareness. And if the moment of our awareness is directed to that which has been, has served its purpose and gone, then what happens is that we, needing the energy to experience the abundant good of the moment, we lose it and, therefore, do not experience the good that is our birthright. Does that help with your question?

Thank you.

You're welcome. Yes, please, the lady there.

We can't see the people on the other side of the veil, usually. Can they see us in a physical sense? Or how do they perceive us?

Yes, depending upon which realm of consciousness in which they reside. We understand that there are eighty-one levels of consciousness. Therefore, there are eighty-one realms of consciousness. Now if a person on what we call the other side, one who has passed from this physical world—passing from the physical world is not a passing from the mental world. The mental world, our world, is dependent upon the Law of Identification: what we identify with, we experience. And so it is that if we have spent our life here on earth identifying only with a mental world, then that is the world in which we live.

Just because the physical suit returns to the earth, from whence it has been composed, does not free us from the identification that we have with a mental world. Therefore, there are those souls residing in mental worlds, astral worlds, spiritual worlds, and many other worlds of consciousness.

They perceive us through the vision of the body in which the soul is presently encased. For example, if the soul is still encased in a mental form, then they perceive us with mental sight. If it is evolved to a spiritual body, then through spiritual sight do they perceive us. Now when we perceive something with spiritual sight, then we perceive that which is of a spiritual nature; and that which is of a spiritual nature, of course, can only be experienced or perceived by spiritual sight. So that, of course, would be dependent upon what realm of consciousness, having left this physical world, that the soul presently resides in. Does that help with your question?

Yes. Thank you.

You're welcome. The gentleman here, please.

How can one come to know and harmonize with their subconscious?

"How can one come to know and harmonize with their subconscious?" Perhaps we should take a few moments in reference to that question because of all things that is not in our best interest to harmonize with it is what man refers to as our subconscious. Now why does man—why is it not in man's best interest to harmonize with his subconscious? Not to know his subconscious—it is important to know what is stored in the memory. That is indeed important. To harmonize with it is to live in that which has been, denying one the experience of that which is.

Now we understand in this philosophy that the subconscious lives and expresses through a magnetic field. All emotions are magnetic. The soul faculties express through what we call a conscious mind or conscious vehicle. Reason does not exist in what we call the subconscious mind. Only emotion exists in what we call the subconscious mind. Now, for example, we have many thoughts and we have made many changes. Most of those, our emotions did not choose to make. We look out at life and we see consciously that it is in our best interest to change certain attitudes of mind, to change certain experiences that we are having. We know within our self what to do to bring about these changes that we consciously desire. When it comes to applying the effort to bring about these changes that we consciously desire, we ofttimes find great difficulty, great difficulty in bringing about these changes because our emotions will not permit us to bring about the change.

Say, for example, one desires to lose a hundred pounds of weight. They decide in their conscious mind that that is what they want to do. That is a firm desire for them. And they make the effort to do just that. Perhaps the effort will last a day, an hour, a week, a month, three months, six months, possibly a year and then the next thing we know, we're back the way we used to be. Usually worse than we were when we started. Now this happens in all things that we wish to bring about a change with, consciously. When we understand how the subconscious mind—our subconscious mind—really works, then we will understand how all subconscious minds really work because we are all an inseparable part of the so-called human race.

Now a thought isn't just some nebulous thing that just passes through our mind. A thought is a birth. We give birth to a thought, and birth of anything is form of anything. Out of the so-called mental substance we think we have a thought and that's as far as we go, usually. Out of that substance we create a form and we call that a thought. Now we create that form with the energy that passes through our being by directing our attention to this that we call a thought. Now this form, existing in a mental world, is given birth. It does not have a soul, but it has access to the source; the source being our mind. We gave it birth, and that that is given birth from something has the potential of all that gave it birth. Therefore, the thought is now a form. It breathes; it lives in a mental world, being created in a mental world. As long as attention is directed to it, it has the necessary energy to live, to breathe, and to move.

So we look back at life and we, if we're honest with our self, we see that we have created an untold number of thought forms. We have given them birth. We have directed energy, through the Law of Attention, to them, and they have grown up and become very, very strong. They live in what is known as our mental world, our aura. When we, later on, depending [upon] how much energy we have directed, through attention, to the thought form, we want to make a change, that change, our other thought forms view as detrimental to their existence. They look, they see—for they have all that your mind has to offer—that you will now be placing your energy, your attention on new thought forms, depriving them of their survival. They rise up to stop you from doing that. Unless you are aware, awake, and alert and you make the effort, through the powers of concentration, to gain control over the armies that your mind has already created, not just in this life, but through the entire evolutionary path, then they have their way and you change very, very slowly over a period of years and centuries.

Now, one placing their attention upon their subconscious is the great—greatest of all—danger. Until we learn to separate truth from creation, the formless, free Spirit that we are from the form that we believe we are, then it is not advisable, without awakened guidance, to tamper with, to attempt to learn about the forms of one's own subconscious mind.

You see, my friends, there's such a thing as what is termed the mass thinking. Now stop and think. A thought is a form that we alone have created. A thought is the expression of a form we have already created. Therefore, we find some of our thoughts very strong, and we find other thoughts in our minds very weak. It depends on how much energy or attention has been directed to them. And so we have untold millions of people upon the planet and they begin to think a certain way. These forms, they rise up. They live. They move. And we experience what is termed the mass-thought vibration. We don't have to experience the mass-thought vibration if we will make the daily effort, through the powers of concentration, to gain control over our mind. Until we awaken to the truth that freedom is the effect of the control of self, that self is the house in which all thought forms live, go out from our aura, and return like-kind to us, then we cannot gain control over them.

Many philosophies have taught that you have been given charge over all creation. Thought is creation. It is something that we create. Man *is* a law unto himself. We must be honest with our self and ask our self what we are doing with the law that we are. Life indeed demonstrates that it is ever the way we make it; it is always the way that we take it. We are never left without the divine right, the right of the Divinity, the divine right of choice. But choice is not something that we think about when we're in the depths of disaster. Choice is something we think about moment by moment. If we are not aware of the thoughts in our mind, then we are far from self-control and, yea, even farther from truth and freedom.

We spend our lives, usually, most of us, in a realm of distraction. It is rare that we pause and become aware of the thoughts in our mind. It is rare that we awaken in the morning and place our house, our world in order before confusion sets in. We spend much of our time in what is termed indecision. But when you understand what indecision is, you will no longer ever again be indecisive. A house divided cannot stand. And when the thought forms within the human consciousness battle for supremacy and survival, then man indeed has lost control. 'Tis better to make a seeming poor decision than to live in indecision, for you have taken control and have a right to the experience yet to come.

The minds of men are controlled by what they call fear. The device used by thought forms is what you experience as fear. No one has to live that way. That is an error that we have made along the path of evolution. By over-identifying with a mental world we have become the victims of a mental world. Yet a mental world, its survival, is dependent upon a spiritual essence, a divine principle. And whoever moves beyond form, moves from personality to principle. And a principle of the law is what a wise man will apply in all his thoughts, acts, and activities. I do hope that's helped with your question.

The lady here, please.

Could you speak on the connection between fear and judgments?

Yes, thank you very much. The lady has asked, Could we speak a moment on the connection, if any, between fear and judgment? When you understand that there are these multitudes of forms that are living on the energy that flows through your being—for example, take a person whose mind is filled and cluttered with a multitude of thoughts. Slowly but surely, they become aware of how exhausted they are. Think about your problem for a week and don't stop, and you'll truly see how exhausted you will become, emotionally, and your vitality will be at its lowest ebb.

The connection, if any, between fear and judgment. Now say that you have an army over here in the consciousness and another army over here. And you have made a choice and that army of thought forms, they look at the choice you have made. They're an inseparable part of your mind. And they make their decision that if you go by the choice you have made, they will lose such a percentage of energy flowing through the being; and some of them will die, for there will not be enough energy for them to survive. They rise up within the depths of your being and they prompt you to make a judgment in keeping with their own selfish interests of survival. They know they do not have life eternal, for they know your mind. And they know, beyond a shadow of any doubt, that that is eternal has no beginning or ending. And they know they had birth; they had beginning and therefore they have ending. So they rise up and prompt you to make a judgment. If you go contrary to that judgment, their final and greatest defense for their survival is what you call fear. If you do not react and respond to the fear flowing through your being, then you have freed yourself and no longer are the servant of creation.

The law teaches clearly that creation is a tool designed to serve the eternal being. And when the tool (the mind) no longer serves the worker (the soul) then the worker begins to serve the tool. Now we are all intelligent people. None of us like the thought, the possibility of serving some mechanical, computerized robot in the factories of our country. None of us like the thought of that possibility. None of us like to play chess with some computerized robot that can demonstrate a greater degree of intelligence than our self; yet, we know it is only a machine that man has created. These are the manifestations, in a physical world, of what has been going on, is going on, continues to go on in our mental world. We do not like to think that we are serving something that we created years ago that is no longer beneficial to us. We don't like that thought. Yet, our lives repeatedly reveal that that is what we are doing.

How many people are married and divorced and continue to live with their husband who is long gone and married to someone else and vice versa? How many of us continue to live back in the thirties of the so-called depression? You see, my friends, here in this day and age of 1982 we permit our minds to think of what it was in '32 and '33 and '34 and earlier. Why do we do that? We do not consciously, consciously want to make that choice, yet we find that happening to us. Think how that works. Like attracts like and becomes the Law of Attachment. We have an experience contrary to the way things have been. Something rises within us and we make a judgment. Little do we realize that that judgment is the expression of forms that have been sleeping for a long time. They have awakened and they realize how hungry they are. Having napped for so long, they're hungry when they awaken. They haven't eaten for a long time. So they rise up; you experience a judgment and you begin to serve them. And if you don't serve them and they don't eat, you experience what you call fear. Think, my friends, is that freedom? Surely it cannot be. For he who is a victim to what has been, certainly is not demonstrating the principle of freedom. He who fears what is to be, certainly is not demonstrating the principle of freedom.

Only when our attention is placed upon the eternal moment of now can we be freed, only then can we perceive truth. To look at what has been from a realm of objectivity can serve its purpose without entrapment. To look at what is to be from a realm of objectivity—that means no emotional attachment, no magnetic field operating in consciousness, to look with the pure light of reason from an electrical field of consciousness—can be beneficial. But when a person looks to the future and experiences fear, he is serving that which has been. When a person looks to the past and experiences fear, he is serving that shadow that has gone.

And so judgment, a tool of the mental world, fear, its final, final defense, is something we are all striving in our way to be freed from. But we cannot be free until we stand guardian at the portal of our thought, that we are aware of the forms that enter and send them back to the nap that they should be in. Remember, once a thought is recorded in consciousness, it exists in the memory par excellence. It sleeps only to be reawakened and it's reawakened, unfortunately, through the Law of Association.

We walk down the street: we see something with our eyes; we hear something with our ears. Our senses react and we do not trace that feeling, that experience ever inward on the inward journey to see what is happening. Why do we feel this way? Why do we have this compulsion to do these things? Why do we react the way we do? Because there are things out of our past that are controlling us because we have not made the effort to control them.

Whenever we permit our mind to go backwards, then we must accept the demonstrable truth that we are not only serving what has been but we are establishing new laws based upon what has been to repeat the same, identical experience in principle.

It is stated in this philosophy that repetition is the law through which change is made possible. And so it is. To introduce change into the human consciousness, it takes a phenomenal amount of directed energy. Because you must create new forms, and the birth of those new forms must battle for their energy against forms that are very mature, very strong, and very adult. And so, for us, until we awaken within, it is very difficult; we have made it difficult to experience new horizons. Yet, in spite of the difficulty, in spite of the struggle, we are evolving.

But the divine plan is not evolution through disaster and through discord. The divine plan is evolution through the divine principle of harmony and beauty. Change and new horizons can be, for us, that way when we make the daily effort on the inward journey to awaken. And the first step in flowing in the divine principle of harmony and beauty through evolution, the very first step is the acceptance of the demonstrable Law of Personal Responsibility: the ability to respond to all experiences in our life. The ability to respond personally—that means personally! Going inward to find the cause and, in so finding it, establish a new law for new experiences, for greater good, for greater abundance.

But we listen to the news and we read the papers and unfortunately—and whether we like it or not, it's from sheer laziness—we accept so much of what is said. We accept it because we don't want to make the effort to research and investigate it to see if it's true. News is not interested in truth. That's contrary to its purpose. News is interested in facts. It has no interest, nor concern, with truth, only with facts. But what are facts? The effect of someone or many people's judgments. That's what facts are. And what is a fact to one is certainly not a fact to another. A fact is totally dependent upon our judgment. And if we believe in our judgments and that such and such is a fact, we make great effort to make sure that all our friends agree that that is a fact. And the reason that we make such great effort to get all our friends and acquaintances to agree that what we say is a fact is because something within us knows that truth is not a fact [and] has nothing to do with facts. And we feel that insecurity in our self. And as I have often said, may God ever save me from the reformers, for reformers have their facts. They know what's best for themselves. It's too bad they're not strong enough spiritually to keep it to themselves and not try to reform the rest of us.

Thank you kindly.

SEPTEMBER 5, 1982

Church Questions and Answers 30

[The audio recording of this spiritual awareness class begins after Mr. Goodwin had started his lecture.]—person in life, one sees things one way and someone else sees the same thing some other way. So it only reveals to us that we see in keeping with the censorship of our mind, in keeping to what we judge or judge not and, of course, in keeping with our own limits and our own degrees of intolerance. Now as we view, hopefully, objectively with what has been, we see that we're certainly eating more than potatoes and beans for a change, that things aren't perhaps what they were three years ago, but they're better than they were thirty years ago. And if we don't think so, sometimes we get into those realms of limited viewing and we sigh for the good old days. Well, I've always said to my students, "If the days of old were so good, how come you ever left them in consciousness?"

Now we all know that with every seeming good in a world of creation there is the opposite. So it behooves us to look at everything more carefully, and in so doing we can see the good in everything. But that, I admit, takes a little bit of effort to see the good in all experience. But if we understand that good is God and we understand that God is an infinite intelligence ever present, never absent or away, and is the very principle of what we call life, no matter what form the life may take, then we cannot help but see that God (good) is in everything. And if we have sufficient patience and if we're willing to make enough effort, sooner or later, regardless what we may think about the experience that we are having, sooner or later we can find the good, that is the principle of its life, that brought it into being.

So often in life we are deluded by the form, the personality, which is the form of anything, and it's difficult for us to see the principle that sustains it. Now, of course, if we all saw the principle of everything, if we all did that, which means we would first do it to our self, because we cannot offer to others what we have not first offered to our self, then I don't think we would long be in a world of creation whose law reveals duality or opposite. So let us make the best of what we have and, in so doing, have even more of the best.

And if the best is a new dress or a new suit, then let it be. I've always tried to encourage people who make the effort to work for a living. I'm still working on my tolerance for those who choose not to work for a living. But I do try to make some effort to encourage a person to declare their divinity: that if getting a new pair of shoes is what helps you to feel good, then you must not permit your mind to make your God so small that your God would not permit you, after working so very hard in life, to have a new pair of shoes. After over forty-four years of this work, I have had the opportunity and many occasions to view some of my clients and friends go over to the other side of life. And one of the greatest difficulties that people have when they leave this mundane, physical, material world is the regret that they denied themselves the goodness in life that they desired because they would not permit themselves to have the good things of life.

There is nothing wrong with a physical, material world. If there's anything wrong, it's how we think about it. When we permit in our thinking that it is the most important thing, that it is the highest on our priority, then we lose sight of eternal life. We lose sight of the peace that passeth all understanding. We lose sight and contact with the very Power that sustains us. That's the only error. And if there's any wrong, that is the only wrong.

Why we do not experience more good in our life is because we won't permit more good to enter. And the reason we don't permit more good to enter is because we permit our mind to dictate how it's going to get in. And so, we are the obstruction:

our mind, in its error. Our cup overfloweth because we won't let it flow through us.

Here we are, a principle in a stream of consciousness. We cannot block the flow because we are not greater than that which sustains us. And yet, in our error we constantly make effort, great effort, to block the flow. We want it to come into our life and we have a terrible time letting it go. So our cup is overflowing and no more can come in. If you have a house filled with furniture and you keep filling it and filling it and filling it, you have a choice. Expand the house, broaden its horizon, [and] let more furniture in. And then you continue to pour more in, and the day comes you have to let something go, if you continue to desire something else to come. But fear, the great crown and king of the mental world, it does not allow it to go. It seeks forever for it to come but will not allow what is there, in our home, to go. It fears because it knows (our mind) that it is limited. It is not the Power itself. Our mind knows that it is sustained by something that our mind cannot control. And so, when we think of self, our mind, our fear, becomes the captain of our ship and the master of our destiny. It won't let go and, therefore, is ever in want and ever in need.

Our soul knows better, for our soul is inseparable from the Divine Principle, the Oversoul. It has no fear. It knows that, moment by moment, it is being sustained by a power greater than the thought of man. Therefore, it has no fear; it knows that the moment of our awareness is our eternity. Yesterday is not our eternity. Tomorrow cannot be our eternity. Only the moment of our conscious awareness is our eternity. And so it is when we take control of our mind and we keep it into the conscious moment of now, we enter the realms of eternity; we enter the realms of possibility. We're freed from limit. We are freed from lack. We are freed from the shadows of yesterday and what it had to offer us.

Our own president of our country has made it clear, and how true it is. It is fear that is putting the brakes on what you call financial recovery. But even in spite of the fear, it is happening. It's not happening as quickly as it would have happened or will happen when the fears go. Because, my friends, you multiply one person by millions and you take a look at what the mind offers. And it thinks, even though it was not in physical form on earth at that time, it thinks of the thirties. It thinks of those years. It's heard about them. Millions experienced them. And so when we enter the mental realm, we enter those fears that we're going to be without, and we establish the law not only for our self but we become instruments to establish it for an entire country, and then a country for a world.

We do not consciously desire to live that way. But we do that to our self and to others. And the only reason that we do it is because we are controlled by what has been and not by what is. The human mind, the great computer, relates to its experiences, to others' experiences that it has accepted as true, as fact.

We do not move ahead, we do not evolve until we let go of what has been in consciousness and accept the possibility of something that we desire to be. As we place our attention, our energy, on what we want to become and we diligently, religiously take our attention, our energy, off of what we want to overcome, we soon experience what we chose to become. For he who sees the obstruction is the creator of the obstruction.

We can only see what we alone, in a mental world, create. We think we see what others have created because we do not understand that everything exists within. We view it and *think* that it is outside. It never was outside. It never will be outside. It is all taking place within the limits and the restrictions of our mental world. It isn't what someone else does to us; it is what we *think* they do to us, based upon our own limited, personal experiences.

Because it is demonstrably true that all experience, all thought exists within our consciousness, that because it is our consciousness, we have the right to do something about the thought that exists within our realm of control. Then it's up to us to make the conscious choice to do something—whatever we choose to do—about our thought. It is not important what our thought is concerned with. It is important what our thought does to us. So if you find that your thought is bringing you feelings that you do not like, if you find that your thought is bringing you experiences which you judge to be disastrous, then only you can make that change in your consciousness. If your mind, from its past experiences, has set up restrictions and limits, that it is necessary for someone else to do such and such, and such and such for you to feel better, for you to have more, then you have established that law for yourself; as man is a law unto himself and you must pay the price of that law that you have established, for that's the only way *you* have chosen to allow what you desire into your life.

So if we go out into the world and we're seeking ever a better employer, one that treats us better, a better wife, a better husband, one that will do more what we tell them to do when we want it done, and a better this and a better that, the place to start is on better thought with better understanding, with less need to control outside until more effort's made to control inside. Why spend so much of our life, why spend so much of our energy looking all over the world for something better when it's not there, unless we're willing to let the something better come up here?

Everything starts at home—and you can call the mind whatever you want—but most of us, most of the time believe we are the mind. We don't like to believe it, but when we think we're feeling terrible, we believe we are feeling terrible. If you tell a person that's feeling bad, "That's only your thought. Have a new thought and you will feel better," well, if they get a chance, they'll probably kill you. *[Many in the congregation laugh.]*

You see, it's not so easy to change our thought. And why isn't it easy to change our thought? The number one error: we believe the thought is us. But we've already lived so much of our life knowing, "These thoughts couldn't possibly be me. Well, if they are, they should send me up to one of those places to take care of me. I couldn't possibly be this kind of a person. Changing every time I turn around. Never knowing what I want or I don't want. And if I think I do know what I want, it's changing moment by moment, week by week, day by day." When we're honest enough with our self, we very quickly see that it's really a delusion to believe that we are the thought that's passing through our mind. Because most of the thoughts that pass through our mind, if we're honest with our self, we would not permit our self to be so embarrassed to admit that they're ours, let alone that they are us. So we know very well, first off, we are not the thought.

And when we know we are not the thought and when we understand how thoughts rise in consciousness, then we start to gain control over our thoughts. We become consciously, moment by moment, aware and we choose thoughts and we see that they are the seeds establishing the law unto our self. And we take a look at them and then we watch them go out into the universe. And we take a look and we see what they bring us back. Then we start choosing thoughts, thought patterns, attitudes of mind, rates of vibration that bring us back the good that we all seek in life. And when any of those other thoughts rise up, we have enough value for the good in life that we are experiencing, well, at least a little of it, that we move those out of consciousness immediately!

No one wants to be sick. No one wants to be hungry. No one wants to be deprived of the goodness of life. Because feeling good is indispensable, an inseparable part of the principle of life.

For good is God. And if you are out of goodness, of course, we understand we're out of the God within our self. And the work of this church, one of its many jobs in this life, is to help us to see how we get back on the track to get the goodness flowing again.

Now if I listen to all my students, then I would say to myself, "I'm not too good a person, because I'm not able to please them all the time." Why, if I listened to all of my members, I could just feel totally rejected and be in the depths of self-pity. Because, you see, my friends, when you do what you know is right for you to do, then you must be willing to accept that not all people at all times are going to agree with you. Now if you spend your life working to please people, to tell them what they want to hear when they want to hear it, you're on a terrible roller coaster ride because you will never please them all the time. And you will live to see the day [when] they have, of course, no respect for you. Why should they? You don't even have enough respect for yourself to declare your right to do what you know is right for you to do. So don't live, my friends, to please someone else, because by so doing you sacrifice pleasing the true you, the God, the goodness within you.

People will like you or they won't. But why should that be such a priority to you? If you are doing what is right for you to do, someone, somewhere desires it. You don't have to worry about people. You don't have to worry if they're going to be or not going to be. All we have to do is take care of our self because the law is very clear: we can only grant to another what we first grant to our self. So if we grant unto our self caring for the good that is within us, why, that's all we can grant to anyone else. So why should we be concerned about anyone else? We already know what we're granting to them by knowing what we're granting to our self. Then we won't have to look to someone else to bring us goodness, because we're already making the effort and experiencing the goodness that is within us.

If we cannot in life find the goodness that is within us and we are dependent forever looking to find it through someone else, then we are forever the slave of so-called circumstances. We're the victims. We are the puppets. Surely none of us really want to live that way when there's such a better way to live.

I didn't intend to give a speech, although I didn't speak that long. So now is the time in keeping with our regular tradition, here, over these past years of giving you the opportunity to raise your hand if there are any questions that you have. *[After a short pause, the teacher continues.]* If not, of course, I don't have to work anymore—oh, there's a—yes, please, the gentleman there.

Could you describe the process of what we get out of arguing?

Well, many people—in reference to the process of what we get out of arguing, we get something out of everything that we permit ourselves to experience in consciousness, even the common cold. We get something. The human mind is not a mind that is wasteful unto itself. It is a mind that gathers and garners everything it can get, including the common cold. Now, dependent on a person's, of course, personal experiences, dependent upon their own limits and judgments of what they got out of arguing when they were very small, that is instrumental, of course, what they get out of arguing when they get bigger and they get older.

A person who becomes emotional in any experience is revealing unto themselves, though they may not be aware of it yet, and to all those around and about them, they are revealing the little child within. Now this little child, this little kid that did what it did when it was three, four, five, when it did what it did even when it was two months old—so few of us are yet ready to see that the human mind and all of its emotions are acting and reacting before birth, all during this nine-month time. And so, of course, all children are marked unto the third generation, as even the Bible teaches us.

We get out of arguing—of course, we get attention. Would you not agree? It may be negative, but we do get it. The law demonstrates to all of us that energy follows attention. Now say, for example, [when] we were little children, we felt like we needed some energy. We very quickly learned how to get it. Ofttimes a baby knows how to get energy, even though you just gave the baby its bottle. It does what has to be done to get energy, which flows through attention. Now we grow up and ofttimes we have a need for energy because we're grounded out. Self-thought grounds out our universe electromagnetically. And we find this *[The teacher sighs dramatically.]* depletion of energy. Now energy we must be receptive to or we do not exist on this planet. And so, if our mind, we have programmed it to get the attention, the energy which follows it, through the means of arguing, we will argue and argue until we have our fill.

Ofttimes little children will burn houses down that they may have the energy that they feel that they need. It is not something that I or this philosophy recommends, of course, *[Some in the congregation laugh.]* but we see these things happening all of the time. And yet, we say, well, we're adults [and] we wouldn't do such stupid things. Well, we may not burn the houses down, but we burn down a lot of other things, thoughts and things, and feelings to get the energy, the pure, unadulterated energy, the goodness, that feeling, inside of our self.

If you understand the need of a person, if you understand their need to be contrary, if you understand their need for energy, though it expresses through the vehicle known as arguing, through the vehicle known as emotional upheaval (if they don't have their way), if you understand that, you will, slowly but surely, start to awaken your soul faculty of tolerance, duty, and compassion, begin to understand that what is being expressed lies, potentially, within your own consciousness, and only by the laws you alone have established, it does not express its need in that way. [Does] that help with your question?

Yes.

You're welcome. The gentleman in the back, please.

Yes, I would like you to really explain to us what it is that makes us seemingly sleepy and bored during times like this.

Yes, it's an excellent question. *[Many in the congregation laugh.]* And most all churches have some kind of a stick or something to tap the people awake. This is one of the rare churches that doesn't go to those extreme measures. I have other measures: I take care of them privately. Why do people during these times—you mean church service, I'm sure.

Yes, sir.

Especially while I'm giving a lecture or something. Yes, I understand. A little bit of water here. *[A great many in the congregation laugh.]* Being human, I like to clear my thought. I wouldn't want you to think I had any resentment to your question about sleeping while I'm trying to work. *[And still more in the congregation laugh.]*

Well, of course, we understand we get bored. I mean, I used to get bored myself if the lecture went too long, but I haven't even been twenty minutes. So I don't really think it's quite fair to go to sleep so early.

However, when we become aware that there are in truth, demonstrably, eighty-one levels of consciousness and that some of these levels that we permit our self to get into in consciousness do not appreciate hearing anything that will be instrumental in them making changes, there's many things that these levels do to us. That doesn't mean we're not responsible for them, because we're the ones that created them. One of those many things, if we don't want to hear something because we don't want to make any changes and we don't want to feel guilty about not making the changes we know we should be making, is to get a little bored. And once you feel yourself getting a little bored (that you've heard the story before), the next step is to get a little sleepy. And the next thing, you go to sleep completely. I'm glad my workers are awake, this time.

So if we understand that, it doesn't mean that we work and let the people around us snooze because they're in levels that are not in harmony with what is going on around and about them. It's like children being forced to come to church. That's why I'm so grateful for this little church. It's very little. It's very small. You saw the members, at least some of them that were here. Because we don't have that policy: that you must go to church. Because I wouldn't want to spend my time and effort with people who sit and feel, "Oh God, another Sunday! I have to go to church again!" Because that's a bummer vibration. Why should I expose myself to that stuff? *[Many in the congregation laugh.]* I do understand that some of the men in the congregation, and some of the ladies, they either go to church or they never hear the end of it from the lady or the man. But see, that's a very personal thing and I try not to involve myself in that, until they involve my church in that, and then there's a different situation.

But I do hope that that's helped with your question. Certain levels that we permit our self to get into through self-thought—now remember, friends, we cannot enter those levels that control us from past experiences without the thought of I. There is no way possible you can enter the control of past experiences (to control your life in this moment) without the thought of I. Not the I that you are, but the thought of the I that you have formed. And that's the only way we can enter disasters or any experiences that are gone, you see? Does that help with your question?

Yes, sir.

If not, I could be more specific, but I don't think this is the time or place. Yes, the lady here, please.

Can you please explain how it works, that unto the third-generation phrase?

Well, of course, you understand that three is the demonstrable Law of Manifestation; that it takes the divine Law of Creation and it takes, for conception of any form, it takes that trinity. Without that trinity, there is no manifestation, there is no experience.

Most people think, "I had one thought." Well, that was the manifestation of two opposite poles of consciousness, the electric and the magnetic, that come together and you experience the form of what you call "thought." Now people say, "Well, I thought about going to the store." Well, that's a form. You see, you created that. Now say, for example, you thought about driving your car. Well, when you think about driving your car, what rises in consciousness—that most people do not see and it comes right out in front of you—what rises in consciousness is the form of the car. The one you have. The one you had. The one you lost. The one you want. And the one you're going to get and on down the list. They all exist the moment you permit your mind to think "car." All of those things rise up.

Now, what is so important about that is not just the forms rise up, but those are the seeds that go out into the universe— that like attracts like and becomes the Law of Attachment—and return unto you as an experience. So when you think a thought, you are opening up the door to all that has been in form, all experience associated with it; and all of those laws, they go out and they return unto you. So, you see, my friends, it is so important.

What benefit is it to talk to a mental world so much about soul and spiritual and hereafter, until we understand a little more about the world that we're identified most all of the time with? If we understand the world that we're all familiar with, believe me, we won't have too much of a problem accepting the possibility of a world that most of us know little or anything about.

It is the form that the thought creates, associated with all the forms that have been and all the experiences that have been—for example, say that you want to go out and buy a new coat. Well, what happens when you have the thought of buying a new coat? The form rises up of every coat you ever bought, of every coat you ever desired, of every coat that someone else had that you liked or disliked, and all of those things rise up into consciousness and are the seeds to establish the law.

And this is why a wise man, gaining control over his mind, speaks his word forth into the universe knowing that it shall not come back to him void, but accomplish that which he sends it to do. Our word returns to us void because the energy necessary to bring it back fulfilled is dissipated to give energy to the forms of the dead in consciousness that rise up from past experience. When we understand that, my friends, when we apply that law, we will speak our word and we will know the word is God. And we won't have to wonder which word it is because it is the word.

Thank you very much.

OCTOBER 3, 1982

Church Questions and Answers 31

As our chairman has stated, this is the one time a month in which we have our question-and-answer period.

And before getting into that, I would like to share with you, for a few moments, the way of taking good from all experience. For there is no experience in our life that good is not lying within. For either we believe in a divine, impartial, neutral, intelligent Energy, called God, or we believe in the old God of duality, of good and bad, the God of creation. Over these many years I have listened to some people (some of my students) share with me how grateful that I should be—not that I am not, I hope—how grateful I should be that I don't have the struggles of the human frailties to work through, considering that I was so fortunate to be the son of a medium and to have grown up in a spiritual atmosphere. And I have often thought of that and considered my other seven brothers and sisters.

And so, how fortunate we are when it comes time for us to share our understanding to merit whatever experiences are necessary for us to gain the understanding before sharing it. And so to demonstrate once again to myself and to those around and about me, I managed to demonstrate, a short time ago, what one surely would consider a human frailty. I think we all will agree that stupidity is a human frailty. Certainly, it is not a divine attribute. And so I walked from the car to the door and walked into the gun that's outside. *[Devotional services were held at the American Legion log cabin in San Anselmo, California, outside of which were two howitzers.]* I don't need you to believe it. All I need is for you to have eyes to see. *[Mr. Goodwin's encounter with the howitzer resulted in a noticeable injury to the side of his nose, but he declined to have a Band-Aid applied.]*

So we all have what we consider a self-conscious, that is, a conscious awareness of self. And we all have the feelings that that grants unto us. So we have our choices: we can try to cover up the damage or we can live with it knowing that it is in the process of being healed.

Surely, no one would think that I consciously chose to bang up my nose in order to share some understanding with you. But it does reveal that it, indeed, pays to look up or at least straight ahead. I happened to have been looking down for other reasons, which I am well aware of.

Now what is the good, of course, in such a simple experience? Not just the awareness of one's own self-consciousness, which we understand to be the ego, our ego, clothed in the garment of pride and crowned with the crown of self-pity. We all have had our experiences and know where the pity of self takes us in life. It certainly doesn't bring us the good that we seek. But let us pause in these many experiences we encounter in life and let us look for the good that is there. As I have said, I've tried to tell some of my students, especially the ones who are constantly looking down, to look up. Well, I think it would be much better to look straight ahead. Because, after all, we can walk into a gun or anything else looking up just as well as we can looking down. So it does seem that, after all these years, looking straight ahead, at least in my present state of evolution, would be the wisest thing to do.

Now we read the papers, we listen to the telecast, and we hear the radio. And so often we find our self in harmony and in rapport with the constant fears and the constant, negative projections that seem to be around and about us. Many things seem to be around and about us. We don't have to be a part of them because they're in the world in which we live. We can only be a part of them when we make that world our world. We just sang one of the finest hymns that I have ever heard: "Destiny at My Command." It is so clear and so definite in its explanation of who destiny, our destiny, belongs to. If we still believe that we are subject to and, therefore, the victim of any force or any power that is beyond our own conscious control, then we will constantly be the victim of circumstances, not the captain of the ship and not the master of our destiny. When we understand what thought is and what it does to our world, when we make the effort to understand what it is and what it does, then we will have qualified our self to slowly, but surely, consciously gain control over the thoughts, the feelings, the vibrations, and the attitudes in which we choose to live.

None of us, I'm sure, feel that we are perfect. Some of us, I am sure, feel that we are very close to it in certain areas of our life. And I'm sure many of the ladies present would agree that they have met those type of people. Close to something is not the something. It is a miss by a mile as well as a miss by a hundred miles.

But what we are trying to find in this life in which we have found our self is the way to live with it harmoniously, to experience the good that is really in everything that we encounter. We must realize, sooner or later, the only good we're ever going to find is the good we consciously choose in our own consciousness. We look out and see many things. We look out and have many experiences. How often in the experience do we pause to find the good that it has to offer us?

If we speak to someone and they disagree with us, we speak to someone and they argue with us or attempt to do so, we speak to someone and they do not react the way we think that they should react, where is this experience taking place? It is taking place within our own mind. We know that it's our mind. We're having the feelings and the experience. It's not someone else's mind. It's our mind. We can do something with that mind that is ours. We can do nothing with that mind that is someone else's. Someday, some moment they may choose to make a change. We may or may not be instrumental at the moment they choose to make that change. But we are not doing it for them. That is contrary to the demonstrable Law of Personal Responsibility.

What we do is for our self. Now we may think we are doing something for someone else. We may even have that motivation, but we must go beyond that. We are doing it for our self. For the law herself reveals that to all of us. Someone else may share in the harvest of the effort that we are making, but we consciously chose to do it. And we are doing it for that conscious choice that we alone have made in our life. We may feel that the conscious choice says we're doing it for this person or that person, we are doing it for God, we're doing it for nature, we're doing it for the animal kingdom, we're doing it for the trees, we're doing it for the government. That may well be what our minds are telling us, but we must be honest with our self and we must see that we and we alone have made the choice. And we made that choice based upon what we decided was in our own best interests for what we wanted to do.

A person gets married in life. They didn't marry the other person because the other person wanted them to marry them. They married them because that's what they wanted to do no matter what they tell themselves. Now if we understand and are honest with our self—that what we are doing *is* for our self and hopefully for what most people call the higher self, considering when we identify with a mental world, we identify with creation, and in identifying with creation, we experience the black and white, the day and night, the higher and the lower. But we can move from identification with a world of creation and, in so doing, move to a divine neutrality that just is. And that that just is, that which we truly are, has no motivation, for that which is, is. It has no need; therefore, there is nothing to move it.

We cannot believe in a God that is, in truth that is, and then dictate terms and conditions on how it is. For the moment that we attempt to define anything—truth, God, neutrality, intelligence, infinity, etc.—the moment that we attempt to define a thing is the moment that we bring it into a world of contradiction, a world of duality, a world of creation. And so that which is formless and free, in that moment for us, becomes form and limit.

And so now it is time for you to raise your hands, if you have any questions. The lady in the front row, please.

Thank you. Will you speak to us on guardian angels?

Thank you. The lady has asked that we might share a bit of understanding on guardian angels. I think, in discussing that subject, that we should ask our self the question, "What is it within us that needs guarding? What is it within us that needs to be guarded, to be protected? And from what?" I think in asking the question about guardian angels and what is it within us that needs to be guarded, to be protected, to be cared for, I am sure we would all agree it is that spiritual sensibility within us known as our conscience. That which knows and does not have to be told, that which needs no justification or defense, it's our conscience. It knows.

Some people, they say they hear a voice within them and it tells them what to do or what not to do, but it especially tells them what not to do. But let us stop and think. Is this the spiritual conscience within us or is this the educated conscience that we have formed and developed in keeping with society, in keeping with the dos and don'ts that we believe is right or wrong? Those questions we must ask our self. "Which is this voice within me that tells me to do or not to do and especially not to do? Is it my educated conscience? Is it the way I was taught to believe when I was a child? Is it the way my parents have believed before me and my forefathers before that? Or is it that still, small voice of my own spirit that knows beyond a shadow of any doubt what for me is the path to take?"

True, in keeping with the law that like attracts like and in keeping with teachings throughout the universe for ages untold, there is no soul on earth that does not have, at the moment it enters conception, its guardian angel to help it, to guide it, to inspire it. And I tell you, we are indeed fortunate for these angels who have been given charge over us, who must patiently, with great compassion and understanding, watch the multitude of times we insist on stumbling from our errors of ignorance: their struggle, from my view, is indeed the greatest. Thank you. I hope that's helped with your question.

The lady on the aisle, please.

Would you please speak on what some people call spiritual plants? And in particular, one gentleman said, "It's my way of finding God and I find people who oppose are in judgment."

Well, many people have found many different methods of finding their God. Now, I [would] like to clarify: each person that chooses to believe in God finds, usually, a God that is not opposed or obstructed by the judgments of the human mind. So often in life we pray to God and we wait and if our experiences reveal to our satisfaction that our prayers have been answered, that God in which we believe becomes stronger in our conscience. And more of our energy, by more of our attention, more of our faith is directed to that God.

There is the God that is formless and free, that is not dependent upon the faith and the belief of man. And then there is the god of the form that the human minds have made so. If a person finds their God in a plant, a tree, a flower, a cat, or a dog, that, of course, is the right of the individual. For we understand that God is good. And if one finds good for their life by believing in a rabbit's foot, who is so great in their judgments to deny the goodness to a soul who brings no harm to others? These are the questions we must ask our self. Do we have the right—does everyone have the right to find their God in their way in keeping with the demonstrable Law of Personal Responsibility? If so, then we have established the Law of Freedom for our right of belief.

In reference to what you are referring—"spiritual plants"—I have not heard it in those particular terms, but I find that there is no thing in all of the universes that is not spiritual.

For it is the intelligent, neutral Divine Energy that sustains all things. So where can we find something that is not sustained by this infinite, intelligent Energy?

What we find to be bad, for us, is ofttimes, for others, found to be good. Therefore, if each and every one of us demonstrate the ability to personally respond to all our experiences, to all our thoughts, acts, and deeds, then all souls shall live the freedom which is the right of their own divinity. I hope that's helped with your question.

The lady over here has been waiting. Yes, please.

Mr. Goodwin, recently I heard you say that someone had gone to spirit consciously. And I didn't quite understand that. I wish you would elaborate.

Thank you. When we leave this physical body, this physical world, usually what takes place is we consciously go to sleep and we are awakened in another dimension, which the Spiritualists call the spirit world. It is rare, indeed, that a soul is sufficiently awakened and in control to leave this physical world and be consciously aware of the process of passing from the physical body. As I say, the usual process is that we go to sleep and awaken over there.

Ofttimes in sudden, so-called sudden death, there is also a spontaneous, conscious awareness of the process. However, in those cases usually the astral and mental bodies remain at the scene of the so-called accident and, unless help is received rather quickly, experience the trap of what man calls earthbound spirits.

We all want to be prepared for the inevitable. We set aside, some of us, a few pennies to try to take care of that which is inevitable, and in this country it's taxes and death. None of us seem to escape that inevitability. We often work diligently to postpone it, but we do not escape it. And so, because no one amongst us knows the exact day, hour, month, or year when they will face that inevitability of leaving this world, it does, indeed, behoove us to make a little effort, just a little bit of effort, to be prepared. To be prepared for that which is inevitable is not only wise—and even to the human mind, surely, is logical. And how does one prepare themselves for the things that are inevitable? By accepting that which is inevitable.

The struggle and the difficulty with so-called death or transition—it's not the process; that is not where the pain or suffering is. It is the refusal to accept the process. Because we do not work with our mind daily to view the inevitable with a different perspective—to study and to apply and to know beyond a shadow of any doubt our mind remains the same. Life has already taught us that. We've experienced many shocks and many disasters already. It didn't change us, our thinking, completely. Death, so-called, does not change our thinking. It does not change our interests. It does not change our desires. It does not change the things which we hold. The refusal to accept it is the mind that is holding to physical things of this planet. If we don't want to leave the person that we're with, then we must face what that offers us when we are forced to do so by what is called the inevitable transition from this life.

Is it not better and would it not behoove us to prepare our self by accepting the possibility that someday it's going to be and it might be this moment? When man accepts the possibility of the worst, then he is prepared to experience the best. Because he has already, in the process of accepting the possibility of the worst, he has already prepared himself and his mind to accept. And when we prepare our self to accept, when we are ready and we are willing to do that, then all the fears and all the pain and all of the struggle, it just disappears. And we find that it really wasn't so bad, this process of leaving this world. In fact, it was like putting on a new suit for a new day. In fact, it was a joyful experience. Because, my friends, when you have no fear, life, then, is beautiful. Whether it's the life that you are viewing through a physical form in a physical world or it is the life you view in a spiritual world through a spiritual form, it is beautiful when you no longer fear.

Hell is sustained by what man calls fear. Without fear, there is no pain. Without fear, there is no suffering. Without fear, there is no struggle. And without fear, there is no hell. So then, let us understand what fear is, if without it life is so wonderful. And I assure you it truly is. Fear is man's belief in the mental world. It never was anything else. So man must ask himself, "What is my mental world composed of? If the mental world is what fear is and if fear is what hell is and if fear is the obstruction to all the beauty and abundant good that is my divine right, let me understand the mental world which is fear." Our mental world is all of the experiences, all of the judgments, all of the rejections, all of the denials, and all the acceptances that we have already had. That is our mental world and that is our fear. That is our hell.

We look through the process of self-identification. We experience our mental world only when we entertain in our mental world the thought of I. Now the thought of I is a very clever and subtle thing. Ofttimes we are not aware that in our consciousness we are experiencing identification with the thought of I because it is so subtle, so habitual. We can enter the mental world, hell, fear, only when we think in our consciousness and, by thinking, identify with separation, which is the thought of I. The angel fell from grace the moment it thought of and identified with separation, the thought of I. For truth cannot be separated. God cannot be divided. And our division in our life (our house divided) only takes place when we permit our mind to identify with the delusion that is known as the thought of I. For it is that curtain, that separation from the divine Source that we are that is the hell that we experience, that is the pain, the suffering, and the struggle.

As we pause in our thinking this moment, and we claim to believe in a God that is, Truth that is. And to us God, therefore, is good. Therefore, that *which* we are—not which we *think* we are, but that which we are—is good, is abundant, is free, is limitless, is formless, is all of life.

Man looks out from the thought of I and sees division and destruction. Man looks from the thought of I and experiences comparison. Without comparison, there cannot be the functions of jealousy, there cannot be the functions of envy, there cannot be the functions of greed. But comparison is a function born from separation, the thought of I. The I which we are is whole and complete. And because it is whole and complete, it cannot experience want and need, for that which is, is! There is nothing to want. How can there be when you identify with your true being?

As long as we insist on identifying with the gods of clay feet, with the god of form, with the gods created by the mental consciousness, then we must plead and cry for the fulfillment and the satisfaction of our desires. For it is our error, for it is our division. It is our ignorance that we pay so dearly for. Why choose to live in separation, when it is so painful, when it is such a struggle? But that, my friends, is what denial offers us. For when we choose to live in separation from the Source of which we are an inseparable part, when we make that choice we establish the Law of Denial. And the result of denial is our destiny. So in that respect, indeed, we are the captain of our ship and the master of our destiny.

But through an error in our consciousness we have not chosen, yet, the way, the path of freedom. We can do that this moment if we choose to. But a wise person, in freeing themselves from bondage, does not choose the most difficult way, but chooses the simple and the small way, for it is the small things in life that bring to us the opportunities of growth.

So we look at our life and we see what we are willing to no longer identify with in the feeling of personal possession. And I'm speaking of the greatest of all possessions; the things we hold more dearly than precious jewels: the thoughts of our mind. Which thought are we willing to give up? Are we willing to give up the thought of eating a certain way? Of brushing our teeth a certain way? Of dressing a certain way? Which thought do we not have so precious in our mind that we're willing to give? For those are the ones to work on, to slowly but surely free our self from the bondage of a lifetime. If we're willing to do that and we're willing to make that effort each day and every day, sooner or later we cannot help but see the transformation take place in our life.

Many years ago I gave to my students a little exercise to help them grow and expand in understanding. Surely, we will all agree, without tolerance there is little, if any, understanding. Can man understand what he cannot tolerate? So if we are truly seeking to expand in understanding, then let us look around—and we won't have to look far—for someone that has or says something that we cannot tolerate. Then that, the stone we have rejected, is our golden opportunity. We take a good look at what it is we see them express that we cannot tolerate. And because we are the ones who cannot tolerate it, we are the ones lacking in understanding. Therefore, we are seeking to grow and expand in understanding.

It is our thought in our mind that we call intolerance. And because it is our thought in our mind that we cannot tolerate, we say that person is intolerable to us. It is our thought of what that person does that is intolerable to us. It is not that person. It is our thought of that person. And that thought of that person was given birth in our consciousness in our days and years of ignorance. We are the ones who suffer from our thought that we cannot tolerate, for that is the truth of the matter. It is not the person out there; it is our thought of the person out there that we, in our own mind, cannot tolerate. So we are the ones who suffer, we are the ones who struggle, and we are the ones with war instead of peace in our emotional being. The person that we think we cannot tolerate, they're having no problem at all, which only proves to us it has always been our thought that we cannot tolerate. Think, my friends, we are our own worst enemies. We can be our own best friends.

Thank you.

DECEMBER 5, 1982

Church Questions and Answers 32

This morning, with your questions and answers, I would like to take just a few moments to speak on that which has been, these past few years, of great concern, of course, to all of us.

So many changes have taken place within our country, so many new avenues of expression and endeavor by our government; in keeping with the Law of Abuse, we all have, to some degree, of course, been affected. I wish to take these moments to once again encourage all of us to the demonstrable truth that the economy of the United States of America is not only turning around in this year of '83 but we will all benefit. We will realize the benefit of the struggle when we are freed from it.

Nature teaches us the demonstrable Law of Balance. But ofttimes we do not relate that balance is the effect of poles of opposites, known as creation. And so it is when we go to look at our budgets in life, we ofttimes see, at the expense of the other pole, we ofttimes see only one end of that scale. And now in this year of 1983, if we will open our eyes more than we have in the past, we will see that balance (our budgets in life), be they money or health or whatever our interests and choice, will [then], through the light of reason, once again, harmony, wealth, health, and happiness will flow. They flow through the natural Law of Balance. The tree sheds its leaves to nourish the soil from whence its roots benefit, to continue to go through its cycle.

We are, when identified with form, it is then that we experience the flux and flow, the tides of creation. And because most of our earthly life is identified with form, creation, we are constantly affected by the rise and fall, the Law of Duality, the demonstrable truth of creation.

Our teaching has always been to separate truth from creation. Our teaching has always been to be in creation—that we are well aware of—but never to be a part of it; to be with a person, place, or thing, but not to be a part of a person, place, or thing. What does that mean? To be in a world of creation and not to be affected by it is to awaken ourselves, our consciousness, to understand beyond a shadow of any doubt that creation (the body, the tree, and all the forms we see) are vehicles through which we, the eternal being, are temporarily expressing our self. When we awaken to that great truth, we will then, indeed, be the instruments through which balance may be restored in our life. And in keeping with the law that like attracts like and becomes the Law of Attachment, we will demonstrate what we know as personal responsibility: the ability to personally respond to all of our experiences and reap the great harvest, the effect of personal responsibility, which we know, in truth, is our freedom.

Let us not deny creation. Let us not deny our responsibility to it. But let us no longer be deluded and deceived to think that it is us. Who would enter his automobile and believe that the vehicle, which we are driving, has the right to tell the driver where it's going, when it's going, and whether or not it is going at all? The automobile, a vehicle of form, of creation, has been designed by man to be a servant through which man may fulfill some or many of his personal desires. Shall we permit the hand to tell the head it does not care to move? Shall we permit the foot not to do as we have the right to tell it to do. Let us think and think more deeply, for in so doing not only do we awaken within our consciousness the fullness of responsibility but we enter the consciousness of the formless and free which we are. And in so doing that which serves the Light becomes the Light.

As water cannot pass through a pipe without depositing the varied minerals that it contains, so the formless, free Spirit, that which we are, cannot express through form, our body, without a deposit of its vibration and in so doing and in so making that deposit is our body, our form, and all form, evolved.

We have not come to earth to be the victim of that which is temporal. We have come to earth to understand and to demonstrate the Infinite Intelligence that is, has always been, shall always be. It has revealed unto us for centuries, all creation, you have charge over. But he who does not take charge over the creation which he lives in (our own form) does not qualify themselves in any way to take charge over the multitudes of form of creation.

Let us, in awakening within our consciousness the truth that is—that deep inside of us we all know, for we cannot help but know what we are. Let us awaken through pausing, through gaining control over the vehicle known as our human mind. Surely, we would not permit the vehicle (our automobile) to go at any speed that it chose to go at, to go in any direction that *it* chose to go, for to do so would be to tempt disaster. Let us use the tools as they have been designed to be used: as tools to serve us well. Let us free our self from the bondage of serving the tool, when, by the Divine Architect, the tool was designed to serve us.

And now, my friends, it's time for you to ask any question that you find of interest to you. And if you will be so kind as to raise your hand, I will get to as many questions as time will permit. The lady, here, in the front row, please.

Can you explain the meaning of kundalini that I've heard in the spiritual teachings?

Thank you. *Kundalini* is a term used in ancient teachings from the Far East, originally from ancient Egypt, before it was known as Egypt. It is, what is known, kundalini, as the prana or life force. It, of course, is within all form, for it is the force that sustains the form. It is not limited to the human form, nor is it limited to animal, fish, or fowl, for the tree releases its life force when the branch is cut; without the sap, we know it as death. And so it is with that particular word, known to the ancients and many, of course, of the present. But let us not permit, in our knowledge of its existence, [ourselves] to be so concerned with what it's doing, for nature and her demonstrable laws know best how to care for the form in which we temporarily reside. I do hope that's helped with your question.

Thank you.

Yes, the gentleman on the aisle, please.

I recently heard in the—from the news media that sports has become America's newest religion. I wonder if you'd define religion and how Spiritualism relates to that concept.

Thank you. It is, indeed, most interesting. And, yes, I have been aware of some people who believe that sport or sports has become the fad of the day.

Religion, its understanding in this philosophy, means that which binds—binds us to. Now let us pause in our mental activity and let us, hopefully, see clearly. That which we serve serves us. And so whether it's sport, a rabbit foot, or anything else, we reap the harvest from our efforts in keeping with the divine, demonstrable Law of Continuity. If man chooses to find his God (meaning goodness) his peace, his health, his wealth, and his happiness through a vehicle known as sport, that is not only the divine right of all souls but it is, to that man, of great benefit if he makes it so. Therefore, I see no difference in man finding a sport as his religion, as man finding a temple as his religion if in so finding that "binding to" benefits himself, for in so doing shall it benefit all those around and about him.

I know of no God, in Spiritualist terms, Infinite Intelligence, that dictates to man that we can receive the benefits from this divine Infinite Intelligence only if we do certain things. That is not a God that I have ever known of, nor is it a God that I could possibly believe in. For I understand the will of God to be total acceptance, for I look at all creation; I see the life. I see nothing is denied. Therefore, I could not possibly believe in a God that gives to one and takes from another. I could not possibly believe that the will of God would be limited in any way.

I know that many of us have limited how we will permit good to be experienced within our consciousness. We are the ones who suffer from that limit and censorship. Some of us must go to a baseball game to be uplifted and feel good. To another, they must go to an opera, a play, or something else to feel uplifted. There is nothing wrong in the going to that which we have a right of choice to go to. What is the struggle for us is that we have told the goodness, which is the Universal Intelligence, that we will experience that goodness, which we have a divine right to, only if we do certain things that the vehicle, known as our mind, has limited us to do in keeping with past errors, past experience, and the darkness of ignorance. It is the shadows of the past, of things that have been, that limit the God of our present moment.

When as children we had desire—and no form is free from desire, for desire is the divine expression—but in our evolution, little children on this planet Earth, we desired and were educated on how the desire that we had in our consciousness would be fulfilled. We have merited, in our evolution, the limits in which God can enter our consciousness, or good.

But let us never forget, we have eternity—and by *eternity* I mean the moment of which we are conscious: the conscious awareness of any moment is our eternity. So in our eternity is the possibility. In the present, this moment, is the power available to us not in our thought, in a vehicle of that which has gone, a shadow of what has been, but in the moment of which we are consciously aware. In that moment is the power of the universe available to us. Not in the moment yet to be. Not in the moment that has been. But in this, the moment eternity. We may choose in this moment, moment by moment, to permit, by identifying with the present, we can choose to no longer be controlled by the limits that we have set before us from past errors and ignorance. This is our right, the right, the divine right to all souls.

So when we look out in the world and we see a man experiences good or God in playing baseball, jogging, or any other sport, if it is good they experience, there is harm to no one. If it is not good, then there is harm to many. For man cannot experience good or God without being the living demonstration in that moment of personal responsibility. For when we begin to blame God for our struggle, we also blame God for what crumb of goodness we experience. Let's stop blaming God for the good that we may stop blaming God for the opposite. Let us accept personal responsibility and know beyond a shadow of any doubt that God or goodness is everywhere present and never absent or away, that we and we alone make the choice moment by moment.

But let us be aware of how we arrive at our choice. Is that choice in the light of reason, in the moment of eternity which we are? Or is that choice dependent upon what we think others will think? And we always think that way from past experience. When we are no longer concerned with what someone thinks, then we are no longer in the bondage of what has been. When we are no longer concerned with what someone else will do, we will begin to do what we know in our heart is right for us.

I have always found—it has been my experience in these forty-some years that one who is not secure in their belief works diligently to gather and to garner to convert someone else—the more the merrier for them—to believe the same way. It is our own insecurity that demands that upon us. It doesn't need to be that way. It does not need to be. When we know in our consciousness, we become secure and stable. It is one thing—and a personal responsibility of all souls who experience the goodness of life—to share when it is solicited by the Law of Presence those whom they love and care for by showing them where the river they have found flows. That's where it begins and that's where it should end. Beyond that point it is fruitless and a demonstration of weakness (the lack of security in one's convictions) to go any further.

For, my friends, if it is goodness that we have, then beyond a shadow of any doubt do we accept and respect the right of difference. Do we fully accept, as we view creation, God's beautiful diversity? Shall the rose be permitted in the garden to deny the daisy because it's not the same? Who can be so great to rise in judgment, the bondage of hell itself, to tell the humble daisy it has no right to life? My friends, when we do those things, we establish the Law of Denial; we become superior to the very Power that sustains us. And in so doing our denials become our destinies. It is only an error in our thinking that does such a foolish thing.

There is no law that says we have to, but let us remember and let us ask our self the question: man, we see, is a law unto himself, then let us think, "O God, what am I doing with the law that I am?" We cannot possibly, in the light of reason, deny that we are a law unto our self. Our life has already revealed that to us so many times. For to deny that truth is to cast that pearl of truth to the swine and pay the price thereof, for we no longer, in that type of thinking, accept personal responsibility.

So, my friends, let us be of good cheer. Let us accept God's will, the right of the power which sustains us, to sustain all life, to sustain all choice in keeping, of course, with personal responsibility.

Perhaps, with such great interest in sports as a new religion, perhaps—all things to God are possible—man will begin to accept, once again, that there *is* some Power, some Energy; that it is intelligent; that it is not partial; that it is good, if we permit it to be by not standing in its way; that it is everywhere. And that if it is a movie or a sport, a play or an opera through which the limit and error of our thinking will permit this great Power to flow through us in a conscious awareness of it—because it flows all the time, yet we consistently deny it. We deny it because it does not do what we want it to do when we want it to do it. Because you cannot tell that which sustains the thought that you don't want it around anymore and still have the thought.

So let us accept the divine right of all to find God in their way. And let us not tell our self that what they have found is not

God. If [with] our eyes we view that they are a better person, those around them are benefited and improved, they are not instruments through which others are hurt and destroyed, then it cannot help but be good.

If religion, as we commonly know it, and if the churches of our world had truly been about the business they're supposed to be about (showing people how to find God without telling them there's only one way) perhaps, then, we would not have merited sports being the new church, sports being the new religion.

I see only good in it. I see only good that can possibly come from any avenue through which man permits Infinite Intelligence to flow unobstructed, uplift his soul, and bring good to everyone around him. I do hope that's helped with your question.

We, perhaps, may have time for one more. The lady on the aisle, please.

Could you speak about the difference between the soul and the spirit?

Yes. Spirit—we don't mean spirits when we say Spirit. I do not mean spirits. I mean Spirit as formless and free. Now perhaps it's still on the back of your program; so many things go on, I can't recall. "I am Spirit, formless and free; whatever I think that will I be." We are formless, free Spirit. To have the awareness that we are formless, free Spirit requires the Law of Identity. The Law of Identity is the effect of the law and the process of individualization. And so man, what he really is, formless, free Spirit, identifies, individualizes and we call that soul. And that that we call soul, on through its journey in this great eternity, in keeping with the Law of Attraction, attracts unto itself these various forms or bodies. And so we understand that we have celestial bodies, universal bodies, astral bodies, mental bodies, physical bodies, and on down the list.

But it is unfortunate that we over-identify with the vehicle, the body, and when the time comes for us to take off the suit, the dress, for ladies—by "he" I mean all humanity—and the suffering and the pain is in our error; through over-identification, we are the body. We're not the driver of it. We become it. And because in our consciousness we have made *[The teacher coughs at this moment.]*—Excuse me—that great error, because of that we suffer pain.

All great philosophies have taught the Law of Disassociation, the Law of Redirection of energy, the Law of Identity, and certainly the Law of Personal Responsibility. If we believe we are the hair on our head, when it begins to change in keeping with nature's law, we are not peaceful, let alone happy. *[Some of the congregation laugh.]* Its color changes and we're furious. And so we try many things to keep it the way that it was because we spent so many years identifying with it that way. Change is difficult for man only because man is over-identified with the automobile that he's driving; that's the only reason it is difficult. Our legs, as time passes, don't move, perhaps, as rapidly as we want them to move, as we have identified for years of how fast they can move, and we experience discordant, unhappy thoughts in our consciousness. And yet, my friends, it is inevitable.

Does the tree cry as it ages? Does the cat or the dog get emotionally upset because a few white hairs begin to appear around its little mouth? Does it get all upset because it can no longer, as time passes, do the things it naturally does—the birds and bees—during its season? For that, too, has passed. So my friends, our bondage is our attachment, which is over-identification with the vehicle we're driving. That's all our bondage is. That's all our suffering is. That's all it ever was. That's all it ever will be. Now we are in the process, whether we like it or not—and most of us don't like it—we are in the process of change, for that is the Law of Evolution. And repetition is the law through which change is made possible. So as one gray hair appears, there's a repetition, and there's two, and there's three.

And from gray to white and go on down the list. And how beautiful the law, demonstrable, is.

One should not have blind faith. We're filled with that. Tell me what mind is so clear that it knows the centuries or years ahead. That is not within the power or the domain of the human mind. The mind is simply a storehouse in which we have stored many facts, based upon experiences that have passed. And when our faith is so great in it and those things that have passed are brought to the present and we see, "Oh, that's no longer a fact. Therefore, it is no longer logical for me." And you get all upset.

You see, knowledge knows much, but wisdom knows better. For knowledge, we can only experience through the Law of Identification with form, for that's where facts are. That's not where wisdom lives. Wisdom lives in the soul faculty of patience. And so it is that, as we spend a little time encouraging our self, each moment, we help this great journey of evolution and we experience it more harmoniously. Then we don't have to follow this piece of clay into the sod and weep; and become attached— so attached we're bound there, in that terrible place—terrible to me.

I do not attend graveyards. And I made sure I set every law possible into motion that I would not have to have that responsibility; for that I am grateful. It would be like me attending a sale at a used car lot! I have never done it! I am not interested in those junk heaps! *[Some of the congregation laugh.]* So why in the name of God should I establish laws to go out in that wet sod and all that foolishness? I respect the right of those who need it. I don't! But I respect their understanding and I certainly respect their right. And in no way do I wish to be an instrument to hurt their feelings when they have that need. It is my responsibility to reveal, to those who are interested, that the soul is not there. For if the soul was there, the form would not be cold and inanimate. The soul has left. It's not coming back to that car. That one served its purpose. It has to go in the junk heap, from whence it was born, you see?

That which belongs to the planet Earth no man can steal. It shall return to the planet Earth, for from the planet Earth did it come. And that that comes from a thing is destined, by demonstrable law, to return unto the thing. Why stand in the way of the little car we're in, that we know came from there, called the dust of Earth, that has to return there? Why over-identify with it and see the process of decay when you can see the goodness, the greatness, the spring of life itself in any moment of your choice?

So, how does one make the change and evolve from the attachment, from the bondage? Well, let's start with the little car that we have. Are the wrinkles getting more? Is the hair getting grayer? Are we not as spry as we used to be? And go on down the list. Have we accepted graciously that is the right of nature? Have we accepted our self in all honesty? And are we freely experiencing in consciousness the real strength and joy and life that we are, that is not dependent upon one, dinky, little vehicle, when there are many through which we express?

Thank you very much. Thank you.

JANUARY 2, 1983

Church Questions and Answers 33

As most of you are already familiar, or have just been told, this is your time, once a month, to speak forth your [questions on topics of a general spiritual] interest. If you'll be so kind as to raise your hands, I will get to as many as time will allow.

Yes, the lady here, please.

In most of the major religions the most enlightened spiritual seekers take vows of chastity. Is this a good practice and, if so, why?

Well, in reference to your question that most spiritual leaders take vows of chastity and is it or is it not a good practice: that, of course, is entirely dependent upon the victimization of identification. For example, this philosophy teaches and strives to demonstrate that there is good, or God, in all things. Otherwise, our belief in a God is a limited belief in a limited god. If we believe that the tree is sustained by the same intelligent Energy that is sustaining the animal or the human, then we understand a God of infinite intelligence, of divine, supreme neutrality.

Now if in our error of ignorance in a realm of illusion, known as form—for that's what form is. And we teach a separation of truth from creation in order to be the truth we are and experience the freedom thereof. Therefore, it is entirely dependent upon man's ability, upon man's effort to maintain a separation between truth and creation.

Now many religions have taught throughout the ages that it is indispensable and necessary (for chastity) in order to maintain this separation of truth from creation. It is not indispensable to the separation of truth from creation. But, of course, it is indeed most difficult until man and at such time [as] he awakens and he knows beyond a shadow of any doubt that in the great evolution in which we are presently in, that this is one planet of many planets; that our being has experienced through many forms, in many times, in many places. And in keeping with the Law of Change, which is indispensable to evolution, that we will continue to experience and express through many forms yet to be.

However, if one, in their present evolution, finds themselves weak in courage, finds themselves weak in strength, finds themselves weak in spiritual conviction of their own, eternal being, then it could, of course, be beneficial to some degree to take various vows until such time as they're able to strengthen themselves and to awaken to the demonstrable truth that they are not the form or forms of mind or substance, but they are the divine, infinite, formless Spirit which is using the form or forms as a vehicle through which to express on a planet of any substance of which the planet is composed. I do hope that's helped with your question.

Thank you.

You're welcome. The gentleman on the aisle, please.

I believe it was Freud that made the judgment that religion is an opiate for the people. Would you care to . . .

Yes, he is only one of many opiates that made the judgment that religion is an opiate. But let us, perhaps, pause for a few moments and, perhaps, in the pause the light of reason may rise that we may understand that which prompted his statement and became, according to history, his judgment.

When man in his evolution looks about the world and finds support for any level of consciousness that he chooses to be the victim of—remember, to be the victim of any judgment we entertain in consciousness establishes the Law of Need to support and to sustain the judgment that is within our consciousness. For, like all form, like all limits, judgments require and are dependent upon intelligent energy for their own continuity. And so we find in this world of creation that we have many judgments, and we have many so-called friends who support and direct life-giving energy to the judgments that we *believe* that we are. And whoever believes a thing, becomes the thing, until, of course, he awakens. And so we find with Sigmund Freud or with anyone else, who, through their great faith in the power, which is truly the force, of the human intellect, they make their statements, their judgments, and those judgments within consciousness require energy for their continuity. So we look out in the world and we look for people who will support our judgments, whatever they may be, and we call that, of course, friendship. So far from the truth, that belief.

However, Freud is no different than any other man. He believes the judgment that he makes and, therefore, becomes it. Remember, friends, misery not only loves company but it is indispensable for its continuity. I hope that's helped with your question.

[It] has nothing to do with religion. It could have been why a cat eats fish, you understand. Thank you.

Anyone else? Yes, the gentleman, here, on the aisle, please.

This philosophy . . .

Pardon?

We are taught in this philosophy that we should not limit ourselves to certain things and to accept the abundant flow and the abundant good. And we're also taught that we must accept personal responsibilities. How do the two harmonize with one another?

Thank you very much for that most important question in reference to the teaching of the divine, abundant flow, which is the birthright of our own divinity, and how does that harmonize or [is] in unity with the demonstrable Law of Personal Responsibility, which is so clear: the ability to personally respond to all thoughts, acts, and deeds that we and we alone are responsible for.

In order for man to experience the divinity of abundant good, man must take charge over his consciousness, which, by the demonstrable law, he has been given right to. The prophets of old taught us that God has given us charge over all creation. Well, what is our creation? We create many thoughts and each thought is a form. And it goes out into the world to fulfill the purpose of its own design and creation. Therefore, of course, it is responsible to us, the creator thereof. And so we not only have charge over all of our creation, we have the ability to respond and to instruct our creations to do what we consciously choose them to do, for they are the servants and we are the master. That's when we awaken and become the captain of our ship and the master of our destiny.

And so it is in our days of error, of ignorance, we have created, of course, many thoughts and many forms. They exist within our consciousness and we have experienced lack and limitation of many different things. Now those are the thoughts and the forms of what has been. And we want something different than what has been. And so we study philosophies and religions in the hopes that we can attain something better than what has been, that our todays and tomorrows may be in harmony with the abundant good, that we don't have to believe in. Nature demonstrates it constantly. Look at the rain that takes care of the trees and the grass, and look at all of nature. It's not left without; it's never been left without because it is in harmony with divine and natural law. The tree doesn't grow and worry whether or not it will rain next year when it's supposed to rain, and, if so, how much rain will there be. And will it be flooded? Will the winds break its branches? Or will it stand on a desert of drought? The tree does not such foolish things. Neither do the birds nor the bees. Neither do the animals or all of creation. Except one! Only one worries and frets, concerns and creates a multitude of forms that stand in the way between that which is truly its being and the Source which sustains it. And that's called the mind of man.

Now it is the mind, the vehicle, through which the infinite Divine Intelligence, directed by our own will, [that] has created these multitudes of things in our consciousness. And so one day, finally, weary of the struggle, weary of the experiences, weary of the disasters, which we are yet to see God in—for they are only directions to make changes necessary for greater good. Someday we'll see the beauty, the divinity in disaster. And so we continue on with all these things and we become frustrated.

A desire rises from our being within our consciousness. It immediately comes up against the censorship of past events, of forms, of creations and it gets shoved back down again, because it looks around in our universe and it does not see all the necessary steps available to us, according [to] and in keeping with, of course, the judgments we have made so long ago.

Now there is one way, of course—not a shortcut. But it is a way. For man to take the time, in a world of illusion, and the effort to go step-by-step through some type of analytical process of the psyche is going to take him a few centuries, considering how much is already in the mind. And as this philosophy teaches, it's not what you need to put into your mind to free you; it's what you truly need to take out of your mind that will free you. There is a way, however. These events of yesteryear, these obstructions on our path that cause us to stand in our own light and move not forward, these obstructions we can control, for they only exist in consciousness when we open up the door to that realm of consciousness.

And so for many, many years the Living Light has taught to the students and those who come to it, that self is the house in which this mass of thought forms and obstructions truly exist. They are an illusion. And they are the instruments to which we are responsible while we insist on entertaining or entering the house of self. Now, like all houses, it has a roof to keep out what it does not choose or want to enter. Like all houses, it has at least one door, hopefully two; so often we want to escape out the back way because we know what's coming in front. And it has, hopefully, some windows to let some light in. Now that's what we call this temple of God, this house, this physical and mental being.

Remember now, our physical being is only a reflection of our mental being at any moment; that it reveals our mental being and its evolution throughout all eternity. And so here we have this roof on our house. And man—this house of self—and man calls that roof pride. And that poor roof is constantly in need, it seems, of repair. If any house has ever been reroofed as many times as the house of self, the roof of pride, it's man. He's constantly trying to cover it up and put untold numbers of shingles upon it in order that he may feel good.

Now many religions, throughout the ages, have taught that pride is the greatest sin. This religion does not teach that pride is the greatest sin. This religion teaches and demonstrates that all functions, including pride, can and are designed to serve a great and beneficial purpose to the divine Spirit and truth, which we are. Pride permits the opening into our consciousness of God through the judgments and forms that we have made in our life. Now all form requires, for its own existence, good or God.

At one of our meetings here, one of the congregation asked, "What did we think about this new religion called sports?" Well, what can one think about goodness? If man finds God in playing baseball, then baseball is what man should do. For as long as he does not transgress the divine rights of another soul, then he's doing what's necessary for him to find God. It is not within the right or the domain of the minds of men to dictate and, in so doing, establish the law to suppress all people because they judge that God can only be found one particular way. How would it be if the daisy in the garden said, "God, you will shine because I need sunlight on Monday, Tuesday, Wednesday, Thursday, Friday, Saturday. You could rest on Sunday, but that time only!"? What would happen to all the flowers with their divine right of different types of weather conditions? And so it is with man and his finding God or goodness.

Let us understand that pride can, and ofttimes does, serve a most useful purpose. It is the very instrument through which we accept the divine Law of Encouragement. It is the very instrument through which we enter the great power known as enthusiasm or to be in God. It also has its great balance in the soul faculty, known as humility. You don't have to worry about praying for humility. It's known to the human mind as humiliation. And God knows, we get plenty of that in the world in which we live. So humility is not something you need to pray for; you'll have plenty of it if you are imbalanced at any time in what is known as the function of pride.

Now that simply—and truth indeed is simple. It is falsehood that is complex and deeply hidden. That is simple: to pause and to think [and] say, "Just a moment. These experiences in my life, I certainly don't appreciate them. Things are not going the way I would like them to go. I have a choice to make. I am capable of making that choice in this instant. I can go on the long, dreary path and try to find out, while I'm feeling so bad, what laws I set into motion, what thoughts I created and look to see how many chickens are coming home into my life to roost." Well, when you're feeling bad, that means there's a cloud between you and the Source; you're not feeling good. That certainly isn't the time to go through that kind of analysis. So the better way, of course, is to pause for a moment, [and] say, "That's it. I've had enough of that. I don't like feeling bad like that. I'm going to put the brake on. Get myself out of self [and] go do something that I like and enjoy!" And therefore, you'll be amazed how God will get in. And abundance and the goodness it contains, you won't have to be concerned about. Does that help with your question?

Thank you.

Thank you. I realize the answers are a bit long sometimes. The lady in the back, please, first.

I would like to ask this: Is there a special place for people who commit suicide?

In reference to your question, "Is there a special place for people who commit suicide?" if you dictate that a realm of recovery is a special place, then in that respect, of course, it would be called, that realm of recovery, a special place.

I think it, perhaps, would be best if we took a few moments to understand what suicide really is. We are often tempted in the difficulties and the struggles that we alone set into motion in this life. We are often tempted to escape, of course, from them. Some of us, perhaps most of us, it seems, take a look at what avenues we have established to escape from something that we find distasteful. Not stopping to pause, to awaken that whatever in life we find distasteful is a reflection of a level of consciousness that is within us. Because if we stopped to do that, the distastefulness would soon disappear. But we don't usually do that.

We don't usually, when we experience or find something distasteful, we don't usually pause to think. We don't usually, in pausing, awaken to the demonstrable, divine law of the ability to respond to what we think is distasteful. And in that responding to awaken within our consciousness that we are the captain. We are not the slave. We are not the crew. We are the captain of our ship. And therefore, if we find something distasteful, we have the power within us to change within consciousness, and therefore no longer experience that which is distasteful within our consciousness. Because it's within our consciousness where everything takes place. The great delusion is to look outside and say so-and-so did something. It's our thought. We are captain of it when we choose to be captain of it.

And so, some people, not awakening to that demonstrable truth, finding life's experiences unbearable to their consciousness, they become instruments through which the physical body returns to the substance from whence it was created, to this Earth planet. There is absolutely and positively—I assure you from over forty-four years of working in these other dimensions—there is absolutely and positively no escape from what is established within consciousness. They enter realms of recovery, if there is someone there to guide them to those realms. If there is not, they remain earth-bound, because it is the bondage of mental substance that they can no longer bear. And the laws are infallible; they are demonstrable: we shall, in our wandering from the Source, we shall be free. And that means exactly what it says: truth crushed to earth shall rise again. It doesn't matter whether or not we are the instruments through which our physical body returns to the planet Earth, because truth shall not be crushed without rising again.

And so there are untold numbers of people who have left this planet who are in the realms of recovery, who are facing, with the divine soul faculty of courage and hope and possibility, their own growth and awakening.

And let us look beyond such a short span in eternity. Let us go beyond this simple, limited few years, not even a pin drop in eternity [is] an Earth-planet experience. We are in truth the captain of our ship and the master of our destiny. And if in the final analysis these experiences we make necessary for our own truth and our own freedom, then for us they are necessary. And so shall it be. I hope that's helped with your question.

Yes, the lady here has been waiting.

Can I ask you a question, please, about marijuana inhaling in this respect; a friend of mine has said she wishes to go on the spiritual path and she asked me if she would have to give up smoking marijuana or, like in the ancient Indian religions, could it ever be used for enlightenment?

Thank you. It's a wonderful question. The lady has asked in reference to going on a spiritual path, would this person have to give up marijuana or could it be used, as ancient cultures have used it in times past, as a benefit for them on the spiritual path. As long as there is need for it, the path is not spiritual. It is in truth mental, for the light of our spirit is freed from want, need, and desire.

However, it could be beneficial to anyone, if, having been freed from the need of it, in their evolution it was used in the light of reason, as an instrument through which they may enter other realms of consciousness and they were not dependent upon its use for that purpose, then there are times when many crutches are useful for a time, until we're strong enough to walk with God. Now, any form, *any* form, all form is a reflection and an illusion. It is not truth. It is not freedom. It is not the Spirit that we are. It is not the infinity. It is only limit, which is illusion. Any form, any limit, any illusion that is necessary, that we make necessary for truth no longer is truth. We must remember that the convenience of truth is the falsehood of man. It certainly is not truth.

And so dependence upon form for spiritual awakening, for freedom, for joy, and all that is, is an illusion and a crutch. Along our path of awakening, it seems that in our evolution through form, through the illusion and delusion and self-deception, it does seem that we require, at times, many different crutches. And wise is he who knows that it's a crutch, and it's only for a time, and that it changes in keeping with the law of change of form. Does that help with your question?

[Thank you.]

You're welcome. *[After a short pause, the teacher continues.]* We're not finished yet because some of my students just sighed. The lady has a question here, please.

I believe that we're taught that the soul goes to the other side on the mental body. Is that true?

Well, thank you very much for that statement. The lady says that the soul goes to the other side with a mental body. Well, if that's the only body the poor soul has to transport it after the physical one goes, yes, indeed, of course, the mental body takes us to the mental world of consciousness.

Here we strive to study and to apply that which we study to open our soul faculties to hopefully bring some degree of balance into our life with our sense functions. You see, my friends, this academy, this church, this school offers you the opportunity to study and, hopefully, apply its understanding of soul faculties, because I believe beyond a shadow of any doubt that it is demonstrable that we are not lacking in sense functions. And so, the infinite, intelligent Energy, directed by the will of man to sense functions, at the sacrifice and imbalance of soul faculties, creates for us, in a mental world, a very strong, a very forceful mental body, very forceful emotional body, which, of course, is composed of mental substance. And so when we leave the physical body, here of the Earth planet, the strongest body we have is the one we reside in.

However, through some degree of effort and some conscious choice of our will, this great power of God that flows through us, we can send that infinite, intelligent Energy through an expression of soul faculties and, in that process, from spiritual substance, create a spirit body. So that when we leave here, having been so very familiar with a mental body, we may enter this other body that it will be sufficiently created so that it can be a substantial vehicle for our conscious awareness in spiritual realms.

Now the purpose, basically, of the Living Light Philosophy is to show you the way to bring about balance in your life so that you may not be limited to mental and astral bodies for your expression and, hopefully, create, to some degree, a spiritual body while yet encased in flesh. Because, you see, my friends, if the effort is not made while in the flesh to create a spiritual body through inner spiritual awakening, there is no spiritual body to take us on to spiritual realms. There's only the bodies that are already capable of moving around. And we all know that our mental bodies have no problem at all in that respect. So I hope that's helped with your question.

Yes. The lady here, please.

Yes. There's been a lot of talk about the nuclear waste. I was wondering if there's going to be a solution, if we're—someone, somehow, they will discover what to do.

Oh, you're asking the question, Will there be a solution to the disposal of nuclear waste? Why, yes, of course. Because if there wasn't a solution, it would be contrary to the demonstrable Law of Truth. There is no problem that does not contain within the form of the problem its own solution. So look at the problems that—small problems—we have in our life. Sometimes the problem appears to be very great. We go to sleep with the problem and awaken with the solution. Well, we don't need to go to sleep with the problem to awaken to the solution that is contained within the problem. That can be done consciously by the power of the will, which is our divinity and our right to use it wisely.

See, my friends, as we conclude this short time here, we understand that the will of the Divinity, that's God's will, divine will, demonstrably reveals to us that divine will is, in truth, total acceptance. Show me the blade of grass, the divine will, in its acceptance, does not sustain. So it is foolhardy, stupid, and ridiculous to think for one moment that good will, divine will, God will does not and is not total acceptance. [It] doesn't leave out anything, any place in any universe. Now that divine will doesn't leave us out either. It sustains every thought we think. It sustains every emotion and every judgment we choose to have. In fact, it sustains everything we do and everything we do not do. And we call that Energy.

Is the energy intelligent? Well, it's self-evident that the energy is intelligent because it does exactly what *we* will it to do. You want to move your hand? The will moves it. You think its automatic. It is this great Power, called God, that moves it. You want to speak? It is this Power, intelligent Energy, that moves your vocal cords. You choose to do that and it responds. This is why the God of the Living Light is the greatest servant man will ever know. Because it leaves nothing out, serves everything, and that's just the truth that is.

Now we come to man's will. Same Power. Same Intelligence. Same Energy. Now man, he chooses to direct the will of God. This he has become and is receptive to, as all forms are receptive to it. But man has the one thing that makes him a little different animal than all the other animals: and [with] that one thing, man then judges he's no longer an animal. He's now a human being. Because man now has self-awareness, choice, reason, dictate, judgment, and the power to create his own destiny. And so man's self-will, the will of God trapped within the house of self, roofed with the roof of pride, directs the will of God in the way that man chooses to do it.

Unfortunately, man has yet to learn the lesson that the will of God is total acceptance. It doesn't have any judgments in the way. It doesn't restrict the will, the Power, the Intelligence. It doesn't do that. Only man does that through man's own ignorance. And because he does it in ignorance, he becomes very emotional, very frustrated, and very upset. When the law that says clearly like attracts like and becomes the Law of Attachment, when all the chickens come home to roost, man becomes very upset. Instead of stopping to think, "My God, my God, just look at those chickens! Look how many, through my great self-will, I have created! And now I must pay the price, like it or not." Man's other choice is to procrastinate, to distract himself. He'll always have to face the chickens that he alone created that are coming back because they know their creator and they're not about to stay out there in the cold and [be] hungry.

I do hope that's helped with your questions.

Thank you.

FEBRUARY 6, 1983

Church Questions and Answers 34

Well, in keeping with the Living Light Philosophy, a philosophy of evolution, which is demonstrably a philosophy of change, expansion, and growth, we shall make a slight change in our schedule this morning of questions and answers. And instead, we shall take this time available for a spiritual class. Now if there are any moments after that, I'll be more than happy to answer your questions. Please take this away. *[The teacher asks that the lectern be removed from the top of the table.]*

I realize, perhaps, to some of you present—the rest of our service, of course, will remain the same—I do realize to our first-time and new visitors that, who have never attended one of our classes, it may be a bit different, but that's what life is all about. If it isn't different, we soon find we're dead. And we don't believe in death; so change, of course, is the Law of Evolution.

We all are familiar with what we call desire. We have, within our consciousness, from moment to moment, desires for many things. Some of us believe or understand that desire is, of course, ever a normal thing. It is a natural thing. Animals desire to eat; they eat and survive. People desire to eat and they survive. And people desire many different things in the world which we all view, the world of form or creation. So man, we see, is never left without desire. Man believes that the satisfaction of his desires makes him feel better. We understand that desire is the expression of the Divinity, God, or goodness. And so man in this earth experience frequently becomes frustrated because his desires, it seems so often in his life, are not satisfied. And, of course, better they be fulfilled. And so we're ever working with our minds to find ways to attain this, to gather that, to garner something. And the desire for things never seems to end, for there are so many things that we believe we will feel better if we have.

No one can deny desire, which is the expression of the Divinity called God, for the thought of man sustained by God, the Light of Eternal Truth, is not greater than that which sustains it. Consequently, man is obliged to do something with the desires that impinge upon his consciousness, and, if not fulfilled, seem to be a great, compelling force to do something with—whatever desire seems to plague him.

We understand in the Living Light Philosophy that not only is desire an expression of God, the Divinity, but a wise man should not suppress desire for, in so doing, mental substance (his mind) is attempting to rise supreme over God, the power which sustains and is, of course, the desire, the power which sustains his own mind. So suppression is not the path to freedom, nor is it ever the path to truth, the light. For that which is suppressed is concealed; that which is concealed is falsehood. That which is revealed, that which is simple is truth and demonstrable. So a wise man does not suppress desire.

He has two alternatives left, in reference to that, and that is the fulfillment of the desire or the education thereof. Now, having so many desires in the course of one, simple day, multiplied many times in what we know as sleep, existing beneath the conscious level of awareness, man seems to live a life of frustration, anxiety. Certainly not a life of the peace that passeth all understanding. Certainly not a life of abundant good and fullness, for we view in this old creation, not heaven, which is a state of consciousness, but ofttimes its opposite. Not being able, in a world governed by the laws of mental substance, to fulfill the many multitudes of desires within the consciousness, man, in his evolution, has earned restrictions or limits. He has earned those and has learned to abide by those restrictions and limits for that is known as the law that his soul has earned in his evolution. In reference to law, divine law, we also understand that freedom without law is, indeed, license. And so the Bible teaches us the value, of course, of fidelity—fidelity to that which we are responsible to.

So man, not being able to fulfill the many desires within his consciousness in the course of a day and not being unwise and attempting to suppress them, man learns, in time, to educate them. Now to educate something does not mean, in any sense of the word, to eliminate it. To educate means to transform, to transfigure, to change the form, which the divine expression, desire, has taken. Not to attempt to annihilate it. For the principle of anything is the power of the thing. It is the principle of the automobile and its design that is the movement of the automobile. It is not the wheel, nor is it the hood. But it is the principle of the design that moves the automobile to where *we* decide we wish the automobile to take us. And so it is with desire. It is the power of God. How we choose, in our designing, to permit that power to flow through us, the form that it takes in the design within our consciousness is what type of a ride we're going to have and whether or not, in entering the vehicle, which is the form of the desire, the power that is flowing through us, whether we will go with it out into the universe and return with the fullness thereof, which is the power contained within the vehicle that we are now being transported by. For it is our consciousness that moves in the form that our mind designs, the vehicle through which the Divinity, called divine expression, flows.

We have at our disposal, at any moment, the divine, demonstrable immutable Law of Choice. We are never left, in any moment of consciousness, without choice. So man looks into the universe, to old creation, this great illusion, and he has a desire for this, a desire for that. Say, he has a desire for apples and he would like an apple. And he goes to the market and he sees apples—red apples, green apples, yellow apples, all types, shapes, and sizes of apples. And he experiences a desire for the fullness of the eating of the apple. And he chooses apples and he goes to purchase them. And he finds that those apples are too expensive, that he cannot afford those apples. And so he goes back and he looks at all the other apples [and] chooses a different apple and that apple is within the law that he has established. In other words, he decides and he judges that apple he can afford. Now there is no difference in principle with the red apple or the yellow apple, for they are all apples. Just like a rose is a rose no matter what you call it. So to the mind who has dictated the form of the desire and forgotten the design and the principle of its purpose, man indeed does have a problem.

It's just like the desire to be comfortable. Adjust the heat downward, please; we want to stay up, where it is comfortable. *[The teacher instructs the vice president.]* It is the principle, my friends; it is not the form. When we believe—and we do believe—we believe we are the form. In that belief we are controlled by the form, for as a man thinketh in his heart, believeth in his mind, so man becomes. But man is not the thought. The thought is the vehicle available to man to use at any moment. Now he may have the thought of a hammer or the thought of a saw. If he goes to saw a plank of wood, if he goes to cut a plank of wood, how foolish would he be to use the hammer instead of the saw. For all these tools, or thoughts, which are forms within our consciousness, are available for man to use. However, in our ignorance we do not use the tools that are in the divine design of the Eternal Being, called God. No. The tools, they use us!

For example, we have a job, as I stated, to saw or to cut a plank of wood. In our lack of effort in our consciousness we think of the plank of wood and we have to do something, and we stop and the hammer rises through the Law of Association. For the hammer, too, a tool, has been used in past experiences to do something with a plank of wood. It pounds a nail into it or other things. The hammer rises and we leave to take care of the plank of wood. We get to the plank of wood and become aware we don't have the saw. And the hammer in consciousness, the thought form rises up and we use the hammer. And the cut in the wood certainly is not one of quality. It certainly is not a tool that is serving us. It is, however, a tool, therefore, that we are serving.

Is that the way we truly desire to live? Moments to moments of seeming satisfaction, never fulfillment, and no days without frustration and no days without anxiety. The eternal being, known as man, was not designed for such foolishness. It is the error of the human mind that has twisted and turned the eternal truth, the divine plan, known as design, and created so many problems from a simple lack of awareness.

Whatever it is you want to be, stop wanting to be. Pause in consciousness and awaken to the truth that you are. And if you are not, then, of course, you do not be. You only hope to be. So we find with our desires, oh, we hope for many things. And we wait and we wait. And we diligently work with our mind and we create many forms in order that this desire, whatever it may be, that our mind has dictated, has formed in consciousness—when will this happen? We are the victims of mental substance, the human mind, that is a tool, an effect, not a cause. The mind in and of itself does not survive. It is the divine, intelligent, infinite Power of the universes that sustains and supports mental substance, the human mind.

If we were the thought, we still would be crying like babies, for we have the baby thought form from many years ago. Now some of us, suppressing the baby thought form, cry in different ways by our acts and deeds. It is known in this philosophy as the pity of self, the most destructive force in the universe.

A wise man, seeing that the human mind believes many things and that its beliefs are in a constant process of changing—dependent, of course, upon what it judges and creates as circumstances and conditions. We believe in one president—that he's going to bring us the prosperity that we have a divine right to—and then only to be disappointed. And then we believe in another president; and he's going to do this and he's going to do that. We believe in our employer—that he's going to give us a raise—and then he doesn't give us a raise. We believe in the boss we work for—that he's going to start showing some kindness to us and he's going to give us a ten-minute coffee break every hour on the hour—and then it does not happen. And then we believe that we only have a half hour for lunch and that that boss of ours certainly must make a change and grow spiritually someday and give us a two-hour lunch break. And so we *believe*, of course, in many things. And because we believe in many things, our days are filled with disappointments, discouragement, etc., etc., etc. Is that life? No, that's what *we* have made of life. For life is ever as we make it; she is always as we take it.

So we have the divine right of choice, moment by moment, to make and then to take. We're constantly taking life. And it is constantly revealing to us what we are doing with an infinite, intelligent, divine Power, what we're making out of it. Do we make something that we consciously desire to consume? Ofttimes we're making something that we choke on. And then when we choke on it, somebody else did it to us. The greatest bondage the human being will ever know is denial of the ability to personally respond to life, which *is* eternity.

So when we pause and we look around and we say, "If he or she had not done that, I would feel wonderful. If he or she would do this or something else, I would feel God. For I, my mind, my love of self, dictates that the form of this divine expression, called desire, can only be fulfilled in this form; that I, in consciousness, dictate that God shall fill my cup only through that particular form within my consciousness. Now that form within my consciousness is a separate being. And they are not responding to my dictate and I'm driving myself crazy. Because that form—I so believe in my love of self, and that is a form that my love of self has created within my consciousness." Don't you see, children? You have told God, the power that sustains you, that

God may flow through you, deposit the eternal goodness and joy of life, that it may enter one way and one way only.

Just like apples. If you insist that it be a McIntosh and there are no McIntoshes, but there are one hundred other types of apples at the store, then you must go to the store as often as necessary, look at all the apples, and see the bin, where the McIntosh is supposed to be, empty! Always empty! It's known as the great void of total self, which offers discouragement and emptiness. God, the divine, eternal Power of Goodness that ever is, [is] never absent or away. The absence of God or goodness is ever dependent upon our willingness to accept the principle of the Divinity, known as divine expression, called desire, to stop the insanity of trying to tell the Power that sustains us, to tell that Power how that Power may enter our life and fill our cup. Surely, someday in eternity we will stop the error, the ignorance, the blatant stupidity that we are greater than that which is our very life.

We are not the thought of yesterday. We change it constantly. We look around the universe; it's one thought, it's this thought, it's that thought. From moment to moment and day to day our beliefs are in a constant process of changing. Well, in one step on the ladder of eternal progression, millions believe, until the light of reason shines and they begin *being* faith, the power that is far, far superior and greater than all beliefs of all things. For faith, the power that is, truth, the light you be, is greater than the human mind that is in a constant process of changing, for that is the Law of Evolution.

Why, the strands of hair upon your head, they are not the same they were ten years ago, five years ago, thirty years ago. Man does many things to keep them similar, hopefully, the same color, [and] finally decides that green is better than red. Or, perhaps, yellow is better than blue and on down the list. That's man's divine right of choice, but the principle is still the same. It's still hair. Some with a lot. Some with less. And no matter what you do, you cannot change the principle. But the form through which the principle expresses, ah, that changes before our very eyes, moment by moment.

Remember that love is nothing more nor less than the reflection in another of the goodness in oneself. So who wants the mirror when the being is the value? Many mirrors, they crack; they change. They're so fragile they're easily broken. So look at life. Let life be the mirror reflecting the God or goodness that you are. Now it can only reflect that to you in keeping with your own control of self.

God has given you charge over all your creations. Take charge over your creations. You are captain of your ship of destiny. Throw the crew overboard that dares to mutiny against you. For that is the demonstration of reason, the power of the Light that transforms us. That is your right. Now that takes what man calls the power of will.

Everyone has the power of will. We use it for many things. We use it to hold this form, hold that form, and hold all kinds of things. Our human mind is designed to gather and to garner. Wisdom reveals truth is like a river; it continuously flows. And when we permit the human mind to gather of the rivers of life and not to release the rivers of life, the day comes that we explode. The dams are broken—the dams of our own dictates, the dams of our own judgments. That is certainly not freedom because it is not flow. The truth reveals: that which we hold destroys us; ah, but that which we give unfolds us. And so joy is in the giving. Only destruction is in the holding. For no matter what you try to hold, you can only be deluded and deceived for a time. By the very law you have transgressed, what you think you hold shall do what the law, infallible law, has designed it to do: it will destroy you in consciousness.

For man is the greatest borrower the universes shall ever know. He borrows everything from pencils to paper and who knows what. He certainly does know how to borrow. Man owns nothing. That's the greatest con game of all con games. Man owns nothing! For if he did, he would remain eternally on earth to defend what he holds and owns. No, man owns nothing. He borrows everything. And he makes the debt very, very high. With all your desires in life, check the going interest rate before you purchase, for creation is a price tag. Its debt may be, for you, too high. Thank you.

Now if you have any questions, we can go on with that. If not... Yes, the gentleman there, please. Yes.

I saw a video tape regarding the predictions of the sixteenth century prophet, Nostradamus.

Yes.

And he made a number of predictions all through the centuries, including some disconcerting predictions for the remainder of this century.

Yes.

Famine, earthquakes, and nuclear world war III.

Yes.

What is your opinion of these predictions?

Well, I would be happy to share my understanding. I have no opinion, for all opinion is based upon judgment. And may God free me and keep me free from judgment, for it is restrictive and, therefore, could not possibly be truth. That which is limited cannot be true. In reference to my understanding concerning the predictions that you have spoken of, it is my personal assurance, number one: this so-called great disaster of nuclear world war III is not what it appears to be, for the minds of men, with all their scientific technology, are not greater than the power of peace. And though [there will be] many skirmishes and battles, there'll be no war as one the minds of men may think. I hope that's helped with your question.

Now, in reference to famine, why, of course, famine is ever amongst us. For thousands upon thousands of years, through the abuses of the mental substance of the human mind, we know famine. Wise little creatures, without the great intellect, they don't know famine. Only man makes them know famine. The squirrel gathers and garners and does not eat it all up in a day. It saves it, cares for it, protects it, when it knows, by the divine laws of nature, there won't be any. And so, it doesn't starve during those months. Famines are ever amongst you.

Creation is a Law of Duality. Flood and drought, feast and famine, that is the Law of Duality; that's how man knows difference. Without creation, man would not know difference; without difference, man would not be form. Therefore, it is difference or duality that is the curtain of illusion and man identifies with that which he thinks he is and loses that which he is. Therefore, he knows falsehood and truth, he knows good and bad. That is the descent that man has chosen by thinking he is the I and not *being* the I. Does that help with your question? *[After a short pause, the teacher continues.]*

Yes?

Well, what are your comments regarding his predictions in general? In other words, is he . . .

Do you mean do I believe he's accurate or inaccurate?

Yes. Apparently, the interpretations of his past predictions are rather accurate.

It has nothing to do with accuracy or inaccuracy because he is not here to speak with us. It does have a great deal to do with the falsifying hands of the copyist, of what he was supposed to have intended. You see, hell itself is paved with good intentions, and indeed it is loaded with broken promises. So it is not just, right, nor fair, to say the least, to speak for a soul who is not present to give to us exactly what *he* meant at the time that he spoke the words. We have only the copies—the falsifying hands of the minds of men. And so we see the struggle of all the great books of all times. One interpretation this way, another that way—whatever suits the self-motivation of the copyist. Does that help with your question?

Thank you.

You're welcome. Yes, the lady here, please.

Yes, can our—when you awaken, for instance, and you're depressed, can you appeal to the guides to help you immediately?

Why, of course! Absolutely! Because the thing they have to do are remove the shadows of past events. One cannot be discouraged without thinking of an event that has passed. You see, being in the eternal moment, the truth that you are, there is no disappointment. How can there be? There is no reference. You are! And so, if you have no reference for what you—what has passed and you have no reference for what is yet to be, you cannot be disappointed, you cannot be discouraged; you can only be that which you are: truth, abundant good, freedom, the love of life. So it is only the removal of these shadows, you see—that through the thought of I we enter the shadowland, the twilight zones. And only there do we suffer. Only there are we not so wise, to say the least. Does that help with your question?

Yes. Thank you.

Because we must understand, you see, the tree of knowledge. Because before biting of the fruit of the tree of knowledge, which the books have revealed—a little changes, of course, in interpretation through the years of falsifying hands of the copyists. But, you see, before the thought of I, there was not the knowledge of the difference, duality, comparisons of creation. Therefore, there was none of those things. There was, as even the Bible reveals, the paradise, the peace on earth that passeth all understanding, you see? It is when we know—ofttimes we've heard one say that ignorance is bliss. Well, ignorance may be blissful. Wisdom, then, is ecstatic! *[Many in the congregation laugh.]* For knowledge knows much and wisdom, certainly, knows better.

Thank you, friends. I see our time is up. Thank you.

MARCH 6, 1983

Church Questions and Answers 35

And each day, of course, is a special day to any of us who, in our own awakening, make it so. But traditionally this is a day of rebirth or renewal. *[This class was given on Easter.]* The renewal of anything is the return to the source from whence it cometh. And so a renewal does not mean a reliving of past events as shadows that have passed through our life, but it does mean a return to the Source, to that which we are, of course, not that which we just think we are. If man was only what he thought he was, then man would obviously be, indeed, a very unreliable being. For we go through but the course of one day and see how contradictory our thoughts can be and often are. Therefore, we know that we are not what we think we are, but we are what we are. And our quest in life is to, of course, awaken to what we are. We have certainly spent many years already in thinking what we are.

And so we come to this time each month where it is your opportunity to ask questions of a general nature of interest to all of us. I will be happy to reach as many as time will permit. And so, if you will be so kind as to raise your hands if you have a question—otherwise, this part of our service can be quite short. *[Some of the congregation laugh.]*

Yes, the gentleman on the aisle, please.

Yes. I'd like you to answer the question: How do you resolve the conflict between being attached to the fruits of your action and wanting the fruits of your action and planning and working towards your goals?

Thank you. The question is, How can one free oneself from attachment to their fruits of action and to be free to fulfill their goal or goals in life? Well, of course, we experience what we call attachment to the fruits of action. We can only experience that by the registration in consciousness of what we all know as need. Now man needs what he thinks he needs, and man thinks he needs because he has the awareness within his consciousness that he is not fulfilled.

You see, we all know where our home is. Getting there has been our question throughout all eternity. We know from whence we cometh and we are destined by the law of coming forth to return to the Source, which is, in truth, our own home. So man, in his quest to return to that which he is, constantly registers what we call need. And so he searches in his consciousness, for all things do take place within our consciousness. It is our lack of awareness that believes that we need something that is beyond our power to control, it is beyond our grasp and beyond our reach. Consequently, we continue to search without, for we have yet to find where it is—of course, within our self. And in that quest, in that search to fulfill our being, for we know it is lacking, lacking in the awareness of what we truly are, we search out. And in that search we grasp, we hold, and we tempt to make it our own.

We all know from our own experiences that God disposes and man proposes. We all know from our own experiences [that] that which we hold tenaciously to destroys us. We all know from experience that that which we free from our being unfolds us. So we understand, of course, at moments we understand that to forgive or to give forth is to free oneself from the bondage of the illusion created by our own mind. So man goes out and he works. And he attempts to hold that which he receives, and in that attempt he is destroyed by attachment to that which he holds. For that which is held is not freed and does not fulfill the purpose of its true design.

The divine, infinite Spirit, known as Infinite Intelligence to the Spiritualists, is not something that can be placed into a vessel and held for all to view. It is beyond form and therefore it is beyond limit. Man can only hold to that which is limited. And by holding to that which is limited, man binds himself, for the limit exists within our consciousness. All things that our eyes see, all things that our ears hear, all things that we sense, feel, and touch take place within our consciousness.

We believe and because we believe, we, therefore, become bound by our own belief. It is our mind that believes; it is our soul, our spirit, that is faith. And it is faith that frees us and returns us to that which we are. But our minds, which reveal unto us only form, therefore, only limit, do not contain truth. Truth cannot be contained for truth is that which is. One cannot contain the air one breathes. One is receptive to the flow of the air and therefore man knows what he calls life. For man to attempt to hold to the air he breathes, he would not long be in the vehicle of the human body. Therefore, man looks and never reaches his goal. He is ever, ever working towards it, for that which we attain our minds grasp and hold and guarantee its own loss. A wise man, therefore, knows beyond a shadow of any doubt that he is, in truth, the river of consciousness, that upon the river which he is many things are flowing. In his effort to place a dam across the river of truth man enters the convenience of truth, which, in truth, is falsehood. I do hope that's helped with your question.

Thank you.

You're welcome. Yes, the gentleman in front, please.

We associate religion with God and with truth. We know truth is individually perceived. We also have been told that more wars have been fought over religion than for any other reason. Would you define religion?

Well, whenever we tempt to define anything, of course, we bind it, for we place it into form. All thought is form, and all expression of thought, therefore, is a bondage to the thought that is expressed. However, one does understand, by the living demonstration, the word *religion* in our world simply means to return to or bind to.

Now anything that is understood by the human mind to be bondage is fought over. One fights over all types of bondage. For bondage offers to us, whether it's a bondage we make of religion, philosophy, or a bondage of anything, it offers to us what man, in his thought, calls power. And therefore, if man registers within his consciousness power, then you may be rest assured he has already registered need. And registering need, he already has the temptation to control. Therefore, man searches throughout the world, through many religions, for security. He searches for the security outside because he has yet to find it inside. We all know, beyond a shadow of any doubt, that we experience a type of insecurity. For every yes, there is a no. And for every day, there is a night; for every good, there is a seeming opposite of bad. We want—all of us—to be freed from that. What we do not realize [is] the freedom from it is in viewing, not in seeing.

Now our minds see, but they do not view. Our ears hear; they do not listen. And why that is so—and all prophets have taught that simple, demonstrable truth—is that our mind, when we are conscious of the thought of I, we are limited by all experiences that we have already had. For example, if we have had the experience of eating an apple and the apple was sour and not tasteful to us, then we have, within our consciousness, the registration and the memory that the apple is not something desirable. Therefore, we do not desire the apple. If we are trained that there are other apples, then in time, perhaps, we will eat the apple. If we are not, we refuse to eat the apple. We learn these things when we're very young, little children in life. So when we see, we are censored by past experiences, by the shadows over the light. When we hear, we are censored by the shadows over the light. Therefore, our reason, our lamp of honesty does not shine brightly, for it is dimmed by the shadows of whatever has been within our consciousness.

For man to experience freedom, man must realize, sooner or later, that freedom is eternity, that it expresses beyond time and space, that its expression is infinite, that God is Infinite Intelligence eternally expressing itself. Now man has that experience and man has that awareness in the conscious moment of his choice, but it is moment by moment. The shadow exists only in what has been, and it casts its shadow only in what is to be. For example, you look out at nature and you see there is, seemingly, a shape upon the meadow. There are many shapes. And you look up to the light and you see, why, that's a tree. That is a tree—or many trees. You look down, you do not see the tree, but you see the reflection of the tree. To man, that is known as illusion, for that's what it is. It is illusion. It's not the tree. It's the reflection of the tree.

So we stand and we look in the mirror, and if we look too much or too often, we call that vanity. But what are we looking at? We are looking at the reflection of the temple of God; that is called our body. Now we're not looking at the temple of God, but we are looking at the reflection. And so it is man is vain, not by looking simply in a mirror. We are vain by looking at the shadows of life and not at life itself.

So, whoever looks up is in keeping with their return home. Now looking up takes more effort than looking down. For, you see, it is easier to fall than it is to rise. It is in the thinking of man, for man believes that he needs to sleep. And depending upon his own belief and attachment thereto does man sleep. But it takes faith to look up, to see that we are what we are, the way that we are. That takes faith. It takes faith in the true being to be honest with oneself.

We seem to take pleasure in trying or attempting to be what we think our friends want us to be. To attempt to be what we think our friends want us to be is to reveal to our self that we have no friends. For true friendship is a principle of use, not abuse. It respects the rights of all difference. It weathers all storms. So when man no longer has the need to tempt himself to be what someone else, *he* thinks, wants him to be, then man shall be and peace shall reign on earth supreme. Now I hope that's helped with your question.

Yes. The gentleman over here, please.

You spoke of man and illusion. When Jesus was resurrected, was he resurrected physically and spiritually?

Well, in reference to your question in reference to Jesus' resurrection, Was he resurrected physically and spiritually? It is my firm conviction that the Nazarene was resurrected in the sense of the Spirit that is. The spirit of the Nazarene rose to the light of truth. I do not believe that the Nazarene demonstrated falsehood. Illusion is falsehood. It is not a reality. It is the reflection of truth, but it is not truth. Therefore, I am firmly convinced that the illusion or form of the Divine Spirit known by man as Jesus the Nazarene, that the illusion was not resurrected because I am firmly convinced that you cannot mix truth with falsehood and have freedom. Does that help with your question? Thank you.

Yes, the lady here, please.

Is the living word, the nom, a kind of transcendental or intuitive hearing, a sound?

The living word, yes. All words—truth, truth is expressed, of course. That which is living, we understand as life. We understand the Light is a living Light. Because, you see, it is life. Now the living word is whatever word that flows through the human being that is not dimmed or obstructed by shadows, illusions, which are not truth, which are not reality. And so that is a living word. We have in this understanding and philosophy, the Living Light Philosophy, that "I speak my word forth into the universe knowing that it shall not return to me void but accomplish that which I send it to do." You see, when we know beyond a shadow of any doubt that the word we speak is not dimmed by the censorship of what we have already spoken, therefore it has the life of the Light that is flowing in the moment. Does that help with your question?

[Thank you.]

You're welcome. The gentleman behind you. Yes, please.

If what we speak now isn't necessarily in keeping with what we spoke at another time, will it be dimmed still?

Oh, of course, indeed it will, if there is the thought of I. The thought of I is the form of the I. It is not the I itself. You cannot put the I, which is eternity, the I, which *is* truth, into form. And the moment you place it into form, then the form limits it; therefore, it is not truth. So if you speak a word forth into the universe and it is not in keeping with the word you have spoken before—it is not in harmony and, therefore, it is not in accord—then consequently, it is dimmed by the shadow of what has already been, if in speaking the word you are identified with the self, which is the thought of the I and not the I. Does that help with your question?

Yes, sir.

You're welcome. The gentleman here, please.

In Serenity's view, is there a connection between self-will and dreams?

Well, there are no dreams possible without the will. We understand the divine will, of course, the will of God, is total acceptance, that the will of man, self-will, is limited acceptance, depending upon what man will permit himself to be receptive to, which is dependent upon what man has already accepted, all right? And therefore, our denials become our destinies.

Now in reference to that and our dreams, of course, there are many causes of dreams. The usual cause of dreams is what man knows as suppressed desire. Because if there was not, by the Divine Architect, that design within the temple of God, the human being, the mind, then man would not be able to maintain a degree of balance in order to function in a physical and mental world. So man thinks that he sleeps and he experiences the release of energy that is trapped, so-to-speak, by forms of desires which have been suppressed by the educated conscience. Now in that respect, of course, there is a direct connection between the self-will of man and the dreams that man entertains.

Now, for example, if—and man does—man says, "I feel good because I was able to do this. I feel good because I experience that." Well, feeling good is not a luxury for man. Feeling good is a necessity because the feeling of good is the experiencing of God. And therefore, it is necessary, for without God, we shall not be. It is not possible. It is the sadness, through the errors of ignorance in our own evolution, that we have limited our receptivity to God or feeling good by the errors of our own experiences. And we, therefore, dictate with our minds how we will feel good and how we will not feel good. Therefore, we have risen in mental consciousness supreme to the divine Infinite Intelligence and placed mental substance (thought) above idea. We have placed perspiration far above inspiration. Does that help with your question?

Yes. Thank you.

You're welcome. Yes, the lady here, please.

In viewing some of these games that are played in the political field and in doing one's part to try to bring about changes for the betterment of the people, how does one keep from becoming frustrated and how does one find a balance between the political and spiritual realms?

Well, first of all, in reference to what we understand, the questioner understands to be the games played in the political arena, the law clearly reveals—the Law of Life—that we cannot grant to another what we have not first granted unto our self. And so in keeping with the Bible that teaches to us, "O physician, heal thyself," we first must qualify our self in order to be instruments through which the good we desire may flow into the world. Therefore, if we see the world as a game of discord and despair and disaster, then that reveals unto us our view of the world. Now, from that vantage point it is not only difficult to be an instrument to help uplift—an instrument because we are never the doers. Only God, the power that sustains us, is the power that frees or lifts us. Our receptivity, of course, is instrumental in that taking place. So, if we see bad, then we are in the level of consciousness within our self where it is registered within our being. Now before moving in consciousness, we must awaken within our self to what is known as the light of reason, for it is only the light of reason that will transfigure or transform us. And we first must qualify our self.

Whoever sees good in all things is awakened to the truth that God, the Divine Power, sustains all thought. The thought is man's choice, but the sustenance and the power that sustains it is the God or Goodness, Life, Light, Truth that is. Now whenever we see the good flowing through form, then we attract, like a magnet, that like attracts like, more of the goodness to flow through the form. So if we see something in the world and it seems distasteful and bad to us, we must realize that *we* are the ones that are doing the seeing, that the Power that sustains whatever the person is doing is the same that is sustaining our own thought, our good thought, our seeming bad thought. Therefore, man must first free himself from judgment and prejudgment, for the law reveals that God, the divine, infinite, neutral Intelligence, is not a judge, let alone a prejudger. So if we want to experience goodness without, we must first awaken to the possibility of the goodness that is within. And then like shall attract like and heaven shall indeed be upon earth. Does that help with your question?

Yes.

There is good in all things for there is no place that God cannot be or is not. Thank you. Yes. The gentleman.

Yes. The seeming economic recovery, which we are having—is this a true economic recovery or is it a false start?

Well, in reference to your statement, the seeming economic recovery, Is it a true recovery or is it a false start? Now, is that which seems or that which appears, is that truth? Well, we know that which seems is not what it is; that which appears is not what it is. We know that from our years of experiences, personally, each and every one of us. And we call that—we justify it as false advertisements. Things are not what they appear to be because, my friends, there are shadows in front of all appearance. Appearance is the illusion, the great shadow.

Now, are you interested in economic recovery for you or for everyone else?

For everyone else.

Well, how about first being interested in economic recovery for you? You see, the law clearly reveals the Law of Personal Responsibility. Man may free himself; he can never free another. But in freeing himself, he is the instrument through which those who are attracted unto him shall be freed, for that is the demonstrable Law of Life. So if man is interested in economic recovery for himself and he is a part of a country, a world, then he is, in that recovery within his own consciousness, an instrument of the recovery. And therefore, all things that are attracted around him shall recover. Does that help you with your question?

Thank you. I see our time has run out. Thank you.

APRIL 3, 1983

Church Questions and Answers 36
[Twelfth Anniversary Service]

And so I thought we might have an exchange of thought and, perhaps, to those of you who are new and especially to those of you who are old, that is, in reference of time being with us, may gain a broader perspective of the true purpose of being here.

For many years now the Serenity Association, through its instrument here on earth, called a church, has shared the Living Light Philosophy. It's called Living Light because we view so many dead ones around, and because we certainly don't believe in death. We know that life is the only way, and anything else is an obstruction to the way. We have taught and shared with you a philosophy that, once applied through the continuity of daily effort, becomes demonstrable. That means that it works for you personally. If an applied philosophy does not work for an individual in a personal way, then it's not worth the personal attention of anyone. That's known, in our philosophy, as being practical.

One, then, makes the daily effort to apply what they are learning. One stumbles many times but does not stop in the continuity of their effort. If that were true, we would never have in the world the great singers, the great ball players, the great scientists, the great composers. We would not have the greatness, which, in truth, is the goodness which we know, of course, is what we call God.

Now each and every one of us have, flowing through us, moment by moment, what we call God or good. Everything everywhere is a living demonstration, an expression of God or good. Now we see things that we do not call good and, therefore, could not be of God. That, of course, is our personal deception and delusion, for if there is more than one God, then there is more than one power. And if there is more than one power, when power is divided, it's known, of course, as force. None of us like to be forced. We have some type of an inner resentment to being forced to anything. And of course, we have this inner feeling not to be forced. Therefore, having this inner feeling not to be forced by anything outside, we certainly awaken within our self not to be forced by anything inside.

And here we have, through all things, all people, all form, the expression of the divine, eternal Light, known as God, the Power, the Truth that is. And then we have the varied forms created in keeping with the divine plan. We have that which is gathered, that which is created, that which is formed. Now we know that as substance. We look at it and see it with our physical eyes. We say, "That is an automobile. That is a cat. That is a dog. That is a person I like or I don't like. Sometimes I like that car; it does what I tell it to do. Then there are times I don't like that car because it doesn't do what I tell it to do when I tell it to do it."

When we experience these likes and these dislikes—that things and people are not doing what we like them to do when we like them to do it—wisdom reveals unto us that it is something inside of us. It is a thought. Therefore, generating within our consciousness a feeling. And from that, an emotion. And from that, a disturbance. From that, a discord. Until finally we're not at ease and we call that disease.

In the Living Light Philosophy, the Light that lives, it is revealed and constantly demonstrated here, publicly, for twelve long years, that we and we alone have the power. It is within us. It is not something we must search for outside, because we will never find it.

We go over the world and we find all kinds of force and all kinds of battles. Most people call that the corporate jungle of life. Well, that's not where truth is, but that is where force reigns supreme. Ever struggling to gather, ever struggling to garner, ever chasing the rainbow that we see and not experiencing the rainbow that we are. Now we cannot be what we do not permit our self to be. But we can permit our self to be what we are by the simple effort of controlling the thoughts that rise in our consciousness before, in keeping with the law, the form of thought becomes the form of pattern, which becomes the form of attitude, which becomes the form of feeling, emotion, disturbance, discord, and disease.

This philosophy reveals a simple teaching: to nip it in the bud. To put God into it or to forget it. We do not appreciate experiencing that which is not good and [not] the abundant joy of life. We must cut it off at the pass, so to speak, as it rises within our consciousness before it becomes a feeling, an emotion, a hurt, a discord, a war, a battle within our self. We have the power, ever available to us, when we choose to use it wisely.

Ofttimes, through patterns of mind, we choose to take the power that is flowing through us and direct it to that which has been. The moment that just passed has been. That moment cannot be changed. It is a creation in our consciousness of discord to attempt to change what has passed. Truth reveals, and repeatedly demonstrates to us personally, "This is the moment in which the power is flowing through me. In this moment and this moment only I can choose to direct it and, therefore, *be*." For those who be are those who experience the joy of life. They are those who view the goodness in all things, for they are in the goodness, the flow of God, within their being, for they have chosen and continue to choose to just be. Whenever we permit our self to direct the great power to what we hope to be, and we direct it to what we have been, we lose the joy of life. We lose the goodness that is the moment that is the Divinity that is our right.

When we permit the great power to pass through us and direct it to a target of our choice and we shoot the missile of our demand and dictate and we hit the bull's-eye, well, it returns unto us and we do not like the return of the morrow. We do not like what is yet to come because we didn't like what has been. Consequently, that reveals the necessity of a change in consciousness. Now if we choose to make that change moment by moment by moment, then we shall indeed experience the abundant good of life.

I have listened for some time to the prophets of doom in this world they call Earth. I listened during the days and years of droughts, and how twenty years or more that California itself would suffer the parched, dry earth. It's so ridiculous. It is so easy to slide and so difficult to climb. It is only easy to slide and difficult to climb because we have judged it to be so. Tell the mountain climber who enjoys the climb to the top and experiences the fullness of his own aspiration that it is better to slide. He will tell you what a fool you are. So it only proves and demonstrates it's what we choose to make it. And so, we have experienced, certainly, not a drought of a twenty-some-year standing that prophets of doom were so willing to broadcast in the world; we have experienced the fullness of God's abundant joy. And so the floods have replenished the lands and have sprouted new the joy of spring, the abundant good. And we have listened to the prophets of doom, over the years, of recessions and depressions and go down the list. And repeatedly I have spoken to you, again and again, that you are paying for the errors and the mistakes of what has been, collectively, as a people. That shall not endure, for that is contrary to the natural Law of Evolution.

We slip and we slide from our own lack of effort. And then we pause at the bottom, where we have slid to, and we look up once again and we view the air—clear and fresh and so beautiful—is at the top. And once again we are encouraged and we start the climb. Some of us climb a little ways and then we rest. And unfortunately, in our rest, we go to sleep; it's called the sleep of satisfaction. A wise man knows that satisfaction is a slide to disaster and despair and, therefore, is not long satisfied. He moves on and on and on. For he knows beyond a shadow of any doubt that it is a sleep; that it's a temporary entrancement. In our philosophy, it's known as the lunatic fringe. It's not the place itself, but, of course, it is the border at which we tempt ourselves.

There is something far greater than the sleep of satisfaction: that is the abundant fullness of life; that is the experience of the joy of the goodness of the greatness of God. Not something you must bend your knees and beg. What kind of a God could that possibly be? Certainly not one that any of us, with our egos, would be tempted to worship.

I have never taught, for any of you, to annihilate the ego. Everything is designed to serve the purpose of good. Should we annihilate what we call our ego or should we use it for the purpose of its design? To move ever forward, to ever climb the mountain and never to reach the top where we can stop and sleep. A wise man ever works towards his goal. It is the fool who thinks he has got it. And so many are the fools. We know they're born every moment, as that man of the circus told millions and still demonstrates. Let us use the wisdom that *is* ours, not something we're climbing around in the world to try to find. It's something that we are. Not something we must agree, of course, that we have been. Not something that we hope to be. It's something that we *are* in the moment that we choose to be what we are and not be tempted, through others' needs, to become something that we can never be.

I spoke to you for a moment here, just the other Sunday. I did not come to please you. I came to reveal. Some of you enjoy what is revealed, and, of course, many do not. But that has not changed our service in twelve long years. For to bring to you what will please you in the moment you dictate what is pleasurable would be so varied and so chaotic, so discordant, there certainly could be no truth and no joy.

So we don't please our self all the time because we're so interested in pleasing others. And because we work so diligently to please others, we've lost the art, the art of pleasing ourselves. Now what is our self? Is it dependent on anything else? Well, if it is, it is not our self. That which is dependent upon something else, be rest assured, is controlled by the something else that it is dependent upon. God, the Light that is, is not a power that is dependent upon man. And therefore, man, for goodness, is not dependent upon God. Man is dependent upon his own willingness to be receptive to that which is. Man has the divine right of choice. He may choose no, he doesn't care to feel good; therefore, he will depend upon that which he knows and has judged is not good that he may feel miserable and, in feeling miserable, may be pitied and, in being pitied, may experience energy, for he has chosen in that moment to close the door to the goodness and the energy that, by divine law, he has the right of choice to be receptive to. Tell me, friends, is that wisdom? Is it even reason? Of course, we know it's not reasonable. Yet, we find many people depend upon their husbands for God. Many husbands depend upon their wives, girlfriends, and etc. for God. Many people depend on many things to experience God or goodness. Therefore, many people are in bondage to, by being dependent upon, many, many things.

For example, a person, a lady is dependent upon her husband for her feeling of good, for her experiencing of joy, for the abundant flow of her life. Well, she's dependent upon him in her thinking of how he is. Now during the early stages, of course, of a marriage, she makes the dictates and judgments based upon her experiences during the honeymoon that this is the way that he is. And therefore, the parameters are made; the judgments are solidified. And the marriage takes place and time passes. And as time passes, she begins to see, "No, that's not the way he was six months ago. Something's happened here. He has to change. He's gotten outside the parameters of my judgments of how he is. And because he has done that, I am experiencing something different. Because it is different to the parameter of the judgments that I have made of the way he is, it is not good. Therefore, I have lost God. Because I have lost God, *he* must change and come back inside the parameter of the judgments that I have made in the early stages of my experience with that particular person." Now the world reveals, because of that basic principle [that has been] established, because of the absolute denial of personal responsibility, because of the loss of the light of wisdom, the loss of truth by the judgments of the human mind, the divorce rate in your world is absolutely astronomical. And it's all based upon the parameters in which the husband has placed the wife and the parameters in which the wife has placed the husband.

Now because of our dependence upon our mind as the source through which goodness may enter our life, we establish these various parameters. And time passes and they're known as has-beens or what has been. Now no one—man, woman, boy, girl, or baby—no one wants to be a wilted flower in an old bouquet. We all want to be as fresh as a spring daisy. No one can tell me that they want to be what has been. Of course, we don't. We all seek the fountain of youth. We all seek the goodness—what we think we were so good—when we were sixteen. Perhaps a little younger for some. But basically, around that time. So no one wants to be, as I said, a wilted flower in an old bouquet. And so we look in the mirror to see if we're wilting or we're [as] fresh as the spring daisy. And if we judge for a moment that we're getting a bit wilted, why, we go through all kinds of techniques, talents—whatever you wish to call them—and make whatever necessary changes that we may look in the mirror and we may say, "Now this is the way they will see me. Therefore, in their thinking I am no longer wilted. Therefore, in my thinking because they think I'm no longer wilted, I think I'm no longer wilted and I feel wonderful." *[Some of the congregation laugh.]*

Now the cosmetic industry has revealed to all of us that that is a phenomenal business. How can it be such a great, successful business if man is not dependent upon it? So it reveals, by its own success in your business world, that man is indeed extremely dependent upon what he thinks he appears to others. So we see clearly here that man, therefore, is dependent not upon the awareness of what he himself is thinking, when he's totally dependent upon what he thinks everyone else is thinking about him, [or] of course, her. By "man" I mean humanity. And so the cosmetic business flourishes in the world.

But what happens to joy and goodness? What happens to peace and harmony? What happens to the beauty of life? Where is the spring daisy? Why, we have given it to those who we want something from. Now, for example, stop and think. Do we care what a person we don't want something from thinks about us? Why, of course we don't. Does a businessman care about the people just walking down the street that don't come into his store and make their purchase and support him? Well, of course not. Does he care, in reference to the principle of his business, what they're doing over in Cambodia or Korea or Russia or someplace else? Not as far as his business is concerned, unless somehow it is related to those particular areas in the world. No. He cares about the potential of those who pass the door and take a look; they may come in and make a purchase. So therefore, a wise businessman, he is interested in those people.

Now we take this business of living personally. Of course, feeling good is a necessity, not a luxury. And we all have the necessity and we all want to feel good. And there's never a moment in our consciousness that we're not trying to find a way to feel good. And so we establish these varying judgments. "This person here, they say things and I feel good. Therefore, I want that person around as much as possible. Because I want to feel good as much as possible. In fact, I have to feel good as much as possible." That is the law. For nothing, in truth, survives without God, goodness. It does not long endure. And so immediately we establish within our consciousness that it is necessary for us to study what this person wants from us that we may appear to give that, that we may, in return, experience the goodness that we judge that we receive when they do and say certain things. And we become dependent upon many people. And those dependencies are in a constant process of changing.

Because the only thing, in the final analysis, that we can control is our own mind and our own thought. And not only is it foolhardy to tempt to control the thoughts and the minds of another being but it is the bondage of all bondages, for it is, in truth, the con artist of all con artists of the universe of universal mental substance. Now when we face that simple truth, we say to ourselves, usually, "Well, I've had it! I've had it with this one. I've had it with that one. I've had it with that one." And go down the list of those who have had it, within your consciousness. *[Some of the congregation laugh.]* And you're going to move on. And so you're going to go out into the world and hopefully attract something better. Well, hopefully in the process you already are something better; you've learned your lesson. A little more, let us say, independence, not dependent and not looking out there to see what they've got that you have judged that'll make you feel good.

Start to go inside—we call that personal responsibility: the ability to personally respond to God, the goodness that is within you in the moment of your choice. And we start the inward journey, difficult as it is, for we spent so many years in our dependence—our absolute, total dependence and reliance upon others for our experience of goodness and God. And slowly but surely, we learn the great lesson to be in the world and never a part of the world. We've had many who helped teach us along the way. And we finally learn that every knock is a boost. "So keep on knocking, I need a higher boost." All right. And then gradually we learn to be with a person, a place, or thing and never a part of a person, place, or thing. To just *be* the God, the goodness that you are.

Remember that true friendship is use and not abuse. It respects the rights of difference; it weathers any and all storms. Now that's true friendship. And fortunate indeed is the one who has one, if only one, true friend. For they are very rare, for it is very rare in our consciousness that we will make the effort—that much effort—to educate our own intolerances. It's difficult—we make it difficult to tolerate ourselves. When we feel bad, we don't want to be inside of ourselves and we turn on the television, we listen to the radio, we run around and do a million different things. We're not good company. We soon learn how to be good company by first finding out whether or not we are good company.

Now we sit perfectly still and we relax and we become aware of how we feel. What kind of thoughts are in our mind? Are they dependent on something outside our control? Forget it. We're still dependent. We're still in bondage. We're still the slave of our own ignorance.

And we sit still; we feel good. We pause [and] become aware of what thoughts are going through our consciousness. [If] the experience of the thought is a good feeling, [then we say,] "Ah, now these are the kind of thoughts that are worth my energy, that are worth attention, that are worth my effort." And you list them all down in your consciousness.

And so, you go along about your business and all of a sudden you feel terrible. You pause. You become aware of what thought that is [and say,] "Oops!" And you kick that out and you replace it with the ones that you already know make you feel good.

Now everyone has within their consciousness many thoughts, both seeming bad and definitely good. Now they have the power, moment by moment, to permit within their consciousness all those good thoughts and act accordingly. For good thoughts are thoughts containing God; they are vehicles through which this great Light is flowing through you. Now if they are good thoughts, they're your thoughts and you can rise them anytime you choose to. They are not dependent on people, places, or things. They are not dependent on bank accounts and girlfriends and boyfriends. They have none of those foolish, stupid dependencies. Because they don't put you in bondage. They free you, your soul, and you feel good.

Now in this philosophy of twelve years of service to the public, we have repeatedly revealed that is your joy of life. It is ever available to you moment by moment. But only you, you alone, in the Light can make the choice at any moment to experience that wonderful goodness that you truly are and in the moment free yourself from what you thought you were. Because what we think we are, if we are honest with our self, is ever dependent upon someone or something. And because it is ever dependent upon something or someone, you never know what it's going to bring.

We all know what we are in truth. And because we know what we are, we graciously and joyously accept, in our experiences in life, what comes to us, for we do not deny the Law of Personal Responsibility. We do not deny the law of like attracts like and becomes the Law of Attachment. Now anyone—we all have some kind of sense. Unfortunately, I wouldn't necessarily call it common. Good sense is not necessarily commonly expressed. It's rather rare. And I think we'd all agree good sense, that's sense that permits us to be receptive to God, to goodness, and the abundant flow of life. But we have that within us.

Why waste our lives? And the numbers of years, they go very quickly. Why waste them so foolishly? For what? For the change in the weather? One moment the sun shines; the next moment it's raining. Are we going to be dependent upon the weather and its fickleness for the goodness of our life? Are we going to be dependent on whether or not she decides to see us or she doesn't? Whether or not he's coming or going? Are we going to be dependent on whether or not our shoes last a month or a year? No. That is, indeed, foolish. Either we're the captain of our ship and we are the masters of our destiny, or we are something else; something that we think we are, that we truly are not. So let us be what we are and we won't have to worry and be so concerned about what someone else *thinks* we are because we are dependent on how they think about us.

Now if this little church, the vehicle of this Living Light Philosophy, was dependent on what everyone thought the way it should be and demanded that it be that way, well, I wouldn't be here. I am, in that sense, quite independent. I never wanted a church! God forbid! I had already been a member of one for many years; and I said, "If that's a church, may God keep me from it!" Well, God didn't keep me from it. I had to face my own adversities, as all of us have to face our own adversities in life. We must face our adversities. This church has served for twelve long years, founded upon the demonstrable, basic principle of personal responsibility.

[When] this one doesn't like that one, [I ask,] "What's the matter with your head? [Have] you lost control? You're in the wrong place. That's not why you're here." I tell my students [that] every day I see them. I tell them on the telephone if they call. And I never fail to tell them. Your God and your goodness is dependent upon how she thinks or how he thinks!? What kind of a God have you got? Get rid of that god. That god is a god of absolute, total bondage. That's not the God, the goodness of the Living Light Philosophy. That is certainly not the God I have ever considered worshipping. Not that type of a god. My good friends, any God that would put you into bondage, dependence, and slavery upon what someone else thinks about you is certainly a very foolish, stupid, ignorant god. That is not the God of the Living Light Philosophy. It is not the God of divine neutrality. It is not the God of balance. It is not the Light that is.

Does the daisy say to the rose, "You're getting all the light. You're getting all the rain. You're getting all the good." Of course, it doesn't! It has the intelligence to share, not compare. How do you suppose I would feel if I started, after forty-two years, to look around and say, "They've got a church building of their own. They've got the gold. They've got this and they've got that." That's comparing! And be rest assured, you're in a mental world that can only take you down to the bondage, the slavery, the total dependence upon fickle thoughts. I'm not interested in that foolishness. That foolishness surrounds me in keeping with the law that I am here with you, but that doesn't mean that I am a part of you. I would not be so greedy to try to take a part of you. Your part belongs to God, the Divine Light. And my part belongs to me. Now to share is one thing. The stupidity to compare can only grant you the absolute dependence on the fickle thoughts and minds of men. That is not the path to freedom. That is not the service of the Living Light Philosophy. That is not the Serenity Church, it's vehicle.

But, you see, my friends, it's available to all of us, moment by moment by moment. And so as all my students and all my members and all my directors, who are few in number because—not that I don't believe in working—but they are a handful, to say the least. And they do a wonderful job, because I am breathing down their neck moment by moment by moment because they think moment by moment by moment! *[Some of Mr. Goodwin's students in the congregation laugh.]* And you see, I must view and I must breathe constantly, because if I don't, the next thing I know I'll be under some kind of a pile down there as they are comparing who's got what and who's about to get something else. That's not the Living Light! That's not Serenity! To free them from the dependence on what someone else thinks about them, that is the Living Light. To free them from the dependence upon a thought that absolutely demands to have its way and takes them to the depths of hell itself. No, that is not the way of freedom. That is not the Light of truth that is available to all of us.

I am so pleased. It was only the other day, after forty-two years, that one of my own students said they finally saw that I was human. I said, "My goodness, they saw me all these years as something divine. God forbid!" I don't want wings. I can't walk around here with wings and do what I want to do. Well, of course I'm human. Does somebody not think I bleed if they cut me? I've been cut many times and I have lots of blood, but I still have got enough left to walk around with. Of course, of course I'm human! I wouldn't even entertain the thought of being something else. Do we all think that somehow because we make our effort to serve God, the goodness of life, that we immediately sprout wings, like ducks? No, that's not what I understand. Are we somehow supposed to be at the bottom of a pond for the observers, like in a zoo, to view us? No, that's not what I understand.

But, you see, my friends, goodness is everywhere, if it is first allowed within our own consciousness. So when I don't please them, I say to myself, being human, "That's, ah, tough!" (I must keep my dignity.) And then I feel better! Don't you see?

Now I won't take up too much of your time, but let us look and see that all the flowers in the field, the light shines upon. None are left out. Total acceptance, the divine will of God. Now total acceptance doesn't mean that we suddenly, here in human form, are divine! Goodness! If we are the totality, which in truth we are, we must accept the demonstrable truth that we're squeezed into a little thing called a form. And how much can one do, squeezed in like that? So let us use the light of reason in this wonderful teaching of the divine will is the totality of acceptance, the abundant good and the wonderful flow of life. Let us, in all of this fullness, let us have the fullness of fidelity to the Light of eternal truth that does not deny that wonderful cornerstone of personal responsibility. Let us fill our consciousness, let us flood our being with that demonstrable truth. And then we shall, indeed, experience the abundant good of life, known as the spirit of joy, moment by moment.

Now I do hope in the time that I have taken that I haven't put you to sleep and we'll go on with the rest of the work.

Thank you.

MAY 1, 1983

Church Questions and Answers 37

And some of the students have prepared some of their questions, and some of you, if you have a question that strikes your mind and your body reacts, then raise your hand, and I'll get to as many questions as possible. So if you will kindly raise your hands, I'll share with you our understanding of this philosophy or any questions you have of a spiritual nature.

I see a hand here. Yes, please.

How does the ozone layer affect the Earth? And what is man doing that puts holes in the ozone layer?

Well, in reference to the ozone layer, which most of us, of course, are familiar with—that without the ozone layer protecting the Earth, the Earth would simply burn up. There would be no life forms left on it. And how is man destroying it? He is destroying it with various chemicals that he's putting into the atmosphere which are detrimental to the very thin ozone layer that protects the planet. The ozone layer, of course, which should be our greatest interest, is the ozone layer of our own universe, of our own mental thoughts. You see, because we have made no effort, yet, in our evolution to gain control over our thoughts, we quickly demonstrate the inability to act in reference to any situation that, by the Law of Attraction, we have encountered. Therefore, our tendency is to blame outside for our lack of effort inside. And the holes in the ozone layer should be of interest to us, the ones of our own protection, of our own ozone layer of our own mental consciousness. I hope that's helped with your question.

Thank you.

Yes, the lady there, please.

In Discourse 64 it's spoken of the womb of satisfaction, five being the number of faith or balance, and two being the number of creation. And in Seminar 2 it is again spoken of the numbers of two and five, stating that the plane on which we are expressing ourselves is known as the fifth plane of the second sphere; that this is a school of the poles of opposites through which we must pass. Could you please further explain the correlation of these two statements, if there is one?

Well, in reference to the number two or the duality of creation, of course, all of our senses register within our consciousness these opposites, the seeming good, the seeming bad, the seeming right, the seeming wrong. Now anything that is seeming or appearing, of course, is dependent upon our faith, for our faith is the very instrument through which we establish our own judgments, our own thoughts, and our own beliefs. As you well know, beliefs, they come and go. Man is in a constant process of changing his beliefs. But faith, the power that is, man does not change. Man calls religion faith. Religion is belief. It's his belief and, therefore, his binding to that which he believes. For example, if you believe in a god that is a giver, then you must believe in a god that is a taker. And whoever believes in a giving god, believes in a taking god. And so when they pray and they want something and they don't receive it, then that god in which they believe, this gift god, they soon discard that god and rarely find another one to take his place. Now those are the false gods of which the prophets have spoken for untold ages.

Our philosophy clearly demonstrates that it is not a matter of believing; it is a matter of knowing beyond a shadow of any doubt. You do not see the air, but without the air, you do not live in the present experience that you have. Therefore, does man have belief in the air or does man have faith in the air? So the question must be asked: Is [it] possible for man [to have] the duality of creation, the experience thereof, without what is known as five or faith? Does that help with your question?

Yes.

Fine. Yes, the lady here, please.

We have been told that the letter of the law demands self-supremacy. Can you elaborate on this?

Yes, thank you very much. In reference to the letter of the law, which killeth, that demands self-supremacy, without the demand of supremacy, then self, as we know self, the importance of self, the need of self no longer exists. Now without an existence of what we call self, that simply reveals there's no identification. It is the identification with the form that creates the belief known as self. And so man is dependent, as long as he identifies with form, on the creation of what he calls self through his belief and, therefore, his judgments. That is his dependence. When man loses that dependence, he best find something to take its place; otherwise, he is no longer identified with form and is no longer form on the planet that you know. Does that help with your question?

Thank you.

You're welcome. Yes, the gentleman back there, please.

What's the spiritual significance of astrology? And is there a method . . . [The remainder of the question is difficult to transcribe.]

Well, in reference to astrology—and we've spoken before on the Babylonian astrology, based upon seven planets, which is incorrect, demonstrably incorrect. It is lacking the two planets. It has basically become, in your world, a suspicion. Worse than that, it has become a crutch. For example, a person awakens in the morning; they don't feel very well. They rush to the morning newspaper. They see that this isn't their day. They justify how they feel; they make no effort to do anything, and therefore they become a cripple and dependent upon circumstances and conditions beyond their control so they don't have to make any effort. I do hope that's helped with your question.

Yes, the lady there, please.

Yes. Does television create forms in the atmosphere?

Why, of course it creates forms. Because, you see, it is a frequency and it goes out into the atmosphere and you call it a frequency or vibration, dependent, of course, upon your own conception. Any sound, which television is—few people realize that it's sound, unless they have a volume knob to turn. Any frequency (sound) is form. Any form is color. Therefore, sound is color and color is sound. And it's all creation. It is beneficial or detrimental depending upon whether or not you are dependent upon it to satisfy your senses and, therefore, sleep in satisfaction. Does that help with your question?

Yes. Thank you.

You're welcome. The lady here, please.

When we came to this Earth, did we have guides and teachers to help us come into this Earth? And as we evolve through this philosophy, do they stay with us or do we get new ones? And as we get older, do they still stay with us? And by the time we go on the other side, are they there to greet us or do they change?

Thank you very much. In reference to God has given his angels charge over thee, lest ye dash your feet against the stone of ignorance, we enter the Earth planet, a soul entering into form, with what we call guides and teachers, God's ministering angels, to assist us in our efforts to perceive the lessons of life. These guides and teachers, in keeping with the Law of Attraction, that like attracts like and becomes the Law of Attachment, they either grow with us as we grow, broaden our horizons, and expand in consciousness, or they go and new ones take their place. Some stay with us throughout our Earth experiences and go on with us because they have and do make the effort to make the changes that we are making.

Remember that a guide or teacher is never more illumined than potentially we are our self, for that is in keeping with the law that like attracts like and becomes the Law of Attachment. Therefore, some helpers, guides, and teachers are with us just like so-called friends here on Earth. Sometimes they prove to have been, after twenty years, an acquaintance, instead of a friend. Because true friendship, as you know, respects the rights of difference and will weather any storm. We find, with our so-called friends, the time comes that certain experiences arise between us and, therefore, suddenly we stop and we think they never were a friend; they're only an acquaintance. Well, it only reveals that *we* were not a friend; *we* were only an acquaintance. For, you see, a true friend doesn't have to tell a friend that they're a friend. A person must learn to be a friend inside their own consciousness, a friend with themselves: to accept all parts of their being and not to be disgusted, discouraged, or adverse to any part of their being, for all lessons of life are necessary to life itself. And so, to some, there is a struggle; to some, it is a pleasure. And it's a constant process of change dependent on how much effort we alone choose to make. Therefore, our guides and teachers, some come and some go, and some stay and some grow. Does that help with your question?

[Yes. Thank you.]

You're welcome. The lady here, please.

What about these machines—I don't even know the name of them—that are supposed to help one to better breathing? Do you know what I mean?

Yes. There are many—thank you, so much for your question in reference to machines to help us in breathing. Now, you see, everything necessary for the perfect health, harmony, and abundant good of the human being already exists within the human being. Now if the human mind makes a judgment that such and such is necessary for the restoration of their health, then in the judgment they become dependent upon that which is beyond their control. Therefore, in keeping with their belief, which is an effect of their own judgments, there are times when it is necessary for various individuals to seek help in their breathing, or anything else, on something that is outside of themselves. However, the Divine Architect has so designed the human body that everything exists within it for its total restoration. That, of course, is dependent upon the awareness or the ignorance of each and every individual, whether or not they shall be dependent on something beyond their control to, once again, regain control. Does that help with your question?

Yes.

Thank you. Yes.

What is taking place in our consciousness when we make a spiritual commitment?

Well, if it is spiritual, the human mind cannot decide that it is. For that which is subject to a thing cannot be greater than the thing to which it is subject; therefore, it is not a spiritual commitment. [A spiritual commitment] is not dependent upon the human mind for the awareness of whether or not it is spiritual. Now the human mind may register in its consciousness that this is a spiritual commitment, but whether or not it is spiritual is dependent and revealed in its own demonstration. That that is spiritual is that that is a vehicle through which good, God, goodness is expressed. Ofttimes we think that we are doing something spiritual and we find the results are far from good, God, or goodness. It only reveals and demonstrates to us that the human mind, being subject to the Spirit, cannot be the authority over the Spirit and make a judgment or decision which is spiritual and which is not. Does that help with your question?

Thank you.

You're welcome. Yes.

In their healing capacity, are plants and animals able to perceive the color of a person's aura? Are plants and animals able to blend the color of purity with a person's aura?

Well, in reference to a plant or nature being able to perceive a human being's aura, they certainly have the ability to react to it. And one cannot react to something that one cannot perceive or recognize. Therefore, it is demonstrable that nature, plants, trees, flowers, etc., indeed have the ability and demonstrate the ability to perceive the varying frequencies and emanations of a human being.

Some people say that certain people, they have green thumbs. Other people try to make a plant grow and they water it, care for it, fertilize it, and feed it, and it just doesn't seem to do well. Then they decide, "Well, the spot, the location isn't right." And they move it someplace else and it still doesn't do well. Until finally, they throw it out. Well, you have to understand that just like another human being or an animal, they have sensitivity. They are sensitive to harmonious emanations, and, of course, they are also sensitive to discordant emanations. So a person who does not really demonstrate care for a plant or an animal, the plant or the animal reacts accordingly in the best way it can, that it doesn't want that person around them. And so, just like we react, either harmoniously or discordantly, to people and things around and about us, the things that are around and about us (mirrors reflecting where we are) react accordingly. Does that help with your question?

Yes. Thank you.

Yes, the lady there, please.

When someone commits suicide, does someone come to meet them? And what happens to them?

In reference to the question, When someone commits suicide, does someone meet them? And where do they go, if they go? Well, the thing is, in this so-called act of committing suicide, the only thing you do—it's like taking off your shirt or your dress—the only thing you do is you take off this physical suit. Now you still have a mental suit. You still have an astral suit. And the temptation for taking off the suit or committing suicide is registered, indelibly recorded in your mind, in your mental body; so you continue on with the experience. However, you do not have a physical world, a physical suit in which to work out the experience, for example. So you have a much more difficult time. It's like a person viewing the world and speaking, shouting, and everyone continues on with whatever they're doing; they don't hear them, you see. So there is no escape from whatever law that we alone set into motion.

Does someone meet them in keeping with the laws of evolution and their own merit system? Of course, there are rescue workers that try to assist them to help them to make changes in their consciousness, changes in their mind, which are absolutely indispensable for their own healing and their own freedom of the transgression of natural law that they alone have set into motion. Does that help with your question?

[Yes.]

Yes. *[Addressing another student, the teacher continues.]*

Yes. *Total acceptance being divine will, and total consideration being divine love, what is total consideration and how does one go about considering totally?*

Thank you very much for your question. What is total consideration and how does one go about considering totally? Well, now let us take—for example, one is driving along the highway; you listen to the radio. Suddenly they have a desire. Well, now that desire is not related to their driving the car at the moment. It isn't even related to the highway that they're supposed to be viewing so they don't have what they call a seeming accident. But it is related to a song that they heard some time ago while they were in the process of filling some other desire. Do you understand? And so they're listening to the radio and suddenly, seemingly from nowhere, they have an unrelated desire to driving the car. Now what do they do with that desire? Do they drive off the highway and head for wherever their mind dictates that that desire may be filled? Well, if so, one can say their total consideration is totally limited to the desire of the moment. You hear?

Now, if one has this particular song and through the laws of association which, man in his mind, when he's self-identified, is addicted to, hears the song, through the Law of Reference, the desire strikes a blow to his mind and his body does not react, [does not] stop his car, [does not] get off the highway, and [does not] go where he thinks he can get the desire filled, then he begins to think more deeply. He begins to consider and he asks himself the question, "Why this and why now?" Now with the question will rise up many answers from his own mind. Some of them reasonable and some of them not so reasonable. And so he thinks and he thinks and he thinks more deeply. Because, remember, desire—a child of judgment because man's mind makes it a child of judgment. Man must stop and consider, "Why do I have this thought at this time? What is it inside of me that has prompted it into my consciousness? Of what benefit to me can it be?"

Now in these things, you see, you must understand judgments come up by the untold thousands. Remember that judgments—our human mind is expert with judgments and justification. We have this wonderful, I guess you might call it a knack, for example, this wonderful knack of justifying anything and everything in order to fill the temporal desire of the moment. And so we must be patient with our self, demonstrate the wisdom of patience that we may gain tolerance with our self, that we may listen to the multitudes of defenses of our judgments to all the justifications. And remember, one thing about justification (to justify things) you will always find in justification there has to be a victim. And be rest assured the victim will not be you. Someone else is to blame. Something else is to blame. You must realize this about justification. For those are the little defenses that rise up from the self and the judgment. "Such and such happened yesterday or the day before. So and so didn't treat me kindly," and on down the list.

The more justifications that we have reveals the more self-identification we have. We have a lot to defend. You see, as we over-identify with our self, we have absolutely, demonstrable multitudes of justifications: why we did this, why we did not do that, and on down the list. Man calls those things excuses.

Never without excuses. Whoever is over-identified with self, you may be rest assured, they are an expert with justifications or excuses. [If you were] supposed to be there at some time, [if you were] supposed to do something, etc., there's always an excuse. There's always a justification. Now that reveals to all of us total bondage.

What does that have to do with consideration? It has a great deal to do with consideration. We are lacking, of course, in the broadening of our horizons. We are not considering, even in our own domain of self, we are not considering other possibilities. We are not considering what is happening to the thought that we alone are supporting and sustaining with this life-giving energy. So a wise man, he pauses and he says, "I see, this desire has entered my consciousness in keeping with the Law of Reference, in keeping with that which I have already experienced."

You see, there's one thing about having experienced something: if you have experienced something and if you have permitted yourself total consideration, which is all your levels of consciousness awakened at that moment, then there is no need to reexperience it. Surely, once is enough! It's recorded in your memory par excellence. It is ever available to you at the moment of your choice. What is the need, with so much experience yet waiting in the universes, to repeat the same old experience, to insist and to demand that things be the way they were yesterday? Why, that's contrary to evolution. Even the tree will teach you the stupidity of that. Yet man insists on repeating experiences that have passed, demanding that those experiences be exactly like the one he had twenty years ago. Does that make sense?

Then we must ask our self, why do we insist on living in the shadows of yesterday? What type of consideration is that? It's like a woman gets married, or a man, of course, gets married and they demand and insist that, twenty years after the marriage, the experiences be the same as the day of the honeymoon.

That doesn't even make sense. Yet, those are the things that we insist on doing. Living in the past because we are over-identified with the self, and the self contains the memory par excellence of all the past events. And, you see, we cannot move ahead because we insist on living in the shadow. No man can see the Light when he stands blinded by it, for he turns around to look—the shadow cast behind us, you see. Do you know of any shadow that is in front of you? *[After a short pause, the teacher continues.]* Hello? Have you found a shadow in front of you?

No.

I have never found a shadow in front of me. But whenever I turn around, I see all kinds of shadows. So wisdom dictates and reveals to us: do not be the fool and turn around; keep thy eye single and look straight ahead.

In this moment everything can be done with total consideration and total acceptance; that the intelligent, infinite Power that is your very breath of life—and if you don't believe me and you don't think so, stop breathing and stop it for at least eleven minutes and let's see if you move after that! This infinite, intelligent Power is in the moment that you are. Now if you insist on being in the moment that you *were*, then all you are doing is sustaining, maintaining, and supporting a shadow of life, the reflector of where you used to be. That is not evolution. That is contrary to the demonstrable Law of Evolution. Change is inevitable. That includes our thoughts, our judgments, our justifications, and certainly our beliefs. So unless we're ready to accept the Law of Life that demonstrates in form, in which we seem to insist on identifying with—instead of the formless, free Spirit that we truly are—as long as we insist on identifying with self, which is this enclosure, then at least use the light of reason: look straight ahead and not back at what has been. For you are dissipating the intelligent life Power that is your breath of life. And no good can come to those who insist on being what has been.

Now we go out into the world and we look around at form and creation, and there's not one of us that want to say, "Oh, I've found a has-been. I'm so pleased." I don't see that in your world at all. Everyone wants something new and fresh, whole and complete and, yet, insists upon having a has-been. That not only doesn't make sense but it is contrary to the Law of Goodness. How do you know what new leaf will appear on the tree if you insist on holding on to the one that is presently on it? There's no way possible. Shall you take glue and glue each leaf back on the tree in the fall? And try to stand in the way of the demonstrable Law of Evolution, which is totally dependent upon change.

Our philosophy is based upon the demonstrable truth: Be ever ready and willing to change. Because if you're not, change will leave you in the dust. Now no one wants to be left in the dust. Therefore, either change or be a little, what you call, dust buster, because that's what you'll turn out to be and those are the things you vacuum the dirt up with. *[The teacher is referring to a hand-held, rechargeable vacuum cleaner.]*

So let's stop and think, in reference to total consideration. Let's totally consider what *is* and not try to make what *is* that which we think used to be. For what it used to be, no longer is. Look at the hair on your head and tell me that every day it's identically the way that it was the day before. I assure you it is not. It may be similar, but it is not the same. So either we accept the laws of nature, because we insist on being controlled by the laws of nature (by our over-identification with self) or we go under with the laws of nature and they say that's planting them six feet deep. Is it or is it eight now? Hmm? Does that help with your question on total consideration?

Yes.

Yes. Any other questions? *[After a short pause, the teacher continues.]* Well, looks like we're hungry for brunch. Yes.

Could you elaborate a little on, please elaborate on health, wealth, and also breathing, which is our breath of life?

Well, I'll be happy to share with you health, wealth, and, of course, happiness. Because I would not want health and wealth if I couldn't have happiness. Therefore, they are inseparable—a triune faculty of life itself. First, of course, we must have health. Forget wealth, if you don't have health, because wealth, for you or for anyone, does not exist. A healthy economy comes first, before the wealth of an economy. So health is the number one priority.

What does nature teach us? Nature teaches us the Law of Health. Health, what we call health, is perfect harmony. That simply means that everything is functioning in keeping with its true design; that it is not contaminated and forced to do that which it has not been designed to do. So man stops and he pauses and he thinks, "Now I'm inside this little vehicle here. What is this vehicle designed to do? Is it designed to lay on its back and sleep for 8 and 10, 12 and 14 hours? Is it designed to walk around, to sit, perhaps to work a few hours? Is it designed to be fed, oh, perhaps every hour on the hour? Is it designed to be constantly having its eyes glued to a picture box hour after hour? Is it designed to get angry and emotional and to demand its own self rights? What is this vehicle that I am using truly designed to do? Well, I'm having difficulty finding out," one says to oneself.

So they take a look at the plant or the tree, perhaps even the animal, the dog or the cat, and they begin to study them. And they see. First, they see so much. They say, "Well, the dog doesn't speak my language. Does it speak at all?" It speaks in keeping with the design of its vehicle, and we call that a bark or a whine. And we study the animal a little more and we begin to believe he has eyes and he can see. But, of course, we insist on believing it couldn't possibly see as well as we could, because if he could, he'd have two legs instead of four. Because we've already made the judgment that those forms which are the most intelligent on the planet have to walk upright on two legs. Therefore, the dog couldn't be as intelligent. Therefore, the dog could not possibly see as well. "Possibly has a pretty good sense of smell, not quite as good as mine," of course, because the animal is not the same in its shape, in its size, in its act, and in its seeming deed. So we see from that type of thinking that we will permit our self to go so far in what we will accept.

We have established for ourselves, through what we call environmental conditioning—more properly stated, environmental contamination—we have established for our self these various parameters of consciousness in which we will permit ourselves to function. Now within those parameters, we have shut our self off, of course, from the universal whole. In other words, we have established, by judgment, the Law of Denial, which in truth, of course, is—its final effect—our destiny. We have closed our self from universal consciousness and we have established a parameter of self consciousness. And within that parameter, there are various harmonious and discordant thoughts, denials, and acceptances.

How do we work in harmony within those limits? The only way we're going to work in harmony within the limits that we have allowed our self is to broaden our limits. And in the broadening of our limits and in accepting the possibility of something greater than what our mind has already offered to us, we, slowly but surely, begin to make changes in our consciousness. But in those changes, we have various experiences. We have identified with this parameter of consciousness and we have called that our self: this is the I, the thing we think is us. And when we start to broaden our horizons, all of those things, known as defenses, rise up and we have emotional traumas and experiences. Something that we had not yet accepted has a right to its existence. That's difficult for most of us.

It is indeed difficult when we insist and demand in the final analysis that we are right. We have this great need to be right.

Because we have such great need to rely on something that does not fail. We have a great need to rely on something that does not fail for day after day we see one seeming mistake after another. And as we continue to see these various mistakes and we experience them as discord, disappointments, and disaster, the need to find something reliable increases within our consciousness. It cannot be filled, this great need for something reliable and dependable, until the moment we're willing, truly, to accept the possibility of some authority in the universes that is greater than the thoughts of our mind that we insist on sustaining and maintaining.

One does not readily accept what they cannot control. One is familiar, to some extent, with their mind. They say, "This is the way my mind works." They never stop and say, "This is the way I make my mind work." A person wants an ice cream; they say, "Well, that's just the way that I am." They never once say, "This is the way I've made myself. And because this is the way I have made myself, my mind, I now choose to make my mind a little different to show my mind that it is still a vehicle that I alone choose to drive; that it is not driving me where it wants to drive me." No, we don't say those things. We insist on supporting this discord, this foolishness that "That's just the way that I am." Like you have brown hair, red hair, blonde hair, etc., or black hair: "That's just the way that I am." No. It is just the way we've made our self. A person says, "Well, I've always been a redhead." No, they haven't always been a redhead. Their limited perspective has always been a redhead. Do they think they started, out of the universe, a speck, just in this short earth-life experience? Life herself reveals that stupidity. No. We haven't always been a redhead or a black-head or a blonde-head or anything else. We are what we choose to be.

Now when we no longer choose to be discordant, when we no longer choose the struggles of life, the struggles of life will no longer exist for us. That's our right, you see. That is our divine right.

But as long as we insist on depending upon something beyond our control—you see, we cannot depend upon something that is beyond our control until first we demand and depend upon the dictate of our mind that someone out there is to blame because things didn't go the way we wanted. First, we must be addicted, as an addiction, to the need to blame something outside of our self, because we don't feel well, or whatever the problem may be. First, that must come. Then comes the victimization of what we call circumstances. Then we are indeed in a sad state or condition. But be rest assured, we will not stay there.

Harmony is the Law of Life. Sooner or later—and we're moving in that direction, through a broadening of our horizons, through a total acceptance, which is the will of God. Does God deny the tree its right to existence? Of course, it does not. Does it deny the ant that crawls the ground, the little lizard or anything else? Oh, it does not. It does not deny that. It accepts the right of all. It does not depend on something (circumstances and conditions beyond its control) because it does not blame anything beyond its control. Therefore, the God that is does not have clay feet. It doesn't have feet at all, for it has everything! Whoever has everything has need for no thing. So man, in truth, being everything, has everything. And it is only in moments of absolute blindness that he says he has not. And when he says he has not, he justifies and proves to himself how right he is.

So it is through denial that we destine our life to struggle, disasters, and disappointments; that we find our self without harmony, which means without health, without the joy of life. Health, wealth, and happiness are not dependent upon anything beyond our control. Health, wealth, and happiness are totally dependent upon a broadening of our horizon, upon a lack of demanding and dictating what the universe shall do to serve us.

God, the infinite, divine, neutral, intelligent Spirit, is the greatest servant of all universes, for it sustains and supports all things, even the thoughts of stupidity. But we shall never be—being that which is sustained—greater than that which sustains us. And so when we learn that lesson, we bow in humbleness. We accept what we alone set into motion. We stop dreaming and thinking about the good old days. We stop loving that which has been and we start enjoying that which is. For that which is, is totally dependent upon our view. And our view is totally dependent upon our own effort to gain control of our own mind and enjoy the abundant good that is so close to our nose, to our consideration and reason, that we blind our self to it. I do hope that's helped with your question.

Now if there are no more questions, I think it's time we have a nice brunch. No more questions. Thank you kindly.

JUNE 5, 1983

Church Questions and Answers 38

As our chairman has said, this is the once-a-month time when you have the opportunity to ask your questions of general interest. And so I'd just like to take one moment to ask my own question, which I think we'll all find of interest, hopefully. And the question is, What is the principle of successful living? Whereas so many of us spend so much of our time in the miracle of life, called survival, it only seems reasonable that we should question what is the principle of successful living.

So many things we find our self interested in, in the course of a day, an hour, a week, or a moment. And so often in life we think we have set into motion a goal, a particular project, and an endeavor that we wish to accomplish and, of course, to experience the success thereof. One of the first obstructions that we meet—first, we have the thought, hopefully the idea. And we are filled, to some varying degrees, with enthusiasm. Well, the enthusiasm, of course, is our anticipation of reaping the harvest of our own efforts. So rare in that feeling, so rare in that anticipation, does the awakening of the faculty of patience rise in our consciousness. So [in]frequently does the soul faculty, indispensable to success, known as tolerance, rise. So we find in the success or successful living that absolute faith in the wisdom of patience is necessary, that absolute faith in the benefit of an expanding tolerance within our own consciousness is necessary.

We also find in any endeavor that we seek to reap its harvest—for that is the nature of the human mind: to gather and to garner—we also find that our mind so often becomes concerned. But what are we concerned about? Are we concerned about the endeavor and the goal that we've set into motion? Or are we concerned that our judgments and our dictates of how it should grow and prosper are not in harmony with what we demand to be? So often in business, the business of living, one looks and one sees that things, in keeping with their judgment, are not going the way they decide that it should go. What does that do in truth? It establishes, in truth, an obstruction to the original thought, to the original idea. Because contained within the original idea are all the necessary ingredients for the success thereof, if we do not permit other levels of consciousness to interfere.

For example, we understand there are eighty-one, separate levels of consciousness through which our eternal being is expressing itself. Now an idea, a thought we are receptive to on a particular level of consciousness, on that level of consciousness where we receive the original thought or idea, there is contained all of the necessary ingredients, all of the ways for that particular endeavor to be successful. However, frequently in our efforts in life we do not remain on the level of consciousness where the inspiration, the idea, or the thought we were first receptive to [exists]. So other levels of consciousness, we permit to rise and to interfere. They really know nothing about the original idea, for those levels of consciousness are not receptive to that. They do have access to other levels of consciousness in our own mind and therefore they are limited by what our mind is experiencing, has experienced in reference to the particular endeavor.

Therefore, we find, demonstrated for us daily in the world, many people whose success is rather difficult. We find others whose success seems to be very easy and simple. But we don't investigate thoroughly to see which one is always concerned of how it's going to go and if it's going to go at all. Well, that depends, of course, on us. That depends on what we're doing with our mind, whether or not we, through our own effort of personal responsibility, remain receptive to the original idea. Now if we remain receptive to, through a control of our own mind, to the original idea, then we can be rest assured that it will serve the purpose of its own origin. And it will serve it well. It will serve it successfully and we will complete whatever the project or job is that we have to do, if we will refrain from interfering. Now to refrain from interfering simply means to gain control over one's own mind and to realize and then accept, beyond a shadow of any doubt, that the law—and man is a law unto himself—has no emotion.

Emotion does not make a successful living. Emotion does not make a successful endeavor. That is not what does it. What does it is our willingness to follow the original law that we were receptive to. Now if we do that, through an expansion of our own tolerance, through absolute faith in the wisdom of patience, and through an absence of mental activity or interference by levels of consciousness that are not responsible for the original idea, then we can be rest assured that time will pass, many changes will take place, and success is absolutely and positively guaranteed.

Now you are free to ask any questions that you have. If you will be so kind as to raise your hand. If not, I can have a real holiday today. Yes, the lady here, please.

You spoke of the levels of consciousness as being—you spoke of them as "they." Do they have color?

Yes. They not only have—they have color because they have vibration. They have vibration because they have form; that which is form vibrates, has sound and color. Yes, does that help with your question? Yes.

The gentleman here, please.

As I understand it, God is a neutral force or intelligence.

Well, we might best say "power" in the description thereof; whereas force is that which is subject to and dependent upon mental substance. Go ahead, please.

Then when it comes to making a choice between good and bad, sometimes it's difficult to know what is good and what is bad. I wonder how you clarify it.

It is always difficult to know what is good or what is bad, when we are identified with the limited computer known as the self or the human mind. You see, we have an educated conscience. That educated conscience is based upon what we have dictated in our own mental substance is either good or either bad. That is dependent upon our environmental factors, our hereditary factors, and it is dependent upon what we are doing with the limited mind that we are identifying with. Then, of course, we have a spiritual conscience. You might liken that to a universal consciousness and it is not dependent upon what a person knows or does not know in mental substance. For whatever is good today is ofttimes, to an individual, bad tomorrow. Ofttimes we have a desire and we make the absolute judgment that that is definitely good. Nothing but good can come therefrom because it is our own desire. And then the days, weeks, months, or years pass and then we decide, "That desire was not good at all. Look what happened to me." And we call that—that was a bad desire. Do you understand? But, of course, we can't call it a bad desire until we blame someone else for the results. That, of course, is in keeping with denying the Law of Personal Responsibility. Does that help with your question?

Ah, not really.

Well, it's on tape, if you'd like to review it. *[Some of the congregation laugh.]* Ask your question again. What is good or bad? God is the divine, neutral Intelligence. It sustains what you think is bad as well as sustaining what you think is good. Now if you want to take it and broaden it to universal consciousness, whoever interferes with natural, divine law, we could consider that to be bad because it is discordant to the Law of Harmony. Would you not agree?

Yes.

Therefore, man chops down a tree. Is that good or bad? Does the tree have a right to another year of life? Or doesn't it have a right to another year of life? Do you understand? Then we totally deny the very laws of nature: everything shall rise and by the law of rising, it shall fall. Do you understand that?

Yes. Only—but to take that to the extreme, then how, if you say something like murder, how do you justify it?

Does murder interfere with the divine right of another individual? Does it interfere with their law and their right? That's the question. Isn't that a good question?

Yes. I'm not sure—

Does it interfere with their life? If someone is murdered, is that an interference with their right to life?

Probably.

Yes. [Other members of the congregation respond.]

Well, I think that's rather demonstrable, don't you?

The same would hold true for the tree, would it not?

That's right. Does the tree have the same expressed intelligence that the human does? Is the tree more evolved? That's the question. Have you talked to the tree to make the judgment whether it's less or more evolved? *[After a short pause, the teacher continues.]* Pardon?

Ah, yes, but I wouldn't—

What did the tree say?

We don't speak the same language, so I—

Ah, there's the problem! We are not reading out of the same dictionary. Is that correct?

Yes.

Well, we want to bridge that gap through understanding. Without understanding, there is no communication, except with one's own levels. So let's make some effort to bridge that gap through understanding.

We asked the question, well, What about murder? Well, now we say, obviously, it is demonstrable that murder interferes with the right to life of another individual. Do we, however, know whether or not that individual established laws—for man is a law unto himself—that he in his own ignorance interfered with his own right to life, in keeping with the laws through which he had set into motion to be exposed to that particular society where those laws are firmly established? Now isn't that a good question to ask?

So, is capital punishment right or is it wrong? What is your own evolution and, therefore, what is your view? What have you earned in your evolution and the law that you set into motion to be in what particular society? Does that help with your question? You see, to deny personal responsibility is to deny the demonstrable Law of Life. Do you or do you not have a right to the thought that is in your mind? That's the question. Do you feel you have a right to it? *[After a short pause, the teacher repeats the question.]* Do you feel you have a right to the thought that is in your mind?

Sometimes, unless I judge it to be bad, then I wonder.

I see. If we feel that we do not have a right to the thought that is in our mind because we judge that that thought is bad, then we must accept that we are a house divided and, therefore, cannot succeed. Would you not agree? That that is divided is discordant; it is separate. It is not harmonious; therefore, it cannot be successful.

However, man in his evolution, recognizing that the thought he has in his mind, he now judges not to be a good thought, he must go within himself and ask himself the question, "Why do I judge that this particular thought is not good?" The next thing that will rise in his consciousness is an awareness of past experiences. Would you not agree? How else could he make the judgment: the thought is good; the thought is not good? The good thought or the bad thought in man's mind is totally dependent upon what man has already experienced. Do you understand?

So, is that the way to a successful life? Recognizing that man has had this limited package of experiences, does man make the effort to broaden his horizon, therefore expand his experiences? Or does he remain in judgment to "This thought is bad because twice before I had an experience and it was not in keeping with my judgment of being good. Therefore, by having this thought,

it is bad." And vice versa, of course, [if] it is good. That is a very limited view. It is certainly not broadening one's horizons. It is certainly not permitting a harmonious evolution of one's own being. Would you not agree? Does that help with your question?
Yes.
Thank you very much. The lady in the back. Yes, please. Yes.
How do you recognize opportunity when it knocks, especially when we resist that path that is before us?
Yes, thank you. Well, we resist many paths that are before us. And how do we recognize opportunity when it strikes, if we're constantly resisting because it's change? You see, opportunity, like the hands of the clock, meets every so often. Whether or not man is ready to stand there at the meeting is totally dependent on how much man is attached to what has already been. The degree of attachment to any thought or judgment is totally dependent, of course, upon past experiences in one life and is ever in keeping with the degree of over-identification with the self, which is the limited computer of past experiences.

So, one resists. Why do they resist? They must ask themselves that question. "I resist this change. The reason I resist this change is based upon these experiences of the past." That's called awakening. You take a good look at those experiences in the light of reason and you say—and you look at them—"Are these particular experiences from years ago, or days, or months ago, applicable to what I personally choose to do at this moment?" Now if you think they are applicable, then you don't make the change, but at least you give yourself a chance. Does that help with your question?

Yes. Thank you.

For opportunity is constantly knocking at our door. And, however, as I said, because of over-identification with the self, we resist repeatedly. Yes, now remember, a forced growth is not a healthy growth because those things that resist will rise, perhaps mid-stream, and do us in. And that's not success. Thank you.

The lady in the front please, yes.

What is helpful in getting closer to the original idea?

"What is helpful in getting closer to the original idea?" First, for example, a person awakens, perhaps in the morning, and they have an idea about something. And they feel very good about that. Would you not agree?

Yes.

You've had many ideas. I'm sure you would agree. Now, one must become aware of what level of consciousness they're on when they receive the idea, their inspiration. One must be aware, through a self-awareness, aware of how their own mind works and why it works the way that it does work. Once making the effort to gain that awareness, then one can gradually, slowly but surely, begin to control it. The mind is not designed to control the formless, free Spirit, the intelligence that we truly are. It is not designed for that purpose. It is designed to be used. And because we have not made the effort to properly use it, we have abused it. And it is the law of our own abuse that the mind now uses us. For example, one says, "I do not think about life the way I did twenty years ago." However, if they have an experience that through the Law of Reference and the Law of Association permits an experience of twenty years ago to rise up, they will emotionally react in keeping with the experience of twenty years ago. Does that help with your question?

[Yes.]

Thank you. The lady here, please.

How can we become less emotional?

One becomes less emotional through less identification with the self. The more we think of our self, the more emotional we become. You see, we must someday accept scientific fact: in the human mind, through its process of evolution, is what is known as the primitive mind. So we study the lizard to see how it reacts and then we know a little more about our own emotions. And we study the various animals and we learn a little bit more about our aggressions and all of those different types of things. Then we make a reasonable decision—remember, the soul faculty of reason only expresses through the conscious mind; it is not something that reacts from the depths of our subconscious. So the less we identify with the thought of I, then we become more identified with the I that we are and we're not as emotional.

What is emotion? Emotions are levels of consciousness that rise up to protect themselves; they feel threatened. Man is always threatened because man insists on being emotional. A non-emotional person is not threatened. You cannot threaten that which is, for that which is has always been and shall ever be. It is only that which you *think* is that can be threatened. If you think that this is the only life you will ever know, then you walk around in great fear. You never know, because it's constantly being threatened. And if you think the judgment that you have is right, absolutely and positively, and the next step you believe that you are that judgment (you believe that's you), then you walk around the universe threatened and one lives in fear.

You see, fear is mental substance—the human mind's control over the eternal being. So when man is experiencing fear, man is expressing his emotions and constantly on guard, constantly working to defend himself, to protect himself. Truth needs no defense because truth just is. Crushed to earth, it constantly rises again. So if we want to be less emotional, more reasonable, therefore successful in life, then we must make the effort to stop over-identifying with the self, which offers to us only emotional reaction to everything to protect itself. Does that help with your question?

Yes. Thank you.

You're welcome. The lady, here, has a question. Yes.

Well, I don't know quite how to word this, but at some time along the path are you handed dreams by your guides?

In keeping with dreams, you see, many people, aware and many not aware, have guides and teachers from other dimensions who, in keeping with the Law of Attraction, of our own efforts, are attracted to us to help us and to try to reveal to us, in keeping with our own efforts, what is to be. Now that is often done so that we can stay true and honest to our original purpose of being. Sometimes these dreams, of course, are extremely prophetic. There are also dreams that rise up from suppressed desires.

We have to understand that nothing in the universe is what we would call alone. Everything is inseparably connected. There is only one Intelligence. One Intelligence, that's all there is. That one Intelligence expresses through all form: the human, the plant, the animal, everything, including, of course, the rock. Now that Intelligence is limited only in expression by the form through which it is expressing; that is its only limit. So therefore, when we—and this is getting to dreams, of course, because life is a dream. What kind of dream shall we dream when we are the dreamer? Now the thing is that [if] a person wants to communicate with the Intelligence in the tree or the plant or the rock, then one must, in their consciousness, go beyond the limits of form. You see, when we permit self-thought, we are limited by form and image because thought is form; it is image. We must go beyond image, beyond self-thought, beyond form to the formless, free Intelligence that we truly are. Now when we enter that level of consciousness, then our communication with the tree, the Intelligence contained and expressing through it, or the Intelligence expressing through anything, no longer is there an obstruction. The obstruction exists in our own error of not making the conscious effort to free our self from a world of limit, of form, image, and self-thought.

Now we go off to sleep and the first thing we are receptive to are all of the suppressions of the day, of the week and they'll rise up with all kinds of dreams. Then there are times when we rise beyond that in consciousness and we are receptive to Intelligence expressing on higher levels of consciousness.

But we have to remember that we our self have risen to those higher levels of consciousness and in so doing that's where we are at that moment and we are helped. Does that help with your question?

Yes. Thank you.

You see? Yes, the lady here, please.

Could you fill me in a little more—fill us in more on singing and emotion? What, what's the . . .

Well, as I have spoken to our own choir, here at the church, singing is like speaking. Hopefully, it's harmonious, but not always is. It's dependent on the form which it's having to flow through.

We know in this philosophy that the spoken word is life-giving energy. Therefore, the question must be asked, what does it give life to? What does it give life to? Well, it gives life to the form, you see, of the thought.

Many people say the word *good* and they think the opposite. So it's like singing. When you go to sing a song, the words you are singing are telling you something. Is your mind seeing what your mouth is speaking forth? If it is not, you are a house divided. And no matter what you say, not being united, there is not the harmony that one might think there is. So many people—singers, speakers, or anything else—are overly concerned, "How did that sound?" They are so interested in listening to what their mouth just said that there is no unity whatsoever between the words that are sung and the thoughts that are thought. Therefore, the mental body is divided in consciousness, and that which is divided is discordant no matter what anyone says.

So if you want to speak and be effective, if you want to sing and be effective for the good, then one first must be the good within, for like attracts like. And one can only grant to another what one first grants to themselves. Do you understand? So if you are singing a song about climbing a mountain, do you see in your mind's eye that actual climb taking place? If you are singing a song about sailing on a river, do you see the river and do you feel yourself sailing? Well, if you do, then your word is united in your mind, and that which is united, therefore, is no longer an obstruction to the good that you are, you see.

The only reason we think we're not good is because we identify with creation and the Law of Creation reveals to all of us the duality thereof. For that which is created (or form) is dual. All of nature teaches us that. And being dual, or opposite, it is not one, harmonious and united. So when man identifies with self, he says, "I feel good," only then something rises right on up and gives him the reason, the justification, of course, the justification why he shouldn't feel good. Therefore, he feels lousy. Because it looks around inside of its computer to find the opposite. That is the Law of Creation. So anyone who identifies with self, the limited computer, has to accept, sooner or later, that every time they feel good, they're going to feel lousy because they're going to make great effort within their own computer for the opposite, which is the balance. Now if you want to be free from that karmic wheel of delusion, then one must make their own effort to enter it, not infrequently, until finally they recognize: "This is the Law of Creation. It says good and bad. It says day and night. It says win and lose. That's what that is. I am not that. I choose now to enter that to move that body which is subject to that law"—you understand?—"and therefore I will be in it for a time, not a part of it." And it will serve the purpose of its original design: to be used, not abused. Does that help with your question on singing?

Yes. Thank you.

You see, if you sing for that which you are, not what you *think* you are, then your voice will unite with your imagery, your mind, and it will come out good. You won't have to worry, "Is this note too high? Is this note too low? Is this note just right?" You won't be all that foolish concern because every time you think you sang the note right, the very next note is going to be worse. Because that's to keep your mind, the Law of Creation, in balance. So by less identification with what you think you are doing, you will be doing what you are. And it cannot help but be successful, because it's freed from concern. The tolerance, of course, is expanded. There's nothing to obstruct it. There's no question about the wisdom of patience, for patience just is.

You see, when you give what you have to give and you care less what the world does with it, then you will live and fulfill the purpose of your being. But if you insist, through self-identification, to do what you think will please others, then you will suffer through life, but you will survive. That's known as the miracle of life. But as far as successful living, do not wish for that and demonstrate the opposite law. Does that help with your question?

Yes.

Thank you. Our time is up. Thank you very much.

JULY 3, 1983

Church Questions and Answers 39

As our chairman has stated, this is the once-a-month time for you to present the questions that you have of a general interest. I will be more than grateful if I am able to establish the necessary rapport with those who may have some light to shed upon your questions. So if you will be so kind as to raise your hand, we'll reach as many people as possible.

Yes, please.

In the taped lectures [of the Living Light Philosophy] it mentions that spiritually evolved people can sometimes see spirits. Does it mean that if you don't see spirits, you're not spiritually evolved?

Well, now that's a very good question. It mentions that sometimes spiritually evolved people see what we call spirits, is that not correct?

Yes.

We do note that it mentions sometimes. For example, many people are spiritually evolved and have yet to ever experience the seeing of a decarnate spirit. There are many frequencies that we are in rapport with. We identify with many different things in life. And our identification is the limit or the censorship that we place upon our own evolving soul. Consequently, many people who are spiritually evolved have identified and dedicated their life to a particular avenue of expression that is not the avenue of communication with decarnate spirits. That in no way implies, nor does it dictate, that they are not as spiritually evolved, or that those who see, or do not see, decarnate spirits are more evolved. Many people see and experience what they interpret to be a decarnate spirit. But unless we understand that we are more than a physical, mental, spiritual, astral body, then, of course, we are limited by our own understanding of our own interpretation of what we see and what we view. Does that help with your question?

Yes. Thank you.

You're welcome. Yes, the gentleman back there, please.

You've explained that this is the planet of faith. However, in the natural order of things, as witnessed with cosmetics, it is also a planet of deception. Could you explain the difference between faith and deception?

Faith and deception?

Yes.

Why, many people have faith in deception. They have so much faith in it that they absolutely believe it. Now that, of course, is ever in keeping with one's own evolution. We have faith when we turn the key in our automobile and we step on the accelerator that the—and we're in the proper shift, of course—that the car is going to go. Now we have that faith. Now does that make that a fact? Or does it make it truth? Which is it? That is the question. So we find in life that through direction of this power known as faith that we believe in many, many things. We also, in our own experiences throughout life, we sooner or later realize that our belief is the very limit and is the instrument through which we are bound to a particular, limited view of the universe. So man can have faith in many things. It is not limited, of course, to goodness or God. For many people have faith in whatever strikes their fancy of the moment.

Now, many people, in fact, all of us spend much of our time having faith in our mind and what our mind has to say to us. And we call that type of directed faith, we call that fear. We're afraid that the world is going to be blown up. We're afraid that the economy is going to collapse. We're afraid that we're going to have another very cold and wet winter. We're afraid that there's going to be a drought. And we are so afraid that we actually believe it! And so, that is a revelation and a demonstration of the direction of our faith to mental substance. Does that help with your question?

Yes, the gentleman there, please.

In The Living Light *in Discourse 37, I seem to have come across a contradiction when he talks about the hands of action, the color of action being red and that of wisdom, divine wisdom is yellow. It seems to say that the hands are yellow . . .*

It seems to say what?

That the hands are yellow and the hands are . . .

No. That is not what it states. But let us, perhaps, take a few moments in reference to your question—Thank you. You may be seated, if you wish.

Thank you.

It is revealed in *The Living Light* textbook, the original book, that red is the color of action. That yellow, or what man calls gold, is the color representative of wisdom. And it reveals clearly, upon further investigation, that the action or movement of wisdom is the indispensable ingredient to creation. Without wisdom, the act of wisdom, there is no formation in any universe at any time.

In reference to contradictions, let us understand, upon thorough investigation, in the study of anything in life we view it from one level of consciousness or attitude of mind at one time. We return to it, ofttimes, with a different attitude of mind. Depending upon our attitude of mind at any moment is our interpretation revealed to us. So man studies any law and interprets that law according to his own state of mind or state of consciousness. However, the demonstration is the revelation. It is when we apply the law (that we study) is it revealed to us and are we freed from the duality of creation or the interpretation of contradiction. Does that help with your question? I'm sure, upon more thorough investigation, you will see what appears or seems to be a contradiction is simply nothing more nor less than the understanding that we have brought to the law that we are attempting to apply. Thank you.

The gentleman here, please.

In January, you spoke of this being a time of there being an uplifting. Did that apply to the whole world or to this society?
Do you mean in the Annual Forecast in December?
Yes, sir.
In December.
December.
In reference to upliftment in speaking of this universe?
Spiritually, economically and across the board.
Well—Thank you. I just want to get to the right part of that particular forecast. In reference to a time of spiritual upliftment and betterment and in reference to the improvement of the economy, it was stated in our regular Annual Forecast that there would, definitely and positively, be an improvement and an upliftment. To those who view our world in perhaps a bit broader perspective already have had that experience.

Perhaps we should consider what happens in our own life from our own thoughts, our own judgments, our own dictates, and our own needs. Ever in keeping with our belief in limit, ever in keeping with our dependence upon something beyond our control to improve our life, does our world appear to us. We compose, as human beings, an indispensable part of the world, such as a tree does, or an animal does, or a blade of grass does. So we have, by that living demonstration, a responsibility to the world, to the universe, and universes, as an indispensable part of it. All things that are, are necessary for the vibration that is at any given moment.

Ofttimes a person believes that they are going through an unbearable struggle, and someone else they communicate with and the other person says, "Yes, I can see that you're struggling with great difficulty, ever in keeping with the needs that you alone insist upon establishing." Now that is an avenue of reason, revealing and demonstrating the Law of Personal Responsibility, but one does not leave one out on the limb where one finds one, for there is the Law of Solicitation. And in keeping with that law, each one has their own personal responsibility.

Now in reference to this upliftment that was forecast last December to our country and the world as a whole, to the economy especially, its improvement, here in the United States, that is in keeping with the changes of attitude of the masses of people who compose the society and the country of the United States. We, unfortunately, from abuse and from the Law of Habit, no longer value the power contained within the form known as a thought. We have long ago lost that value. And the time has come that, slowly but surely, as material science reveals more and more about electromagnetic energy, as the science evolves to understand what is taking place within the human body to cause a discord, which man calls disease, man will gain ever-increasing value for the great power that flows through the form of his own thought. Consequently, in so doing man will move, slowly but surely, to the demonstrable Law of Personal Responsibility, the ability to personally respond to every thought, act, and deed within our consciousness. And when man stands upon that principle of life itself, he shall know the truth, and in that moment the truth shall free him. I hope that's helped with your question.

The lady here, please.

Mr. Goodwin, could you please speak on mercy killing? If you're in the medical profession, at the time of someone's death, you administer a lethal dose of medicine, to help. And also, about abortions, if someone doesn't want a child.

Yes, certainly. The law clearly reveals that each and every evolving soul establishes their own laws and their own experiences. We enter the planet Earth in keeping with our own evolution, in keeping with the lessons that are necessary for us to free our self from the vehicles through which we are expressing. Those laws are established before we enter the planet Earth. Those laws govern form or limit. And therefore, those laws are 90 percent, *90 percent* fulfilled. For that Power which flows through form, which is limit, is not completely limited by the vehicle through which it flows. In other words, there is 10 percent choice at any moment to change any law in keeping with our own evolution. Now, in keeping with that demonstration that we all have constantly, we often find ourselves desiring to change laws that we alone have established. And in that desiring to change those laws, we are indeed impatient, for we want to escape from the payment of the laws we have already established.

A law established, by the law, the principle of it, shall be fulfilled!

When we transgress any law, we all know that we have an experience known as the penalty of the transgression. So we go through life and we find our self, at times, very upset, very hurt, very emotional because of the experiences that we are having. Now we have a choice in those moments to pause in consciousness and make an intelligent decision in reference to accepting the Law of Personal Responsibility: that our experience is not caused by anyone else. It is not continued by anyone else, because it is taking place within our mind, within our own consciousness. Because it is taking place within our own consciousness, we have the possibility, through our own will, to change it. If we insist upon denying the demonstrable Law of Personal Responsibility, then we continue to pay for the law that we alone have established. However, we are never left without that 10 percent free will to choose to change the thought, the attitude, that is taking place within our consciousness. Whenever we deny this ability to personally respond in life, we give to another (person, place, or thing) the power and the control over our life.

Now a person may say, "I want to have more money in order that I may experience more good in my life." Well, there are two laws established, number one: the need to have more money and, most important, the judgment that to experience more good in one's life is dependent upon making more money, which is dependent upon a multitude of other variables, all, of course, under the control of something or someone beyond our control. So man continues to tread the karmic wheel of illusion-delusion, the effect of ignorance in consciousness.

What does that have to do with what the lady has asked in reference to mercy killing? First of all, in order to make that declaration of "mercy killing," we must have someone that supposedly we respect their wisdom that dictates and judges this person is to be killed for it is an act of mercy. The question then rises, is it or is it not an act of mercy? Does the human mind, without limit, understand and apply the principle of mercy? We all know the human mind does not, for if the human mind understood the principle of mercy and was truly capable of acting upon it, then our minds would certainly be more merciful to our self, and we wouldn't be so miserable so often. Therefore, it is demonstrable that the human mind does not—someone else's human mind, anyway—understand and apply what is known as the act of mercy because we reveal personally we do not understand and apply it for ourselves.

And the law states clearly, what you do not grant unto yourself, there's no way possible you can grant it to another, for you do not have it to grant. If you are kind to yourself, then you have the kindness to grant to another. If you are merciful to yourself, then you have the mercy to grant to another. But we cannot give, my good friends, what we do not have. Therefore, someone has to judge somewhere that it is merciful to take my life [and], therefore, take my life. That is always dependent upon a mental world. A mental world is a world of form. It is a world of limit. It is a world of contradiction. It is a world of discord. And we all know it.

Now, mercy killing and abortion. We must not deny the right of choice that we grant to our self. Each and every soul has the right to choose what they understand to be the good for their life, ever in keeping with the Law of Personal Responsibility and non-interference or transgression upon the rights of another. Now we come to 2 people, 20, 20,000, 200,000, 200,000,000, etc. And we now enter the same law in principle in what we call society. Society, in order to survive and to flourish, as we now know society, must be governed by, hopefully, the wisdom of the strongest of the species. All of nature reveals that truth to us. Whether it is the wolves in a pack or the barracudas in a school, nature reveals the truth whether we like it or not.

Many of us do not like to hear that we are governed by, and therefore controlled by, whoever are the strongest of the species of the human race for they are the ones who are in authority and therefore, they establish the laws by which we are going to be governed. And then, we pause and we think, this is a democracy. Well, of course, it's a democracy! We all go and we all vote. What to go for and what do we vote for? Do we go and do we vote for what we believe is the good of the people living in the heat waves of Chicago or the state of Missouri or Kansas? Is that what we vote for? Is that what we go for? No. We don't even go to vote for what we consider would be in the best interests of the thirsty people in the city of Los Angeles. So as we continue to narrow it down, we see clearly, through honesty, that we go and we vote for what we believe will be in our own best, personal interest. And we're often disappointed. So—and sometimes we are pleased, and that changes according to how we choose to think at any given moment.

So society has established certain rules and regulations, certain mental laws that declare we shall have the right of all women to have an abortion by their own free choice. The question then rises, Is that a good law? Will it bring good to society? Or is it a bad law and will it break society down as we know society today? Well, it's an excellent question. What will *we* do with it? Depending on what we do with the law will dictate what the next law will be. Will it be more restricting than before?

Or will it be more license than before? It's ever dependent [upon]—and does reveal—what it is we do with it. We have traffic laws and we see people driving a million different types of ways. And we still have what you call "accidents." There are no accidents; it's an effect of what someone set into motion: two people; then they came together and we call that an accident. Now we have laws that govern all these things. Do we all abide by them? Do we all apply them? So is there in truth any difference?

Do we believe in a God that says, "Women are second-class citizens. Therefore, men shall judge that they have been brought to earth to bear children and it is unthinkable that they shall abort any of them"? Is that what society is asking for? What is the question? The question can only be, Do we believe in a God that says, "There shall be no abortions. There shall be abortions"? Do we believe in a God that says, "There shall be this and there shan't be that"? And then turn right around and reveal that all of nature, all of nature is working diligently to evolve and to express the true purpose of its design. That's the question that we must ask our self. Because if we do not ask our self those questions, then we do not face personal responsibility. Then we go like sheep to follow whichever drum beats the loudest in our ear. Does that help with your question?

[Yes. Thank you.]

You're welcome. The gentleman here. We have just a few moments left.

If we had never accepted the Law of Personal Responsibility, then we decided that that's what we needed to do, how long until such a change takes place?

My good friend, in reference to accepting the Law of Personal Responsibility, we have accepted it; we have just limited it. That's the only problem. Without an acceptance of the Law of Personal Responsibility, we'd not be on the planet this moment.

We have accepted that in order to enter this world, because we were able to personally respond to the law established and set into motion in order to evolve here in the first place.

You see, it's like consideration. It isn't that we need more of it. We have plenty of consideration. I know many people who have a phenomenal amount of consideration. Why, they consider themselves constantly. So, you see, it isn't a matter of having more of anything. It is only a matter of broadening or expressing in more avenues of expression what we already have.

You see, there's nothing that we need. It is only our view. We look around and because we have over-considered this and have not considered that and we turn and we see, "I don't have any of that." Well, how can you have any of that? You spent no time considering that! You spent all your time considering this. You see? So it is not that we need anything, unless it is the final awakening that we already have it. Because—stop and think. The Law of Denial is the Law of Destiny; they are inseparable. So when man says, "I need this and I need that and I need something else," he is expressing the Law of Denial and is destined to the continuity of the experience.

We say, "We have just a little of this." And we keep saying that and we perpetuate the law of little. So, ten years pass; it's a little bit less. Another ten, it's almost gone. And we never stop to think about the Law of Personal Responsibility, that the only thing we spent our twenty years in that time doing is telling our self how little that we had. Until finally we prove, beyond a shadow of any doubt, how right we are! You see, my friends, little or much has less value to our consciousness than how right we are. So if we say we have a little of anything, the higher priority to our consciousness is to prove unto our self how right we are. I've yet to find an ego that loved to be wrong. So we must understand the Law of Self-Identification. Little and lot is ever dependent upon the insistence of our own mind to continue to broadcast the frequency or rate of vibration through which these experiences will take place within our consciousness.

Now if we're at other levels of consciousness, we look out and say, "Well, I didn't get the chance that someone else had. I didn't get this and I didn't get that. And I wasn't born with a silver spoon in my mouth. I wasn't even born with a gold one." And all of the justifications. When you look at another and you see how—what *you* think—how well and how good they are doing in anything, what you are telling yourself is simply this, "What a lucky person they are." And then you justify how lucky they are. Well, we all know what luck is. It's simply a loser's excuse for a winner's expression, isn't it? That's all that luck is. We justify our laziness. So in that sense, we've done a wonderful job! We have directed this great Power—infinite, intelligent, and neutral—to lying around like the toads! Well, if we were supposed to be a toad, our soul would have evolved into a toad form and not into a human form.

So the first thing to do on the path of freedom is to stand upon the rock of principle, known as personal responsibility—the ability to personally respond to all your thoughts, acts, and deeds within your own consciousness, where you have power. Therefore, not to look outside to see how easy it is for someone else, because each time you look outside to see how somebody else is doing, you direct this great Power, this energy, to that person and they get boosted even higher on the ladder. And you go down even deeper because you see them again and they're doing even better. So that energy that you are receptive to, the effect thereof, is how you channel it. If you want to channel this neutral, intelligent, infinite Power, known as God, to a greater abundance of good, then you must use the law that brings the greater abundance of good into your consciousness. And the use of that law is totally dependent upon your ability to gain control over your mind: so you will not lust for what you judge someone else has, that you now judge that you don't have, but that you do need. That's known as growing up. So when we grow up, we're going to see how great our life really is!

Thank you. Our time is up.

AUGUST 7, 1983

Church Questions and Answers 40

Our chairman has already stated this is your time of the month to ask the questions of a general interest to yourself and to your friends. So as much as time will permit, I will be happy to be the instrument through which your answers are received. If you will be so kind as to raise your hand, I will reach as many as possible.

Yes, the lady here, please.

What is the nature of the desire to find God?

The question is asked, "What is the nature of the desire to find God?" The nature of the thing is the principle or purpose of the thing. So whether or not we believe or do not believe in an effort to seek God, it is the nature [of] us to return to that which we truly are. Now all form reveals the demonstrable truth: that it returns to the cause from whence it is formed. Therefore, all men, their very being, that which moves the form, that which sustains it, the consciousness of it, is what we know as God and returns unto itself. Does that help with your question? Thank you.

The gentleman there, please.

Mr. Goodwin, Jane from Sutter Creek gave me a question for you—a good friend of ours. And she couldn't be here today, but the question is, "How does the unconscious affect relationships that one is having? And could you please give an example?"

Thank you. How does the unconscious affect relationships that we are having? And could we give an example? Based upon the demonstrable teaching that like attracts like and becomes the Law of Attachment, we must understand that when we permit our mind to identify with what we call self or self-thought, we are, at that moment, controlled by all experiences that exist in what is known as the memory par excellence. Now the memory par excellence—because few of us have evolved sufficiently out of identification with self, [most of us] are not aware of the untold, so-called bits of information or experiences that exist in our life already that have passed. So man is controlled by, in relationships, in the attraction unto himself of all experiences, by what he has already experienced, if he permits his mind to identify with what is called self.

Now because experiences are the effects and are never the causes, all experiences are in truth a mirror, which reflects and reveals to us the levels of consciousness that are predominant or in control of our life at any given moment. For example, if a person entertains in consciousness a need to have a fulfillment in any particular area of their life and they identify to whatever degree in consciousness with the need, which is in truth a revelation of self-thought or over self-identification, they are controlled by experiences of the past, [and] will call forth to themselves, in keeping with the demonstration that man is a law unto himself, will call [forth] a repetition of experiences in principle that he has already had.

In order to be free from the constant repetition of past experiences, man must make the daily effort to free himself from over-identification with self. For the law demonstrates to all of us that like attracts like and becomes the Law of Attachment. In other words, birds of a feather flock together and we are known by the company that we keep.

For many years I have counseled people with domestic problems. Of all problems that have difficulty in our consciousness to solve, it's what is called domestic problems. Because the word *domestic*, in that sense, means over-identification with self-need. When we are over-identified with self, we are blinded to the light of reason. Consequently, we insist that our problem and the solution for it exists beyond the limits of our control. In other words, it is someone else's thought, act, or deed that is the cause of the problem that we experience. That is one of the greatest self-deceptions that man can possibly entertain. Because that type of deception, self-deception, causes man, in consciousness, to be the victim of another person. In other words, that in truth is the false god, the god, the idols of clay feet, of which the ancient prophets spoke so wisely long ago.

Whenever we permit our mind to make the judgment that our problem and the solution of it is dependent upon what anyone or anything beyond the limits of our control is doing, we may be rest assured we will continue to be the victim of the so-called problem. Therefore, a wise man, knowing those laws that are personally, moment-by-moment demonstrable to him, makes a conscious, reasonable choice: "Whatever I permit in my life is ever dependent upon my lack of effort in consciousness." For example, outward manifestations are merely revelations of our own inner attitude of mind.

Now we have, moment by moment, the light of reason available to us. Man is never left without intelligent choice. If we find our self in a relationship, a domestic problem, we may be rest assured we can make the change in an instant, for it is only an instant in which we make decisions. We can decide to make the necessary changes within our consciousness, to accept personal responsibility, the ability to intelligently respond to the laws that we alone set into motion and, by so doing, free our self from the seeming difficulty and problem. When we do that, that which is manifest around and about us shall do one of two things: it shall go or it shall grow. For the law cannot be transgressed without its own penalty, and the law clearly reveals that like attracts like and becomes the Law of Attachment, attachment to self. Does that help with your question?

Excellent! Thank you.

You're welcome. The lady here, please.

Mr. Goodwin, could I ask you please, why it is 10 percent free will? Why not 5, or 3, or 20 percent? Why is it 10 percent?

The question, in reference on a scale of 100 percent revealing wholeness or totality of anything—and the teaching is not new, that man is governed by the Law of Cause and Effect. That man has 10 percent or 1 to change a law that he alone sets into motion. Man, God, consciousness, being indivisible, inseparable, is one. When consciousness, God, intelligent, infinite Infinity, enters what we know as duality or form, it becomes, in a world of form, its own wholeness, its own totality. For example, the Law of Creation or Form reveals to us that it is dual; it is 2. It is what we call positive and it is what we call negative. It is not 4 or 5 or 20 or 30. But it is direct opposites. And by being direct opposites, it is perfectly balanced.

Now we look at form or creation and we do not see balance, most of us, most of the time, because we are identified with either the positive or the negative side to the sacrifice of the balance or the oneness or the light that we are. Now we become imbalanced in consciousness by our beliefs, for belief is not balance. Reason is. Faith is its direction. Belief is something that we convince mental substance of to the sacrifice of either the positive or the negative. However, we still have the oneness we are. And when we choose to identify with what we truly are and not with what we think and, therefore, believe we are, then we shall be consciously aware of the oneness, the inseparableness, the indivisibleness that we truly are. Now when man makes that effort and that step in evolution, he is no longer controlled by the duality or imbalance by belief in creation. Whoever believes in creation must pay the price or the penalty of the transgression of the Law of Balance, because we never believe in anything that we do not disbelieve in the opposite represented by the belief of it. Consequently, when man pauses in his consciousness, he is not only aware that he is one. He is not only aware in those moments that being one, he is everyone; that being everyone, he is the victim of no one. But then man, awakening in that demonstrable truth, is free. I do hope that's helped with your question.

Yes, the lady there, please.

 . . . *an affirmation upon total consideration and expand* . . . [The questioner spoke very quietly.]

Would you please repeat your question?

I said, Can you give us an affirmation on total consideration and expand on it, please?

Well, in reference to an affirmation on total consideration, the totality of consideration is totally dependent upon the lack of identification with what we call self. Now there is no way possible to consider the totality as long as we insist on identifying with its opposite, with the limit of self-experience. So we know from our own personal experiences, when we make the judgment we're not feeling well, when we make the judgment that things are not going well, [and then] when we choose to identify with something that we desire, in those moments of directing intelligent energy, through the Law of Attention, to the possibility of fulfilling the desire, we are free from the disturbance and the discord. You see, my friends, total consideration takes an expanded consciousness. And an expanded consciousness is dependent upon freeing our self from the limit of self-identification. I hope that's helped with your question.

[The Total Consideration Affirmation is in the appendix.]

The lady here, please.

Would you please tell us what the meaning of the major colors are?

The meaning of the primary colors? Red and blue? Is—

White and yellow and purple and green.

I see. Well, I'm more than happy—and have shared for many years what color, which is vibration, which is frequency, of course, reveals to us. The thing is, it is not beneficial to us unless we do something with it. The world is filled—for centuries—with philosophies. And this church, the Living Light, continues to share the philosophy that it is receptive to from the world of spirit. The next step in evolution is the application, the application of the laws revealed in the philosophy. How often do we awaken in the morning and ask our self the question, "What laws shall I make the effort this day to perceive?" How often do we ever ask our self that question? It is very, very rare. But of what benefit is it, in truth, to learn and not to apply? It's like going to school to learn to be a physician and never apply the knowledge that we have made the effort to acquire.

Now let us pause in reference to color, vibration, which is sound, and let us think about these things. What are we doing with all that we have? We have so much; we become deluded and deceived by the amount that we have, that we have not. Again and again we search the universe trying to find something more. Because we have so much, we no longer make the effort to inventory it, to be consciously aware of what we already have. Therefore, like a great mountain in front of us, we cannot see the horizon. It is blocked by the mountain that we have built. So let us stop and think, my good friends. What are we doing with what we already have? And if we are not having the experiences of the goodness of life, then we can be rest assured with what we already have, we are not using wisely because we are no longer aware of it.

It's like a person that buys a chair. They use it for a while and they decide they want a new one. And they buy another chair. And they use it for a while and then they buy another one. And the chairs keep going up into the attic until someday the roof caves in. And they wonder what happened. They stored so much upstairs that their house became top-heavy and it collapsed.

Now this is what I am interested in. Whoever is interested in the Law of Balance cannot help but see the light of reason. Without a firm foundation, no house can long endure. And so the firm foundation of a spiritual body and a spiritual being is dependent upon the application of the laws of life as we understand them. If we do not make the effort to apply the laws that we have already worked to receive in evolution, then we are transgressing the law. And the transgression of that law is a very severe penalty. Because nature reveals to us that she wastes nothing. One does not work in life and end up with nothing unless they transgress the Law of Working. And so it is in our efforts to work, to awaken our consciousness, to evolve through the various realms from the animal stage, in which we find ourselves so often, to the angelic stage.

We don't find angels in hell. That's where we find the baser animal instincts, not the angelic faculties. That's where we find self; that's not where we find freedom. Now we move up and down through these realms of consciousness by conscious choice, what we *think* is conscious choice. We go out into the world. Someone is miserable around us; we don't pause and think, "I am experiencing a miserable vibration around me. Am I going to look outside and feel sorry for myself that I am exposed to that? Or am I going to make changes within my consciousness in this moment to enter the light of reason, to establish the law for which I am personally responsible, declare the truth, and change the vibration that I am exposing myself to?"

I have always said, for many, many years, one must qualify themselves first to be effective and instrumental in helping those who are seeking, sincerely seeking, help. Ofttimes we believe we want to change until we enter that wonderful Law of Opportunity and we stand before the doorway of opportunity. There, it welcomes us to make the change that we so often said that we wanted to make. And we look through the door. We want to step through, but we know that it's going to take some effort. And so we turn our back to another day, another time. But opportunity will come again, and once again we will face the door of opportunity. Once again we will not deceive our self and try to twist spiritual truth to serve mental substance.

The great danger in the effort to apply spiritual laws is the twisting of them to serve mental needs. There's nothing spiritual about a law that serves limit! A spiritual law is a law of truth and freedom. It is not designed, nor is its purpose, to serve limit. Its very design and purpose is to reveal, and by revelation, to free. So when we study anything of a spiritual nature and it enters only our mind and leaves our heart vacant and empty, we can be rest assured our heart shall remain empty until finally our efforts to identify move from the realm of limit and self to the realms of freedom, of light, of happiness.

So often we seek happiness in life. And we say, "I just want to be happy." But with that word comes thirty million judgments of how we will be happy. What are the requirements to be happy? "This person has to be such and such and do such and such whenever I want them to do it or I'm not happy." Our divorce rate in the world alone reveals that happiness, to our mind, is totally dependent upon what our self-identification demands that another shall do at any given moment under the guise of responsibility.

This philosophy, this association is founded on personal responsibility. It is heartbreaking to me to witness, at times, the errors of ignorance to twist personal responsibility to our eternal being, the human soul, to serve a limited, mental judgment, when mental judgments are designed, by their very nature, to bind us, to limit us, and to enslave us. Show me one judgment that has freed a human being and then I shall bow to the realms of delusion. For there is no judgment, by its very nature, that can free anyone. The only thing that frees us is accepting the truth that what we are is the way we are, for we alone insist that it be that way.

Thank you.

SEPTEMBER 4, 1983

Church Questions and Answers 41

As our chairman has already stated, this is the once-a-month time when you are free to ask the questions that you have which you consider of general interest to all of us. So if you will be so kind as to raise your hand with your question, I will get to as many questions as time will permit.

The gentleman on the aisle, please.

A considerable amount of the energy we consider human intelligence is spent trying to figure out what's important and what's the sense of importance. Would you outline what importance is?

Well, in reference to that question (What is important?) we find in our life and our experiences that there are different things at different times that we consider important. What is important, of course, to all of us [is] that we find within us, somehow, the purpose of being at all. We all ask our self the question at some time in our life, "Why am I here?" "Where did I come from, if I came from anywhere?" and "Where am I going?" Now it is important to anyone, at any time, really, to know why they are. What is their purpose of being? And to answer that question, one must become aware of where they've been in order to consider where they might be going. Now we cannot, of course, become aware of where we have been unless we consider that which has already passed. The dangers, of course, in considering what has passed is that we permit within our consciousness the review of experiences that we find, or had found, distasteful. If we do not have sufficient control over our mind, then we establish the necessary laws to repeat in principle the experiences that have already passed that we found distasteful.

The law clearly reveals that repetition is indispensable to evolution. We look at the world around and about us and we see evolution indeed is inevitable. It is taking place all the time. Change is indispensable to that evolution. When we find difficulty in making changes that we know inside of our self are in our own best interests, it reveals to us that we are attached to the shadows of experiences that have already passed. So in that respect, we can clearly see that what is important is what we are doing in the moment of our conscious awareness.

Now so often in life we think—and our past reveals to us—that we made so-called decisions which proved later in life to be judgments, for decisions consider all areas of our life and are not limited to any particular area. Consideration is a part of making any decision. It has no emotion because it has no attachment. That's the great difference between making a judgment and making a decision. A decision, having considered all factors, present and to be, is ever subject to the wisdom of the Law of Evolution, known as change. A judgment, bound by shadows of the past, does not permit, nor does it contain, the light of wisdom. It only contains the reflected light, known as the shadow. So, of course, it is important what we do moment by moment, not year by year, but moment by moment. I hope that's helped with your question. *[After a short pause, the teacher continues.]* Yes. The gentleman I just spoke to. Does that help with your question?

Oh, thank you. Yes.

Of what's important? Thank you. The lady here, please.

How would you recommend one comforts a child who is afraid of the dark?

Well, first of all, one must realize and understand fear, whether it's in a child or an adult, is indispensable to faith in the human mind. Now we say, "Well, a new baby has fear of the dark." The question must then arise, Do the parents, who are the instruments, mental and physical, through which the soul entered at the moment of conception, do they, in their consciousness, have fear of the dark? Have they forgotten the fear of the dark that they had so many years ago? You see, the child, if it experiences fear of the dark, is simply revealing the mental substance of both of the parents. Therefore, a person, having experiences with a child that has fear of the dark, should first work on themselves to root out and to remove this faith in their mind, for that's what fear is. Fear is nothing more and it is nothing less than faith in the experiences that we have already had. That's called fear; it is our faith in those past experiences. Then, when we encounter similar experiences, we have what is known as fear, based upon what has already been. Therefore, the parents should work on their fears and they would soon discover the child is freed from this so-called fear of the dark.

Now remember that darkness for untold eons of time has represented to all worlds ignorance of the law that is. That's all that darkness is. It is the lesser light. It is the ignorance of the light of wisdom. Does that help with your question?

Yes.

Thank you. The lady here, please.

If a person is a singer on this side of the veil, do they carry with them the same voice on the other side? Or does it become something later or—

Thank you. Well, of course, the voice of any singer is subject to the vehicle through which the voice must travel: the physical vehicle and its obstructions, which are created by the mental vehicle. The obstruction to any talent is dependent upon the mind of the individual and their dictate and demand of how it shall be. For example, many people work diligently to change their hair, to change their features, to change many things. People work to change their voice. Their voice doesn't change. They do create obstructions for its expression, but the voice itself doesn't change.

Now some people work diligently in order that they may remove those obstructions created by beliefs, which are based upon past experiences. For example, man believes many things; they are totally dependent upon what he has experienced. So we find wisdom is not dependent upon belief, for beliefs are not secure. They are not stable. They are not reliable. Many people believe many different things at many times in their life. So a person with any degree of reason does not rely nor depend upon belief.

At onetime certain types of singing are popular in the world, only to collapse and some other type of singing is popular. But what is important? That which is popular or that which is true? The world changes many times in its popularity. It's dependent, of course, upon experiences that it has had. It's dependent upon beliefs. It's also dependent upon this part of us that knows beyond a shadow of any doubt that evolution is the Law of Life and change is inevitable.

So, in singing, as you have asked the question, in reference to that, one tries to improve on anything they involve themselves in. Therefore, they must be honest with themselves. "Am I trying to improve upon what I have earned in evolution? I have earned to speak." He who speaks can sing. That is dependent upon the individual. How well a person will sing is dependent upon the obstructions they have created in mental consciousness and how dependent they are upon their beliefs of what has been. I hope that's helped with your question.

Thank you.

Yes. The gentleman back there, please.

Yes. Would you speak on the process and the correlation of how they work with one another on rejection, retaliation, and revenge?

Thank you. Well, in reference to the question we all experience whenever we believe we've been rejected, it is the way of the human mind to retaliate on the person or persons that we believe have caused us the slight or the injury known as rejection. And depending on how much degree of control we have of our mind will depend on how much revenge shall be revealed. So how does one work with another person—I believe your question is—if they are the victim of rejection or they are, in their belief, the cause of the rejection? Which is it? Or is it both?

I would like to know both.

I see.

Thank you.

All right. First of all, the degree of rejection that anyone experiences is totally dependent upon how much they rely upon what they consider self. If they believe that a person should act this way and not that way to them and the person does not act in keeping with what they believe the way the person should act, then they experience rejection. If they have a very strong belief, through the love of self, which is the attachment to self, then the rejection feeling, of course, is very intense. With that amount of self-love, an attachment to self, we walk on very thin ice with what is known as a china-cabinet ego. It [is] very, very delicate. In our world it's usually called, "We're very thin-skinned." A thin-skinned person or a person with a china-cabinet ego is one who is ever the victim of what is called circumstances, ever the victim upon what some other person thinks or says or does or doesn't do. That is indeed a difficult way to live. There is no freedom in that way of living. There is only slavery and bondage to that belief: the belief of how other people should act to us.

We are, then, not free to give what we have to give to the world as part of our own purpose for being, as a part of our own evolution. We are, then, bound to those types of experiences. We cannot breathe fresh air for we have limited our universe. We have narrowed our horizon, and therefore, life becomes very empty in time and very void. We will always, in that type of thinking, in that—for it's judgment. It's just the epitome of judgment: what another person should or shouldn't do, whether they should smile or not smile, [or] how they should treat us. We are bound in that type of a limited view of life and, therefore, being bound, cannot truly serve the fullness of life that is available to all of us.

A person looks at creation. They see it for what it really is: various forms ever rising and falling, ever-changing, designed to serve a purpose. They've never been designed to bind us into the blindness that they are us.

People who leave this world—and they leave this world daily for these other dimensions—suffer only in their belief that they are the form, the physical and mental substance that is in the process of returning to the source from whence it came. That is, in truth, the only suffering of transition. That is, in truth, the only suffering of the mountain of experiences that we go through day by day. It is our belief that we are creation that is our suffering. This philosophy, the Living Light, clearly teaches and demonstrates: separate truth from creation. For without that separation, you shall never be free.

To be concerned of what someone else thinks is only to reveal how much concern we have in our mind of what other people think of us. It is a bondage. It is a trap. It is a dependence upon mental substance within our own consciousness. To permit ourselves to be hurt because someone doesn't do what we judge they should do is to place a false god within our consciousness, a false god that we can never control. It is to deny the freedom and the abundant good of the true God that is formless, that will ever, ever serve us in keeping with the law that we are, in truth, dependent upon and rely upon: the Light, the Life, that man calls God. There are no manipulations and no bargaining with the Light that is. For bargaining and manipulation is a design of the human mind, because the human mind is a part of creation. It knows so-called good and so-called bad. It knows day and night. It knows and experiences opposites. It is the mind that manipulates. It is the mind that needs. It is the mind that denies and therefore, it is the mind that suffers and never the soul. I hope that's helped with your question.

Thank you.

The gentleman here, please.

Mr. Goodwin, as stated, if where we have been determines where we are going and where we have been, we feel, hasn't been in our best interests, can we change? How can that change—or how long is that change [before it] becomes evident?

Thank you very much for your question in reference to the law revealed that where we have been dictates where we are going as long as we insist upon relying on self. Because that's a mental world. The mental world reveals to us where we have been [and] is the indicator of where we are going. Now, for example, if where we have been is a world in our experiences of rejection and hurt feelings because someone didn't do what we wanted them to do, or people didn't act the way we judge they should act, if that's our type of thinking, [if] that's where we have been and we insist on the love of self, the mental substance, then that's where we are going. And some other experiences yet to be.

Now how long does it take before that changes? It takes the instant of man's effort to no longer identify with the mental world and all that it has to offer of past experiences. The mind says, when we make the effort to free our self from creation, yet to be in creation, "I'm not sure because I can't see. I can't sense. I can't feel. I can't touch." And what is that mind, in all that type of thinking, telling us? "How can I control it?!" Well, that's the whole question.

The human mind experiences need. The reason the human mind experiences need is because the human mind denies. And our denials in life become our destinies. Now the human mind denies and experiences need because the human mind makes its judgments. The human mind makes comparisons. Not the soul. Not the spirit. Not that which you are. Therefore, it is the human mind that denies that it has what it has. Because no matter what the human mind has, it looks out to see that someone has more. If the human mind has a dollar, it immediately sees someone that has ten. If the human mind believes it's able to sing, it looks out and it immediately judges she or he sings better. So it is the human mind that denies and, through the denial, destines itself to prove how right it is. A constant experience of need.

Now is that the way an intelligent person wants to go, once having awakened to the truth? All there is, is what you are. Your beliefs deny the truth. Not the truth in you, but it is your belief. That belief is dependent upon your attachment to the thought that enters your mind. Now many thoughts enter our mind, and many thoughts we reject and many thoughts we accept. And we accept them in keeping with what we have already accepted before. Tomorrow is not a question to man. Tomorrow is a question to those who believe in the shadow of yesterday. And therefore, it is through man's over-identification with the thought of I— what he thinks he is, not what he *is*—[that] is man's bondage. So when we pause in our consciousness and we stop this foolishness of believing in what we think we are, in that instant, in that moment, we shall be what we are. That is, freed from concern, for we no longer believe in denial. Therefore, we no longer have need. Therefore, life is the abundant good.

We're not going to find this great heaven when we leave a physical body. Because by leaving a physical body we do not leave a mental body; [it] goes right along with us. We are in a mental body in evolution as long as we insist on remaining attached to the thought of I. People think they're going to leave a physical world and all of a sudden, they're going to enter up in a spiritual heaven. Well, I have spent forty-two years of my life in this understanding and working with it, and if that's the way it is, then I've certainly been in a lot of delusion for a lot of years of my life. I have seen many people from astral realms and mental realms. And I have seen many souls from spiritual realms. And I can assure you, if we cannot make the effort today and every day to free our self from the thought of I, then we cannot expect, nor demand, to enter a spiritual world while we insist on being attached to a mental vehicle. It just doesn't work that way.

Life has already revealed to us what we thought about the way we were twenty years ago. We don't necessarily think at all that same way today. It is proving to us the Law of Evolution. It is gradually, slowly but surely, changing. The whole country, the whole world is changing. But what is the whole country and the whole world? It is a composite of millions and millions of people. It only reveals, as an effect, that people are changing. They are thinking differently. Different type of music. Different type of understanding. Different technology. That's only an effect revealing that, whether we like it or not, we are changing. But wisdom reveals there's a harmonious way to change. And that is to take control of our own mind that we may find the true I and stop this ridiculous belief in what we thought the I was. I hope that's helped with your question.

We have time for one more. *[After a short pause, the teacher continues.]* No questions? Yes, the lady in the back, please.

All right. I wanted to ask—I understand that in all our getting, we get understanding. But I wanted to know, Is it possible to have acceptance without understanding?

Oh, yes! We accept many things and have zero understanding.

OK.

Oh, yes indeed! We accept colds and we have no understanding of how we got them. We try to justify and tell ourselves, "Oh, that neighbor of mine. If they didn't sneeze,"—and they got in the cold first—"I wouldn't have gotten it. It's September, October, November. It's the time of year. I always get this cold." You see, I've listened to my students; some of them say, "Well, it's that time of year. I always have strep throat. I always get a cold at this time of year." And it's wonderful for me. I just try to reveal to them, "Look how beautiful your law works."

We teach that man is a law unto himself. The question is, What are we doing with the law that we are? Now, we take a look at the law. A person says, "I always have a cold this time of year. It never ever fails." Now if they pause in consciousness, they can say, "Ah, this proves to me that I am a law unto myself. I always have a cold this time of year. I am able to accomplish that!" *[Some of the congregation laugh.]* Look at the principle of the law. You may not like the effect of the law, but let's look at the principle. Now if we put the same energy in a mental world and the same belief into, "This time of year, I always get $10,000. Just comes out of the blue. I don't know how it happens." *[Many in the congregation laugh.]* Wouldn't it be happier—wouldn't we be happier than to say that, "Each time of year, this time of year I always get a cold"? But the truth is the same law is working. With one, we give phenomenal belief; we establish the law and we attract it unto our self in keeping with the law that like attracts like and becomes the Law of Attachment.

My good friends, if you want to be attached to something, choose something with a little reason. What do you get out of having a cold a certain time of year? What do you get out of lying in bed? Of course, maybe you say, "I get some rest. Every year, this time of year, I lie in bed until 10:00, 12:00 noon, maybe 2:00 in the afternoon. I go through this for a few weeks. My nose is all stuffed up. I have headaches. I can't hardly breathe. But I do get to lie in bed." But how expensive, how costly [just] to find a way to lie in bed. When reason reveals you make an intelligent decision. You say, "That's it. I choose to lie in bed at this time of year for this long of time." Why establish laws to have to have these miserable colds in order to accomplish that?

You see, we always get what we really need. We always get that, although we don't always think that we need it. We set those laws into motion. So, a person wants a rest? Now, you see, they get the rest; they get the cold. Do they have any understanding? Does that help with your question? So, yes, I can reveal to you with my own students, some of them, they absolutely, wholeheartedly accept a cold at a certain time of year. And I can assure you year after year after year after year, they prove to themselves how right they are, with zero understanding of how it happens.

Thank you. I hope it's helped with your question.

OCTOBER 2, 1983

Church Questions and Answers 42

As our chairman has stated, this is the once-a-month opportunity for you to ask questions that are of a general interest. If you'll be so kind as to raise your hands, I will be grateful if I am enabled, through this phase of mediumship, to bring the answer to you.

The gentleman here, please.

How can one call upon the light of reason? And how does it interact with the mind?

That's an excellent question. And the question is, "How can one call upon the light of reason? And how does it interact with the mind?" We understand that reason, being a soul faculty, is not subject to the human mind or the dictates thereof. For example, our mental world is limited by the experiences that we have already encountered in our evolution. Therefore, reason offered by the human mind clearly reveals itself to be logic or fact. To call upon the light of reason one must first awaken within their consciousness something that is superior to and not dependent upon the limited mind.

It is, for most people, rather difficult to accept the possibility of something that they do not have conscious realization of. For example, we speak of God, we speak of truth, we speak of light, we speak of freedom. And when we speak of those things, our mind is active and dictates what they mean to us. Therefore, truth to one is not necessarily—[and] usually is not—truth to another. It is dependent upon where we are in consciousness. If we are making the effort to free our self from the limits of the human mind, there are moments when we are freed from those limits; there are moments when we are aware of something that is above and beyond those limits.

We speak of total consideration. And we find many people expressing total consideration: the totality of considering what the mind has to offer. Now the human mind is designed to serve the eternal being, known as the soul. It was never designed to dictate what the eternal soul shall or shall not do. It is through our error of ignorance that we have permitted, through over-identification with the mental world, we have permitted it to become the authority in our life. So when we are offered the possibility of something greater and that something greater does not already exist within our mental world, we find great difficulty in attaining it. Therefore, the light of reason—one wishes to apply the light of reason, of course, in all things. Because it is reason that transfigures and transforms. And what does it transfigure and transform? It transfigures and transforms the mental limits that we have bound our self in.

When we no longer, in any moment, think of self, then we are no longer controlled by what self, or our mind, has to offer. It is in those moments that the light of reason transfigures us. Does that help with your question?

Yes.

You're welcome. The gentleman here, please.

Mr. Goodwin, if someone—if a person is involved in several things and they were seeking to find their God-given talent, rather than what their mind told them they wanted to do, how do they determine what that is specifically?

In reference to your question, in speaking of a natural talent or soul talent, we must realize, of course, that God is not a giver because God is not a taker. We do understand that God is an infinite, intelligent, sustaining Power; does not take, therefore, cannot give.

Now when the question is asked by the human mind, "How can one determine what their natural or soul talent is?" the human mind offers many answers based upon, of course, its own suppressed desires. In keeping with your question on soul talent, it is important to have a basis of foundation to understand how one awakens to what is natural talent within them. This philosophy teaches, and has taught for many, many years, do not suppress desire. Suppressed desire is the first thing to rise at the slightest opportunity to take control over our lives. It is dangerous. It is detrimental, for it is infinite, intelligent, neutral Energy that we have bound into a form of our desire. It is psychologically detrimental. It is an instrument of frustration. It is an instrument of self-pity. Therefore, a wise person does not suppress desire because of the Power that is contained within the form of desire, which, of course, is God. One awakens to speak, to educate, to cast the light of reason upon desire. One does not suppress it.

In reference to a soul talent, so often soul talents, natural talents have been revealed to students of mine over the years. Many times they have not been in keeping with what desire the questioner has. Therefore, that which is natural for them has not been applied. That only reveals the supremacy, for any person, of the human mind over the eternal being. If one truly is seeking to awaken to their natural talent, then one makes the effort to be receptive to something beyond the self-thought. That takes prayer, that takes effort, and that takes the wisdom of patience. I hope that's helped with your question.

Yes, please.

How can a person work on becoming more aware of subconscious patterns and beliefs that keep us from being more in touch with the Light?

That's a fine question. How can one awaken and take control of subconscious patterns and beliefs? Let us understand that we believe many things. And as time marches on, our beliefs change accordingly. Some change begrudgingly. Some change seemingly joyously. Our beliefs change. Not our faith, but our beliefs. We believe ever in keeping at any moment with our needs. So we find ourselves believing many different things at many different times. But our faith, that does not change, for our faith is an expression of our eternal being. Our beliefs are expressions of our human mind.

So when we believe that a person is a certain way, we must understand that we have, within our own consciousness, we have made them that way in keeping with our need. And so we find time passes on. And the person who believed that the other person was a certain way suddenly awakens within their consciousness and finds that the person, in their thinking, has changed. No, the person that they believed was a certain way, that person didn't change; the believer changed. That's who made the change. They began to awaken to the possibility that the way they believed about a certain person, place, or thing was not the way that it is.

We believe today is a good day or we believe it is not. That belief is dependent upon our needs. Now if we awaken to the truth of what our needs are, then our next step is the awakening that they are, in truth, our denials. Because belief fills our need. Our need serves our judgment. And our judgment is our denial. So the bondage continues to perpetrate itself. So we start, not through this self-concern of self-analysis—the world is filled with professionals who do that far much better than ourselves, in some respects—but we start in an awakening of the law that is. The law demonstrates to us our beliefs are in keeping with our needs. Our needs are in keeping with our judgments. Our judgments are in keeping with our dictate of limit, which is in keeping with our denial of the truth that frees us. And when we understand those simple steps of the law that is and in that understanding we accept the possibility of a change within our consciousness, then we shall be freed from the self-imposed bondage that causes us so much grief in keeping with the Law of Denial. Does that help with your question?

[Yes.]

You're welcome. Yes, the lady back there, please.

I recently listened to a cassette [tape of the Living Light Philosophy] that dealt with the fact that you didn't have to follow a mental law through, that you could stop and move on to something else. I was wondering if you could speak on that for a minute.

Well, in reference to following a mental law through, that is totally dependent upon anyone who has established the law. We see that man is a law unto himself. Man thinks a person is good; and in keeping with their desire needs and time passes, and they think differently. So the law they have established, they now change to an opposite law. What we must understand in mental laws [is] they affect us only in keeping with our identification. When we identify with self, we awaken within our consciousness the mental law, the limit, the form. And so we establish many laws, many mental laws for we have many, many, many thoughts. We have many judgments. We have many dictates and many, certainly, many denials. It is possible for us at any moment to free our self from the identification with self or form, mental law, and limit. That is within our power. Some people do it for moments and go back to it and rise again.

That which sustains anything is greater than the thing that it sustains. So the intelligent, infinite Energy, which sustains the thought that we form by mental substance, is certainly greater than the form of the thought that we create. Now we can move from those creations, strengthen our self in the spiritual light and truth, and return to bring about the changes that are necessary in keeping with the light of reason that we were lacking when we established those laws that are so detrimental to our evolution. Thank you.

The lady here, please.

I'm not clear as to what a denial is. Could you . . .

Yes. A denial, of course, is a child of judgment. One judges that this or that is their divine right. One judges that this or that is not someone else's right. And these judgments go on all the time. One judges that a person should treat them in a certain way. When they do not treat them in the way that the person judges, then you have problems. The whole world reveals that to us. Now to form a judgment you must deny. You cannot judge without denying. The sadness is that we have yet to learn that the judgments that we insist on—any judgment—is a denial of the goodness for our self.

We make a judgment that if a certain person would change or act or do what we judge they should do, which is in keeping with the need of our own selfish desires, then everything would be fine. We have created that law. We are the victims of that law. We must pay the price to awaken within our consciousness: that we have made our self a victim in order to free our self; that, in truth, it has absolutely nothing whatsoever to do with anything outside, but that it has everything to do with the judgment, the denial, that law that we have established inside. So whenever we judge, we dictate that God, goodness, abundance, the joy of life shall come ever in keeping with what we decide. That is the law that we have established: the Law of Denial. Consequently, goodness, happiness, the fullness of life, and joy itself can only enter our universe in keeping with what we alone have judged, for in the judgment, we rise, in a mental world, superior to the Power that sustains the mental world. So all of your philosophies have taught: Judge not that you be not judged. They were appealing to your own self-preservation, to your own self-interests: that anyone who judges, in truth, is judging themselves. Therefore, they are limiting themselves; they are denying the goodness for themselves and are deceiving themselves by projecting that out upon another person.

You see, no one robs us but our self. And unfortunately, ofttimes we've learned to be the best robbers in the world. And then we end up in poverty, deprived of the goodness of life and we look out to find someone or something that has robbed us from the joy of life, that is depriving us of the goodness that we seek. And we always find a target somewhere. Whether it's a person or a government or a bank or an insurance company, we find someone. Until the day arrives that we pause and we say, "Personal responsibility reveals to me that I am a law unto myself. What, now, am I doing with the law that I am?"

All of the power of goodness is available to us. We alone, through our error, are keeping our self from the goodness of the Light for we are standing in our own light. And by standing in our own light, we cannot see the Light that is. Does that help with your question?

Fine. We have time for one more. Yes, the lady here, please.

If a person is having trouble being in touch with the God within, what are some of the steps they can take to restore that communication?

Yes. If a person is having, what you say, "trouble" in communicating with the God or goodness within oneself, of course, it reveals to us that our mind is very active. And every time we tempt to get through to that peaceful, beautiful space in consciousness, something's in the way. Is that what you mean?

Yes.

And that something is disturbing. It demands its thought to be expressed, would you not agree?

Yes.

And it plagues us. It bombards our consciousness. We want to think of peace and all we can do is think of a form. Is that correct?

Yes.

For all thoughts are forms, for they are creation. And that's not what we are. Try to understand, if you believe you are your thought, then you believe you are your judgment. And it is that belief that binds us to creation. Therefore, in that false type of thinking we fear death, for, in truth, we fear life. And that's why we fear death. We will continue to fear life, as we fear death, as long as we insist on believing the thought of our mind. There is no freedom, for there is no truth, as long as we insist on believing what thought enters our consciousness.

We know deep within us that there is no death. We do know that. Yet we fear and are a house divided. We fear life the moment we believe we've lost control of it, and that is the bondage of creation. We look and see all creation: the trees, the plants, the animals, the humans. We see them rise only to fall. We see them born and grow and die. And so we fear life because we *believe* we are creation. We *believe* we are the physical body and whenever we believe that, we pay a dear price for it. For fear is demonstrably negative faith. That's what fear is. And so the thing we fear befalls us. We fear we're going to be without and we establish every law necessary to prove how right we are. And then we are without. We fear someone is going to do this or that; we establish the law necessary for it to happen.

The Living Light Philosophy is a philosophy that is demonstrable through daily application. Ofttimes in these many years I have heard the words *personal responsibility*, *divine right* so turned and twisted they were difficult to recognize. This is why I'm so grateful for the recorded, magnetic tape. It is the way it was given. It's not someone's notes that has changed it around. Because when you hear the words *personal responsibility* used to serve the limit of a mental desire, then you have to understand that it is not as is given to free the eternal soul. When you hear the words expressed, *divine right*, to protect and to defend the blatant transgression of the rights of others, there's nothing divine about it. But there's plenty selfish about it.

We can take any religion or any philosophy and we can use it in our consciousness to serve a mental world regardless of its true purpose of being. But if we pause in our consciousness and we study and we consider the whole and not the limit of the self—whoever considers the whole is served by the whole, and whoever considers the self is served by the limit of the self. So it is only reasonable and practical that we awaken our consciousness to serve the whole, not to serve the limit of one's earthly experiences.

So let us encourage our self by not thinking of what has been or what could have been. Now stop and think about that. What has been, we already know, is gone. What could have been didn't happen. So what good is it to think about? You know, we could have had a different president of the country. We could have had all kinds of things, but we didn't. So to entertain the consciousness with what has been, which is gone, and what could have been, which didn't happen, is not only foolhardy, it certainly is far from reason, let alone reality.

Now if we want something to happen, then we have to establish the law for it to happen within our consciousness, because everything that you experience in life is first taking place within your consciousness. First within your consciousness, then is it made manifest in a physical, material world of creation. It first takes place within our consciousness.

Now here's where the problem is with things that could have been. For myself, it could have been that I didn't open up any church and I wouldn't have to get up Sunday morning. All right. But it wasn't. That's not the way it is. So many things could have been that are not. And I thank God that they are not.

So let us stop and think. When you want something in your life, you establish the law within your consciousness, within your own consciousness. In establishing that law, do not transgress, nor tempt to mock the divine law that is, known as God. Do not place within your consciousness, in your need of what you desire, another soul. For in so doing you transgress the law of the right of another soul. So if you want something, remember to work with the law that you can work with: the law that demonstrably is. If you want an apple, establish that law within your consciousness, and you will not have to be tempted to transgress someone else's law to get the apple that you desire. But woe to those who, learning a bit about the law that is, tempt to impose their selfish needs and desires upon the divine rights of another eternal soul. Then you have real problems. You may, in keeping with that law, that law of transgressing the rights of another, you may get what you want for a time, but the payment is very great. For you are tempting to play God and, therefore, must pay the price of that weakness.

Now I wanted to finish up with this soul faculty of encouragement. I find truth encouraging. I have always found it encouraging. Especially, *especially* since I learned that when we receive the light of truth and we find our self a little heavy-hearted, it is that part of our mind that doesn't want to change.

Now you know our mind is a very clever instrument. Study a little baby and you'll see how clever the mind really is. Very clever. Very intelligent and very clever. When it wants something and it demands to have it, it finds many ways of doing many things, even to making us ill to get what it wants. Some of my students, in order to get what they want, they insist, and, true to their insistence, every year around the holidays they either have a sore throat, a cold, or the Russian flu or whatever you want to call it. They absolutely insist on proving how right they are; that it's always been that way. Well, if we lived in the world ever attached to the way things have always been, there'd be no cars to drive. We'd still be taking care of the horses. Now we know we're not doing that. So in spite of what we want for the world, the world continues to evolve.

So in spite of what our mind, when it doesn't want to hear something that will free our soul, and in spite of its tantrum to cause us to feel discouraged—for what is discouragement? The first line of defense to protect what we judge is right. So if we don't get what we want, then we are discouraged so that we can continue on serving the judgments of those has-beens [of] the way it used to be or the way we think it could have been. That's not evolution. That's the hard way of evolving. That's the difficult way. It is just as easy to think and to be encouraged as it is to think and be discouraged. It's just as easy, if we pause and get out of self. If we think of our self, it's much easier to slip down in discouragement and failure. If we don't think of our self, it's very easy to look up.

We all accept: that which is below is subject to that which is above. The law does not fail us. So who wants to look down at what's below, when the Authority is above us? [One] who walks around the world looking at the ground will walk into many obstructions and pay the price thereof. The authority of self, limited as it is, looks down and bows to itself. But when we pause in our consciousness, we look up to where the Authority of the universes is, [and] has always been. So let us look up in what is known as encouragement, for in so doing things get better. But if we don't look up, we must not allow our self to be frustrated because it's the same old thing.

Thank you.

NOVEMBER 6, 1983

Church Questions and Answers 43

And before we get into our discussion this morning, I do have an important announcement for you. Beginning the third Thursday evening of January 1984, there will be limited classes of a personal growth nature. These classes are very limited, if you understand the nature of them. Therefore, registration for these classes must be made not later than the fifth day of January. So those of you [who are] interested, we can take no registrations after January 5th. It will be an 11-week course, Thursday evenings at 8:00 p.m. sharp. And they will be personal growth classes, the first time given by myself to the general public. *[These classes are CC 230 through CC 240, which have been published in* The Living Light Dialogue Volume 8.*]*

Now this morning, we have, of course, our regular, once-a-month question-and-answer [time]. We must try to understand in questioning, in life, that if a question is sufficiently important in our consciousness to be entertained by us, then, of course, for us it is important enough to speak it forth. Philosophies have taught for years to knock and the door shall open, to ask and you shall receive. Ofttimes we want to ask questions of people, or a person, and we are censored by what is called fear. Most of my students understand that fear is simply faith in what our mind is offering at the moment. But when we look at life, we see that our mind offers many different thoughts and certainly many different emotions.

It is only in the last twenty years that material science has been truly awakening to the electromagnetic fields of the universe. And only in these recent latter years is material science studying and accepting the electric and magnetic fields of the human being. This philosophy has taught a balancing between this electric and magnetic field, and that that is dependent upon the thought patterns or vibrations that we permit within our consciousness at any given moment. Ofttimes in our seeking of things in life, the desire (magnetic) is so strong that it goes completely out of balance with the electric field. It is only when the electric and magnetic fields of consciousness are brought into balance does that which we desire manifest itself before us.

We limit our self, in an error of our thinking, that certain acts and deeds are necessary in order for us to experience the fulfillment of any desire that we entertain in consciousness. Because we establish that type of thinking, we set that law, for us, into motion. Ofttimes we want to change a job. We wish a promotion; we wish a change with our employer, and on down the list of desires in our life. When we have that type of thinking—and we're bombarded with it constantly—our mind immediately makes the judgment that the fulfillment of the desire is dependent upon what someone else does. Consequently, we become the victims of that type of thinking, and the desire is not fulfilled until someone else does what we have judged in our minds is necessary for them to do in order for us to experience the fulfillment of the desire. We don't often consciously stop and think about it; it's just the way we've permitted our minds to be programmed. That does not make for a complete or full life. The purpose—one of the many purposes of the Living Light Philosophy is to awaken within our own consciousness that we may personally demonstrate that that is what is truly happening in our lives. For it is only when we awaken (that that is how it works) are we then capable of making the change that is necessary.

The first thing in accepting freedom is, of course, the payment for it. Everything in life has a price tag. That price tag is established by our own mind, by our own thought. The law reveals that the personal ability to respond to any thought, act, or deed—the effect of that personal ability is to be free from the victimization or the error of thinking that our lives are dependent upon something that's beyond our control. So consequently, we go through life in great effort to try to control what someone else thinks, especially what someone else does, and especially if we, in any way, believe that we are dependent upon them.

We must try to understand that we never permit our self to be attached to anything that we have not first judged that we are dependent upon. Man is an intelligent being. He does not attach to anything that he does not first depend on. So we find in life that we are attached to our job. Get fired and we soon find out how attached we are. We are attached to our wives. We're attached to our husbands. We're attached to our children. The attachment reveals to us—and the degree of the attachment—how dependent we are upon them. Now if we are greatly dependent upon our job, our attachment is equal. Therefore, the emotional, traumatic experience of losing a job, a wife, or a husband, boyfriend or girlfriend or whatever the attachment we have made reveals to us our dependence.

Now our dependence reveals to us our own denial. [If] a person is dependent upon someone or something, they must ask themselves the question, "Why am I dependent upon this particular job?" The answer very soon comes into their mind: why, they are dependent upon that particular job because if it wasn't for that particular job, they would not be able to eat, they couldn't pay the rent, and they go down the list of desires. Then the question must be asked, "Is it that particular job? Are there no other jobs in the universe for me?" And if we decide, "Well, that's the job and the only job for me," then we very quickly see that we live in a constant state of fear every time we go to work, every time we think of our employer, of the company, of our boss, of our co-workers, because we never know what moment they will decide to replace us.

Now think about that for just a moment. That's what these classes, for the first time offered to the public in January, personal growth classes, that's one of the many subjects that it will be dealing with. We are living in a constant state of fear.

This philosophy demonstrates and proves to any individual who applies the laws it reveals that fear is the power of faith directed to mental substance, that it is a negative or magnetic field of consciousness, that under the law that magnets attract, the thing we fear the most befalls us. So we find the ancient teachings of many philosophies have revealed that truth to us repeatedly. We have now entered an age of scientific advancement where it can be proven beyond a shadow of any doubt in the material world of material substance.

It is not, for we do not make it so, easy to move this power, known as faith, from the negative magnetic to the positive electric field in order to establish a balance within our own consciousness. When we understand that feeling good is not a luxury, that it is an absolute necessity, that it is indispensable to the balance or sanity of the human mind, when we understand that principle, then we will know beyond any doubt that some time in our daily activities we must feel good. It's indispensable to balance. Therefore, we, in our own errors and experiences in evolution, have limited this, what we call, feeling good experience, we have limited it to certain areas in our consciousness through which we will permit it to flow. And those limited areas, without exception, are dependent upon something beyond our control.

We say, "Oh, I would feel so good, especially at this time of year, if that employer of mine would give me a raise [or] a promotion. I would feel especially good if my husband would demonstrate that he really loves me by buying me this new fur coat." And go on down the list of how we have decided how we can feel good at any given moment. It is always dependent upon, within our consciousness, what somebody else may or may not do. Consequently, we continue to support our fear because we have proven to our self, though we continue to make the effort, we have proven to our self that it is foolhardy to work so hard to control someone else's mind. It's contrary to the law. It's absolutely contrary. Yet, we are tempted to make that effort because there's something else that keeps driving us on, and that something else is that inner knowing for our own stability we must permit our self to feel good.

There are many ways of feeling good. But before one can demonstrate the many ways of feeling good, one must first grow in consciousness to the demonstrable, revealed truth that everything, *everything* we can possibly desire is right where we are. Now when that teaching was first revealed, students—immediately the mind began to think, "Where am I physically?" Most of the time we think we know where we are. And we do know where we are physically. We know where our physical body is. It is not often that we know where our consciousness is. Therefore, we find that we make many mistakes. Our physical bodies make all kinds of errors and mistakes, and we get upset when we're caught. Why do we get upset? Because there's a part of us that knows we weren't there when we were doing the job. We are embarrassed. We are humiliated. We don't feel good. And some of us, at times, even feel stupid because we say to our self, "Well, I knew better." Of course, we did know better. We did know how to do the job. We did know the requirements. But that part of us that knew all of that wasn't in the physical body; that part of us was somewhere else.

And where is that somewhere else? In this philosophy it's known as the past time in the twilight zone. That's where we were. Passing time in the twilight zone. And what is there that tempts us to enter the twilight zone so often in the course of a day? Why, there in the twilight zone we look at, we experience the seeming, *seeming* fulfillment of our unfulfilled desires. That's that in-between dream state. Now in that world, there are many things that are offered to us, for there are many things in our life that we desire. In that world, the twilight zone, there's a shortcut; we get them all. But when we come back to reality, we come back empty-handed. That's a dangerous realm of consciousness.

In psychology, they call it an escape realm. That's where we run off to escape from the weight, what we consider to be the weight of responsibility. Well, the weight of responsibility in life only reveals, of course, to us, there's too much in our consciousness. Our cup runneth over. And we'd better empty it out so we don't feel so heavy and so much weight. How can we empty out this cup that is so filled (our human mind)? Well, only our love of God can do that. Because when our love of God exceeds what we call our weight of responsibility, our cup begins to empty. So that we can put something in there to feel good, to move on, and to have the constructive use of our being and fulfill the purpose of its journey here on earth.

Life is not dependent, and never has been dependent, upon what someone else does. That is an illusion that we enter sometimes. We all know it's dependent upon what *we think* they do. It's never dependent on what someone else does. You see, because it is, in truth, dependent on what *we think* someone else does, it's our thought. And being our thought, it is our servant. And being our servant, we can always tell it, that thought, our servant, what it's going to do, whether it likes it or not. That's the one thing that is encouraging.

So often when the word *discipline*, which is, in truth, guidance, so often when the word *discipline, personal responsibility*, or any of those words are used publicly, even privately in my classes, there's kind of a cringe. It doesn't seem to fit too well on so many people. Yet, without those very avenues, guidance, discipline, personal responsibility, one loses the mastery of life. They no longer, when they throw those precious faculties aside, they no longer are captain of their ship, let alone master of their destiny. They're one of the crew and they can't trust the captain that's running them around through life. Now when you're on a ship and someone in the crew decides they're going to be captain, and you just go take a coffee break, and when you come back, they decide, no, they like being captain and they're going to stay up there, well, usually something happens. You either leap overboard and go get a new ship, if you can get one. Or you get rid of the one that went up and took over your job, your position, and your mastery of life. But we must relate that experience to every time we feel frustrated, to every time we're upset because of what we think someone else is not doing.

Think, my friends, what difficulty, how much of the goodness of life seems to pass us by because our minds are filled about what someone else is about to do, has just done, or may, once again, do us in. The joy of life is the awakening; it's an inside job. It is an awakening that, "Here is a person that I have judged did me in. How grateful, God, I am. I know this person and, therefore, they are but an instrument that I did myself in. And at least I know what they'll do or won't do from experience. God help me if I don't accept the truth with this person who I judge did me in, because you will bring another one much more clever than the one I just, hopefully, within my consciousness grew through!"

This is what people face in this mass divorce rate in the world today. You know what you've got; you not only know what you've got, you know what you paid for it. Well, why throw it out when you've already paid for it and you already know what you've got and you're only tempted with blind desire to go get something else? The change takes place within. Would you pay a great deal of money for a fine sweater that is still useful and you decide there's a better sweater in the store, when you've already paid for that one—you just want to throw it out? It hasn't fulfilled its purpose yet. It's not worn out yet. You haven't learned your lessons yet. So that alone, that awakening, I can tell you, in time in the world, will stem the tide of this so-called divorce rate. Because we'll start thinking, before we leap in the pond, whether or not we want to get wet and how long we want to stay that way.

So, you see, my friends, like everything else in life, you have this job; you know what it offers or should know what it offers. If you go on a job and you're working there and the months pass and you don't know what it has to offer, it has to offer what you permit it to offer. You see, life offers to us what we will allow life to offer. We are not the victims of life. We are the masters of life. That is not only our destiny, it is our purpose expressing on this planet. We are here to demonstrate that. We have not come to earth to be the victims of creation. We have entered earth destined to master creation. Now to master something does not mean to annihilate it, because if you annihilate it, there won't be anything to master. We're here to master creation. How does one master anything in their life? Everyone's been to school. How do you gain the solution to a problem? Through study, through application, through effort.

You face creation the instant you think, for the instant that you think, you form mental substance. If you think red, you form an object within consciousness, whether it's an apple or a coat or anything else. The instant you think, you enter creation. It is by the thought of I, it is through that identification that you enter through the door of creation. Now from that point, you master it or you lose sight of your destiny and your purpose of living, and you become the victims of it.

We know from a life of experience we are not the thought our mind thinks, because if we were, we would be many, many strange things and acting in many strange ways. We are not the thought we think. We enter that realm of deception when we *believe* we are the thought we think. That's when we enter that world. If you *believe* a thought that you're not happy, then, if you believe it, you will not be happy. Because it is through your identification that you experience those effects of creation. But because we have the choice of identifying, we have the choice of forming and deforming the thought we permit to enter our consciousness; because we are never left without that choice, we and we alone make life the way life is for us.

Now I'd like to take a few moments for any questions that any of you have. The lady here, please.

When a dog is—goes to the other side, do the relatives of the owner here on earth take care of it? Or how does that take place?

Thank you. In reference to when an animal, in this case a dog, leaves the physical world into the other realms, do the relatives of the person that owns the animal take care of it? Well, rarely. Because—not that all relatives hate dogs, but there are few that love them quite as much as we do. Now we have to stop and think. Our love for an animal, person or place or a thing is rarely equal to someone else's. However, ofttimes there are cases when a relative, a friend of ours has passed on and they have earned in their evolution, through their own interest and attachments to us, to look in once in a while and see how we're doing. And they may just look in at that particular time and see that you're quite hurt or upset or mourning a little animal going over and certainly do what they can to help you. But let us not forget, here on earth, so it is. There are many people on earth who love animals very much. And there are many people who have gone on who love all animals. And therefore, they are not dependent on whether or not that animal belongs to one of their relatives; they just look after them. Does that help with your question? Yes.

Thank you.

You're welcome. Yes. The lady here, please.

Good morning.

Good morning.

I've been told that it's beneficial to have fresh flowers around for certain reasons.

Yes.

I would you—if you could ask me—if you could tell me point blank, What is the benefit involved in having fresh flowers whether at home or in the office?

Thank you very much. In reference to fresh flowers—and it is very, very important when we study and gain a little understanding, oh, concerning evolution. Now you look out in what you call creation, the physical world, and you see many, many different trees, plants, flowers, grass, weeds, all kinds of things. But let us pause and look at a flower, any flower. Let us look at its intricate and evolved design, for the complexity of the flower, its intricate design, reveals to the observer that it is long in its evolutionary stage of expression.

Something does not come out of nothing. So it is with the human being. Very complex, very evolved, capable of doing more than many other species on the Earth planet (the human being). Through the evolution and the complexity, the flower or flowers reveal to man not only the evolutionary stage of the plant, but they reveal to man a multitude of different colors. We understand that color is vibration. It has been scientifically demonstrated that color is not only frequency and vibration, that color, also, is sound. Now when you hear a sound, there is emanated into the atmosphere varying colors corresponding to the sound. When there is a flower or a color, there is an emanation from that, a frequency, a sound. The human ear—most human ears do not detect that sound, but that sound is very important.

Now this life force, this which we call Spirit, formless and free—we have a little saying; it's on your program. "I am Spirit"—Spirit, that's what I am. "Formless and free, Whatever I think"—whatever I, the formless being, whatever I identify with, through that process of identification I form and, therefore, I be, because I believe. All right.

[The complete saying, as printed on the church program and in Discourse 54 is:

I am Spirit, formless and free;
Whatever I think, that will I be.*]*

Now, the Power, the Spirit, flowing through the flower, as [well as] the tree, of course, but through the complexity of the flower is emanating these different frequencies that are, indeed, harmonious. For eons of time flowers have been used as an instrument through which healing can take place. Now most people, most people will agree that [when] they look at a flower, they may not be a gardener or anything, but there is some feeling that takes place. They see that they're pretty. They're beautiful. And they feel a little bit of good. Maybe not a lot, but a little bit. It depends on how bad they're feeling.

Now what is it that takes place within the consciousness? Now the flower didn't leap out and do that to them. But a change in consciousness within their mind permitted them to be receptive to a more harmonious realm of consciousness. That's what happens. They are instruments through which we may enter a realm of consciousness that is harmonious and, being harmonious, is an instrument through which our health is regained or restored.

Health is totally dependent upon the unobstructed flow of the divine, intelligent Energy. Now [if] we want to be healthy, then we must remove the obstruction, which is [a] discordant frequency or vibration that is a cloud in the way of this flow. Does that help with your question?

Very much. Thank you.

Because, you see, what man knows as disease, what it means in truth is discord. Something within our being is discordant. Now the cure is where the cause is. So we must search within the consciousness to find out what is causing this discord which keeps us from experiencing health. Health is not limited to the human body. There's the healthy business. There's the healthy person. There's the healthy environment. There's—health is harmony. It is the law of the Divine. It is not only the law of the

Divine, it is our birthright. Our divine birthright is experiencing health, which is harmony, which is the wealth or the goodness that life has to offer. But that's entirely up to us.

So many people—look, here, in this day and age; there's so much interest on whether we're underweight or overweight, we're this, we're that, and all these other things. Here we go through life ofttimes and we deprive our self of this and deprive our self of that in hopes to get something else. Then after we've gone through all the deprivation and we get the something else [and] we take another look at it and that that we have deprived our self of all rises up and says, "It's not worth it!" *[Some in the congregation laugh.]* And we go back to another way, instead of going to the cause of things, you see.

What is the cause? What is the cause of what man says is over-eating of this and that? What is the need within us? Are we emotionally balanced in our consciousness? Are we filled with emotional needs? Have we, as little children, been programmed, have we earned the programming that when you have an emotional need, a frustration, and an upset you go eat something? Well, if that's the way we're programmed, then that's what we do. You can't just make changes, force changes, for example, to lose weight or gain weight and not understand the emotional-mental realm. The emotional body maintains and ofttimes retains the fluids of the human body and upsets our whole chemistry. So a person gets emotionally upset and then the balance, the chemical balance, doesn't work properly in their body and they have all kinds of problems. So of what benefit or what good is it to work on the physical and totally leave out the mental world? Now if you work on the physical *and* you work on the mental world, through honesty within yourself, you've got a good chance, through that balance, to let the spirit, your divine being, come through and bring about the balance in your life and the goodness.

Now are there any other questions? I know I've gone quite far overtime this morning. Yes, the lady here, please.

I had so many questions—

That's all right.

... consciousness. I'm going to ask the last one.

Certainly.

Do all great teachers not allow themselves to go into the lower levels of consciousness?

No, quite the contrary. Thank you so very much. Quite the contrary. Now there are two schools of thought and action throughout the eons of time in the physical world on the Earth planet. There is the school of thought in which the spiritual teachers are protected from the auric pollution or contamination or what is, in truth, temptation of the world of creation. Like a hothouse flower, once removed from the hothouse, it cannot weather the storms of life because it has never been given the opportunity to strengthen the weaknesses or temptations of the human being. That's one school of thought where the spiritual teachers are put in their mountain tops and the teachings are passed on through the disciples and out into the world, usually contaminated beyond recognition. *[Some of the congregation laugh.]* However, then there is the other school of thought. There is the school of thought in which the teachers are put out into a world of creation to pay the price of going to the depths of the other realms, to learn what they have to offer, to make the conscious decision that it is not worth it in comparison with the other realms of consciousness, and to constantly live and experience the battle between the two.

Which is the most beneficial? The world has shown the majority of the teachers are placed in their sanctuaries so they will not have to use their energies to battle those realms of consciousness. However, there is something else that takes place and this is the reason why, in these various temples and sanctuaries and monasteries, this is why they have these constant repetitions of affirmations, constantly. Because you may physically remove a person from a world of creation, but you cannot mentally remove them. So they experience the bombardment of what is known as thought force, that is, the predominant force or vibration or realm of consciousness that is in the atmosphere. So you find in the monasteries a constant process of repetition of certain affirmations to help them to keep their consciousness in the realms where they have chosen them to be. Does that help with your question?

Yes. Thank you.

Yes. We have a few moments, if you have any other questions. Yes, certainly.

[After a short pause, the member of the congregation who had just asked what was to have been her last question began at the top of her list of questions.]

I'll start from the first.

That's fine. My chairman always reminds me that I've gone on to a C-60 *[A C-60 is a 60-minute audio cassette tape and a C-120 is a 120-minute audio cassette tape]*. You know, that's your cassettes. But we may go to a C-120. Go ahead.

Do the eighty-one levels of consciousness have all the characteristics of what we term our conscious thought? Do they all possess positive and negative characteristics, color, disease, vibrations, and so forth? And is the balance you speak of a part of the effects of the fluctuations of these things?

Very important question. Very involved and it takes in a good portion of the whole philosophy and we'll try to put it in a small nutshell. There are 40 faculties. There are 40 functions. Now we must understand that a faculty is an evolved function. When we understand that, we'll understand a little bit more about the human mind. In these realms, 40 realms, in which the faculties are (all triune) and 40 realms of the functions (all triune), the true being, that 81, that true one, formless and free, moves in the door which is known as identification.

Now just like a triangle, there we are at the apex entering what we call creation through the law and the door of identity.

As we do that, we bring along with us the left path and the right path. And we, as long as we are identified, we must—and we learn to—be diligent with our thought. For it is only a thought, only an identity, that tips the scale to the left or to the right.

Now we are not the thought. We are the mover of the thought. We are the power which gathers it up from the realms of consciousness; that's what we truly are.

When the negative magnetic field is out of balance with the electric, the field of reason, the field of light, when we are out of balance in the magnetic, we believe. You must understand that knowledge—knowledge and belief are inseparable. We know and we believe. We believe and we know. But there is something that's greater than knowledge, something that is greater than belief. Something that does not change. Beliefs change. Knowledge changes. Wisdom does not. Wisdom *is*. And so, when we permit our self to feel emotion, movement in the water center, in the magnetic field, and that is not stabilized with the electric field of consciousness, we go out of balance and our life is an experience of struggle, obstruction, and disaster.

When you take the power and it meets the force, when this light, this electric field, touches this water, magnetic field of life, when it touches it, you have steam. The power is made manifest. When you are emotional and you get angry, a change takes place within your consciousness. There is a chemical change, a physical, chemical change at that moment that takes place. Of course, it is not the recommendation of this philosophy that when you get emotionally upset with someone and you get angered and then you feel better. No, we don't have to teach that. That's not the path. But to permit yourself to be angry inside, I guarantee you, brings about a change because you've already had those experiences. Ofttimes, from getting angry inside, after you're tired of being emotional about some attachment you have, the result is a change of consciousness and you usually get rid of them. Not always, but usually.

So, you see, when you pause and think of what's really taking place, there are moments that it can be beneficial for you to exercise your determination within your own consciousness—of course, we call that anger—but an exercise of your own determination. Now sometimes a person will spend months in an emotional realm, a magnetic field of consciousness, through their own attachments, which we've already discussed what that is, and all of a sudden, something happens. They get angry inside themselves. And that anger was indispensable to them becoming determined enough to make a change within their thinking. Well, the actual change that took place, they moved from the magnetic field over to the electrical field, a balance came about, and the power moved the mountain.

Thank you kindly. We must finish. Thank you.

DECEMBER 4, 1983

Church Questions and Answers 44

If you will be so kind, this morning, as to raise your hand, if you have a question, and I will be more than happy to serve as a medium to bring you the answer forthcoming.

Yes, the lady on the aisle, please.

Is there a danger, spiritual danger to telling fortunes using the tarot cards and other such things? And is there a danger in mediumship?

There are, like in any profession, of course, dangers of transgressions of natural law. For example, you mentioned specifically tarot cards in the casting of so-called fortune-telling. Well, when we permit our mind to be dependent upon anything outside for the truth we are working to receive inside, then, of course, it reveals to us (that dependency) a transgression of the very law that we are establishing to be a free channel to receive ever in keeping with our effort in evolution. And in that respect and, of course, all the variables involved with depending upon something outside for what is in truth inside, there is, of course, danger. For example, there are many realms of consciousness. I'm sure we're well aware of thought transference, so-called mind reading, astral worlds, spiritual worlds, and, of course, the desire worlds of our own self-consciousness. So in that respect, of course, there would be danger. If one studies, first, the laws governing communication, and then makes the effort to apply those laws that are infallible, that do not fail, then one need not be concerned about danger, for danger, for them, in that respect would not exist. Does that help with your question?

Yes.

Yes. The gentleman over here, please. Yes.

Yes. I was wondering if you would share with us your understanding of the validity of biorhythms.

Well, in reference to the validity of biorhythms, it's as valid as the rhythms of the universe. Everything is in motion. Everything in form is designed to move in that motion or frequency in keeping with its original design. There's the rhythm to the flower and the varied species. There's the rhythm to the human being. There's a rhythm to the trees. There's the rhythm to the animals and, of course, the humans. So man establishes, through his identity with and belief in the thought he chooses to entertain in consciousness at any moment, he establishes the rhythm, frequency, attitude of mind, which is rate of vibration, which is the law that he sends forth in the universe and, therefore, becomes the victim of. I hope that's helped with your question.

The lady here, please.

Could you please explain the value of affirmations and how often one should use them?

Thank you very much. In reference to [the] value of affirmations, we must consider that we all have many affirmations that we flood our consciousness with. For example, we have a desire to attain or to have something, we have a desire to be someone or something and our mind is flooded, our consciousness, with the affirmation of that particular desire. I don't think that's what you're referring to, I hope. I think, perhaps, you are referring to a positive affirmation to gain control of the fluctuating and multitude of thoughts that are in the human mind.

The law reveals that man is a law unto himself. Therefore, man in his own light must ask the question, "What am I doing with the law that I am?" That's where we start. We start with the demonstrable truth of personal responsibility, that all experiences are effects; they are never causes. And because experiences are effects—they are never causes—the cause, therefore, lies within the experiencer. That means, of course, our self and that's known as personal responsibility: the ability to respond to any law that we consciously or seemingly unconsciously, at the moment, set into motion.

Now our mind is flooded constantly with a multitude of thoughts, with a multitude of feelings, with a multitude of desires, (unfulfilled, suppressed), frustration, and fear. Life reveals to us in this world that we attempt to ridicule and to destroy what we fear. All of history has revealed to us the effort of the human mind to destroy, to ridicule, and extinguish what it fears. That is the very nature of the human mind. That's known as survival of the Law of Identity, known as self. What we cannot control, we attempt to destroy or to ignore. It takes a wise man to pause to think, to study, to research, and to investigate what he does not understand. A fool fears what he does not understand and is a fool because he's not willing to make the effort to investigate.

What does that have to do with affirmation? We look around the world and we see one time we're feeling so-called good; another time we're feeling the opposite or bad. One time we're very joyous; the next time we are very depressed. There is a part of us that knows that feeling good is not a luxury. Feeling good is an absolute necessity, for good is God, the very principle of life itself. Therefore, our minds are constantly working to feel good, which, for our minds, is to know God, goodness. The problem is in the limited and narrow horizons of consciousness that we have, through our education, permitted our self. Our horizons cannot be broadened until we gain tolerance. We cannot gain tolerance until we make the effort to understand. We cannot make the effort to understand until we have suffered sufficiently with what we think we already have in consciousness. Then we go to work within our consciousness to bring about a change. But to bring about a change, we must let go of what we think we have. But that is not what our minds want to do. Our minds want to change for the better and hold on to what we think we have, which life has already revealed has not brought us the better that we are now seeking. Therefore, we turn to many philosophies and many different religions. We turn to different studies and meditations, etc., etc., etc., ever in an effort to feel good, to find a way.

And so these laws being set into motion by the thoughts of our mind are slowed down, gradually changed by what is known as flooding the consciousness. Now we understand that to be affirmations. Other religionists understand that to be prayers, etc. Try to understand that though you may not be consciously aware that there are thoughts moving in your consciousness, they are doing so every split second. Because you may not, at the moment, be aware of what those thoughts are in no way exempts you from the law that inner attitudes of mind, created by the mass of thoughts entertained in consciousness, are in truth outward manifestations. For example, outward manifestations are revelations of inner attitudes of mind.

So a person pauses and says, "Just a moment. I wish to change my experiences. I wish to have more of the good of life." First, one must declare the truth: "I have a right to the good of life in keeping with the law that I personally choose to establish." Therefore, a person must pause and become aware of the laws they have established from the experiences they have already encountered, and then let go of those attitudes or laws, let go of those beliefs that one cherishes so dearly. And begin to change our thoughts. By becoming aware of our thoughts, we become the captain of our ship. We then consciously choose the laws that we wish to follow.

For once a law is established by the human consciousness, man cannot escape the law he has established. He may establish new laws in order to balance or neutralize laws already established, but the law is and shall be fulfilled. We all realize, I am sure, that is a mental world, that is a physical world that that law applies to. It is not a spiritual world. But it is a mental and physical world. But we spend most of our time identified with what is known as self, which is the sum total of our mental world. Therefore, in that respect, affirmations, wisely chosen, religiously applied, will, of course, guide a person to new levels of consciousness and bring about a change in their life, new experiences in keeping with their own effort.

The Living Light Philosophy teaches evolution through self-application of the laws revealed. It does not teach, nor has it ever implied, a way of techniques to gain what one seeks. For that is contrary to the very law and, therefore, is a waste of time. I hope that's helped with your question.

The lady here, please.

Please speak on goal being a lifeline.

Goal?

Yes.

Yes. The teaching is that goal is a lifeline; choose wisely.

Everyone enters form, that is, this divine Spirit enters form for a purpose. It doesn't just enter form to move a body or a form around the universe. It has a purpose. That purpose being to reveal itself and, in so doing, to evolve the form in which it is encased at any moment. Therefore, the very basic principle of life is purpose. Without an awakening to our purpose in life, then we, in that sense, are lost, filling up space, chasing one desire for so much of a time or span of our life, to chase another to be disappointed, discouraged, and depressed only to rise and to chase another. Everyone, everything is designed to serve a purpose. Wise and happy are those who find the purpose of their life. Now that's known, of course, to us as a goal; we have set in our consciousness something to accomplish. But remember, in serving one's purpose, in finding one's goal, one must be wise enough never ever to complete it. For once we set a goal and we think we have achieved our goal, there's nothing left to look forward to. Now that's known to most people as retirement, to retire. To retire from activity is contrary to the very Law of Purpose. Everything, regardless of age or sex, color or creed, *everything* has a purpose. There is nothing that stands in the way of our purpose, in the way of our goal but the judgments of our mind that tell us we haven't achieved it yet, we're so far

from it, what's the use? And therefore, we make no effort and the years roll by. I hope that's helped with your question.
Thank you.
The gentleman back there has been waiting, please.
What are the responsibilities of being a godparent?
"What are the responsibilities of being a godparent?" Well, first I think we should look at the word that you have spoken. First [of] all, the word *God* or *good*, we understand and then, of course, we look at the word *parent*. Now we call that a godparent. And few of us seem to understand what that really means. Ofttimes what it means to the parent, it certainly does not mean to the godparent. To some people it means that whenever the parents decide or judge that the child has a need and they don't feel they can fill that need, they turn to the godparent to take care of those needs and they expect them to be filled. Now there's that type of thinking about what a godparent is.

And then there is the god—or good—parent which, in our understanding, is an individual who, by the law he or she has set into motion, has been asked to be the godparent of someone's child. Of course, they're never left without free choice. They choose to be the godparent with the question, "What does that mean to me?" And, most important, "What does it mean to the parents who have asked me to be the godparent?" Therefore, an understanding must be reached before one foolishly accepts the compliment, one might say, of being the godparent. So we take a look and we see—we look at the child and we look at the parents. And then we look at our self. Do we see, with our understanding, is the child being raised to be a benefit to society? Or is the child being raised to be a detriment to society? Is there license? Or is there discipline? Is there love? Or is there self-satisfaction? Is the child being considered? Or is the child only being considered when it suits the parents' need of the moment? All those questions one must ask before taking such a very important step in accepting the great responsibility of being a godparent. Because they may find, as time passes, they, being the godparent, are faced with the full responsibility of rearing the child if something should happen to the parents. So that must be considered. And is the godparent sufficiently evolved in consciousness to suggest, in keeping with the Law of Solicitation, and not transgress the law and interfere? I hope that's helped with your question.

Yes, the lady here, please.

Would you please explain how the soul faculty of humility balances the sense function of sex?

Well, we understand, of course, that function of procreation and the basic animal instinct of the need, which, of course, is to fill the purpose of the continuity of the species. Humility is a soul faculty. And in keeping with that, taken from contents from *The Living Light* book, sex or procreation is a sense function.

The thing is that we have such varied and seemingly strange views of the natural function of procreation. We look at it not as the purpose, usually, for which it has been designed, for procreation. That isn't how we look at it usually, most people. We look at it as something that can be used to fill another desire that we have at the moment. Unfortunately, it is often viewed that way. Because it is often viewed that way, religions and society have brought into being a multitude of taboos concerning it. After all, there was a time, not long ago, it couldn't even be discussed. It's something that just was not discussed. Well, if we don't discuss it, of course, we'll never understand it. Because no one ever understands anything that they do not communicate about.

So we must go within our own consciousness and we must ask our self, "What does it mean to me? Not what it means to someone else. Not what someone else is doing with it. Not what society is doing with it. Not what my neighbors are doing with it. What does it mean to me?" That's where we must begin. Once we understand and are satisfied with our understanding of what it means to us, then we will find a balance begin to take place in our consciousness between the soul faculties and the sense functions.

For example, when we *think* we need anything, in that moment that we *think* we need, we must become aware that our thought of need is a delusion, the effect of denial. Now we say that we need a coat because it is cold. And we have all kinds of emotions if we don't get the coat that we decide that we must have because we're cold. We say we need that. The reason we say we need it is because we look outside and at our closet and our home and we see the coat's not there. Then our mind goes to work through all of the multitude of desires in our consciousness and finally comes up with a decision, a judgment, we'll get the coat in six months because we can't get it now. Well, what is taking place, in truth, is that other desires, long suppressed, they all rise up, for they want to be filled as well as the coat desire. Now when that happens we become, usually, very frustrated. We become frustrated because we are relying and depending upon our mind for the goodness of life.

No one can deny that having a coat when it's freezing cold to keep you warm, to our mind, is good. That is goodness. But because we rely upon a mental world for our sustenance we pay a very dear price, because we deny the truth that all that we have is wherever we are in consciousness. Now when we decide we need a coat, that's fine to make that decision, but we step over the cliff when we permit our mind to tell us that we need it. Because when our mind tells us that we need something, our mind reveals to us that we are the victim, through dependence upon mental substance, and, therefore, have denied the very Source of our life, the very Source of our good, which is the spiritual, divine, infinite, eternal, intelligent Energy that flows through us. And I hope that's helped with your question.

We have time for one more and then we must conclude. The lady over here, please.

The differentiation between—at one point you're saying affirmations are uplifting us [and] giving us positive vibrations, like attracts like.

That is correct.

And at one—I just heard you say a few moments ago about thinking that we need something. How is thinking—

That is correct. Because, you see, you are dealing with a mental world and a spiritual world.

If, you see, you say an affirmation to flood your mental world with positive thoughts, which are positive forms, which are positive attitudes, which the law reveals in a mental world that like attracts like and becomes the Law of Attachment, then you cannot [help but] be benefited and uplifted. So we are speaking of stages of evolution. Now if you are in a spiritual sight within your own consciousness and you see that your mind states it needs something, it is denying the very life and Source that you are. Because if you needed it, then you cannot be identified with the spiritual wholeness that you are in truth. Do you understand?

I guess I'm not clear.

Please speak forth.

What it does is it acknowledges the truth about what you are, which discusses the consciousness that you're at. And if you're stuck in that consciousness, then that's something that you need to see.

That is correct. But, you see, we cannot see, if we have over-identified with the mental world, we certainly cannot see the spiritual life that we truly are. Therefore, the over-identification with the mental world, our little, small world that we have created, the over-identification with that blinds us to that which we are. And we, therefore, experience that which we think we are. And we will experience that which we think we are as long as we permit our mind to dictate need to our consciousness.

I guess I'm hearing different things. At one moment the mind is a channel, and at another moment it's coming from—I hear two different places.

No, the mind is an instrument through which the divine, intelligent Being is expressing. The limit of the expression of the intelligent, spiritual Being is limited by the degree of awareness of the human mind. Now if we permit our self to depend upon the human mind for the good of life, then we must realize that in permitting our self to identify with the human mind for the good of life, we are denying the very thing that we truly are. So it absolutely has to deal with identification.

For example, if you permit your mind to tell you, you are happy because this person or that person is reacting to you the way you wish them to react, then you are denying the very source of your goodness and are limiting it to a judgment that you have made concerning another individual over whom you can never have total control because they are an individual. Now many people fall into that great trap the moment they get married. Not everyone, fortunately, but many people do. They decide and make the judgment that the person that they are marrying is to act in a certain way at all times. And if they do not act in a certain way, then they are very unhappy and miserable, which reveals that they are over-identified with themselves, the mental substance, which has dictated that their God or goodness, happiness or joy, is dependent on what they think that another individual does. Does that help with your question? Pardon?

[Yes.]

Thank you. Thank you kindly.

JANUARY 1, 1984

Church Questions and Answers 45

As our chairman has stated, this is your opportunity to ask questions during this period of a general interest. So, if you will be so kind as to raise your hands, I will be happy to reach as many as time will permit.

The lady here, please.

When you set a law into motion and it comes to fruition, is it ever the case that it was set in motion in a previous life and it comes to fruition in this life?

That's an excellent question. In reference to establishing a law, as man is a law unto himself—there is [a] question concerning the establishing of the law prior to our present awareness of our present existence? That's your question, isn't it?

Yes.

First of all, then, we must question why do we see such a variety of experiences upon entering the planet Earth. In keeping with the Living Light Philosophy, upon which this church is based, there is the teaching and demonstration of evolutionary incarnation. No one in any universe at any time escapes the laws they alone choose to establish. Whether or not they are ignorant of them has no effect upon the law established. And so it is that we enter the planet Earth in keeping with laws in evolution that we alone have established. Consequently, in answer to your question, it is absolutely affirmative. We do not teach what is commonly referred to as return or a reincarnation. We do teach evolutionary [in]carnation of which Nature herself reveals constant demonstration. I hope that's helped with your question.

The gentleman at the back, please.

Could you define the terms idealist *and* fanatic? *And explain our culture's fascination with World War II, the result of an infamous fanatic.*

Thank you very much. You would like our understanding of the word *fanatic*, the word *idealist*, and the seeming or apparent fascination with war, specifically World War II that has passed, is that your question?

People establish within their consciousness what they understand to be an ideal. That is based upon, of course, their own personal acceptances, their own personal denials in keeping with their own evolution. Ofttimes one finds great support for his ideals, for his ideals at times seem to be popular with the masses. In reference to an ideal which one entertains at any given moment, one must also understand anything that is taken to an extreme, that is, that is taken out of balance with the very purpose of its design, is known to us in our world as fanatical or a fanatic, one who does such a thing.

In reference to the seeming or apparent fascination with war that has passed, we must first investigate within our own consciousness what experiences did we demonstrate in reference to a fascination with the experience. For example, we look around the world and we see many people that seemingly are fascinated with one type of disaster after another. We understand that that which stimulates and challenges the senses, indeed, helps the ego to expand. We don't teach it helps the ego to be educated. It does just the contrary; it helps it to expand.

Now as long as man finds within his consciousness a need to express what we understand to be the human ego and not finding or permitting himself sufficient avenues for its expression in constructive ways, the mind frequently turns to destructive ways. For the expression of a thing is necessary for the purpose of its very design. Therefore, one should not consider tempting to annihilate the human ego. One should consider to educate it, to broaden its horizons in such a way that it may express itself in a constructive way. If it is expressed in a constructive way for oneself, and in keeping with the law that we cannot grant to another what we have not first granted unto our self, then, of course, it would be of benefit to humanity. So we find these varying fascinations are fascinations with that which stimulates the senses and the uneducated ego. Does that help with your question? Thank you.

The lady here has a question, please.

[It was] recently stated in a class that if a person goes to spirit without completing the job that that they came here to do, the form remains in the sphere of the planet in which it expressed. Could you elaborate on that?

Why, certainly. In keeping with the demonstrable teaching there is no escape from the law and in keeping with the same teaching that man is a law unto himself and what are we doing with the law that we are, whatever law we set into motion or job that we have established to be completed shall be completed. If that law has been established in a mental world, then in a mental world shall we remain until such time as we have fulfilled the law that we alone have established.

We find in the world, the universes, that in keeping with man's own denial man experiences what he calls need. And that need, which is a judgment within the consciousness that he is not satisfied, let alone fulfilled, binds him to the very need in keeping with the Law of Magnetic Attraction known as desire. If a person judges that, first, they desire something and, second, that they do not have it and, third, that it is attainable somewhere beyond them, then in keeping with those laws established shall man bind himself to the realm of consciousness in which he has established the law. Does that help with your question?

I'm still needing elaboration on how the form remains in the sphere.

The form. Yes. Well, we are, as is demonstrable, we are Spirit, intelligent Energy, formless and free. Thought is that which is formed or created by the consciousness. Therefore, laws established in a mental world or realm of thought shall keep the form of thought, through which we are identifying as a vehicle of expression, to the realm in which it has been created, or law established. Does that help with your question?

Thank you.

Thank you very much. The gentlemen here, please.

Yes. Sometimes I work hard at what seems to be a soul talent. Other times I might—and it doesn't bring much apparent satisfaction. Other times I might do something laborious and it might bring satisfaction. My question is, How do you know? How does one know if they're keeping to their path that would best suit their evolution?

Thank you very much. In reference to one's effort in expressing what is a natural or termed a soul talent, that they do not receive satisfaction from, but ofttimes when they are doing something which they understand is not a soul talent, they feel very satisfied, is a self demonstration revealing to the individual, blatantly and clearly, the truth. First of all, satisfaction is an expression of the senses and is controlled by force, which is known as the human mind. Fulfillment or joy is a faculty, an expression of the soul, that does not require the stimulation of senses for it is in a plane of consciousness where there are no senses, as we know senses. So if we find our self at any time over-identified with the self, the limitation of what we think we are and not what we truly are, then we will find that we are not satisfied in many expressions in our life that are expressions of our true or spiritual being.

Because the obstruction to the divine flow of intelligent, infinite, intelligent Energy, the only obstruction in the world in which we identify is the limit that the human consciousness has placed upon the expression. For example, the flower expresses an infinite, intelligent Being. We look at the flower. We look at it through eyes of form; therefore, we see form. We look with limit; therefore, we see and experience limit. We in time shall evolve beyond these limitations that are established by mental forms. I do hope that's helped you in your question in reference to your natural soul talent.

One does not seek satisfaction in anything until they become aware of the very process through which satisfaction is enabled to register within the human consciousness. Now we have control over our thought whenever we choose to control our thought. So through the control of our thought we can be satisfied with anything we choose to be satisfied with. That, of course, is in keeping with the law that reveals personal responsibility. Man is a captain of his ship. Man is the captain of his destiny if man alone chooses to be. But man cannot intelligently choose to be until man first becomes aware of what the obstructions are. That that we are ignorant of, we cannot control. We place our self and qualify our self to control things within our own sphere or zone of action in keeping with our efforts to awaken and not to be ignorant of. Does that help with your question?

I'm still not clear on how, how do you—is there a way to know what might be a proper path for your—

Well, when we seek to know what is the proper path for us and when we seek to know it with mental substance or mental consciousness, then it shall change from us ever in keeping with past experiences. Because we, from lack of effort, have permitted our mind to be controlled by what has passed, what is a shadow. That which has already passed in our life is a shadow. We have registered it within our consciousness, but it no longer, in truth, is. And so when we look around the world to see what our path is, depending on how much control there is of any particular level of our consciousness, at one time we decide and we judge, "This is the path for me." We go along that path until, in time, from lack of effort, lack of awareness of our own mind, we suddenly see a different path, and we make another judgment, "That last path was not the path for me. *This* is the path for me." And we go along that path so much. That is what over-identification with self offers to all people.

Now if a person wants to know their path, truth is individually perceived. It is not individual; it is perceived individually.

We must first make the effort daily to gain control over our thoughts, which gains control over our emotions, which gains control over our judgments, which gains control over the shadows of the consciousness, which are past events and events that are yet to be that have not yet happened, therefore, they are not truth, nor are they fact. Consequently, through a daily effort of gaining control over our own mind, we will soon become aware of that that we are. Not what we think we are, for what we think we are is in a constant process of change. Man *is* truth. What he thinks he is, is not, for what man thinks he is, is in a constant process of changing. So we must first learn to separate truth from creation. And once we have separated truth from creation, then the path that is our path is clearly revealed within our consciousness. I hope that's helped with your question. Thank you.

The lady over here has been waiting. Yes.

I was wondering what laws in motion are perpetuating the situation in Israel and the problems there with their neighbors.

[A] very interesting question in reference to the country of Israel. The lady has asked what laws have been set into motion by the populace or by the country that has caused so many problems with their neighbors. Well, let us examine more personally, for when we enter into our personal life we get, perhaps, sometimes a better objective of what is going on outside, which is simply an expansion of what goes on inside.

Ofttimes we find in our life a problem with our neighbor next door or a problem with the person who is renting the apartment across the hall. We find problems with the clerk at the grocery store or the department store. There's problems, it seems, wherever we go if problems are what we are seeking. How do we seek problems? The question must be asked. When we tempt to impose our will, our limited views and judgments upon another, we open the door to what is known as problems or trouble. Now one might say, "I am minding my own business. Not imposing my will upon another, yet I seem to have so very many problems." But it is our view and interpretation of how we impose our will. We are the ones that judge, "This is imposing my will on another. This is not imposing my will on another." We take a teaching of the divine right of choice and we take a teaching that is revealing the divine right of choice within a person's consciousness to control that which is demonstrably, justly, and rightly their sphere of action, their zone of responsibility, and we take that and we impose it in many ways upon others.

So troubles, whether they be in the Middle East or the Far East or wherever they may be—to be freed from a problem, we must first find the solution. And to find the solution, we must go to that which grants us freedom. And that which grants us freedom is personal responsibility. There is no difference between the seeming problems in the Middle East and the seeming difficulties over these past few years of the economy in the United States. They are effects; they are not causes. They are effects of transgressing demonstrable laws of personal responsibility. If you're going to move into a neighborhood and you go to view the house or the apartment that you want to live in and you are considering moving to that area, and the first person you meet, you seem to have a disagreement with and you start fighting, the first thing to do is to settle the problem before you make the move. Now the problem must be settled within one's own consciousness. To deny personal responsibility, to say that we are having troubles, struggles, or difficulties because of something that is beyond our control is an absolute, blatant denial of the laws of personal responsibility. Does that help with your question? I do hope so. Thank you.

The lady over here has been waiting. Yes. Yes.

Oh, Mr. Goodwin, would you please speak on the desire realms? Would you—when we leave this earth plane, it's my understanding we go into, we could go into a desire world. Is this desirable? It's my understanding that it's hard to get out of that world. And how can we avoid it?

In reference to the question about leaving this world and entering a desire world, we first must go to what we understand, in the Living Light, as the word *desire*. What does it mean to us? To us, desire means the divine expression, the expression of the Divinity itself, the Divinity being goodness. Now what man does in his judgment and his choices in expressing his divine expression, called desire, is an entirely different question.

When we find in the world in which we are consciously aware that our mind is filled with desire, the lack of fulfilling it, the dependence upon others for its fulfillment, the frustrations of not getting it fulfilled, we may be rest assured when we take off our suit of clay that consciousness does not change. That does not change. There is no law, there is no experience ever recorded in the Akashic records where a person left the clay, the physical flesh, and their consciousness suddenly changed. Now it doesn't work like that. We don't go to sleep one night with a desire bombarding our consciousness because of our ignorance of the Law of Fulfillment; we awaken plagued with it. Sometimes we go night after night, day after day, month after month, and year after year.

It is not desire that is the problem. It is the judgments that have limited the consciousness and have directed the desire, the divine expression, outward to something beyond our control for its fulfillment. Now when we accept personal responsibility, then we can say to our self, "I am experiencing at this moment what I understand and consider to be a desire. My mind is telling me that it contains the experience of need, that it is dependent upon something or someone beyond my control for its fulfillment." Now that's the first step; that's the descent. That is the dictate by the human consciousness of denial.

Now denial in this philosophy reveals our destiny. What we accept, we fulfill within our consciousness. The Living Light teaches and demonstrates that total acceptance is the divine will, the will of God. When, within our own consciousness, we totally accept our wholeness, completeness, for that that we are—not what we think we are, but that that we are is whole and, therefore, complete, for truth cannot be absent of anything. So when we stand within our consciousness, knowing beyond a shadow of any doubt, that we are truth, not our thought that is controlled by creation, but that which we are is truth. "Therefore, I am truth. Therefore, I am free. Therefore, I am not dependent upon anything beyond my own consciousness, which is God, the Divine itself. I am not dependent upon anything that is beyond that; therefore, I do not experience need. Not experiencing need, I do not establish the laws of denial. Not establishing the laws of denial, I do not experience the destiny of want." Does that help with your question?

Yes.

I do hope so. We have time for one or two more only, please. Yes, the lady here, please.

Can you speak a little more on the Akashic records?

Well, in reference to the Akashic records, everything within consciousness is indelibly recorded. Nothing is ever lost and nothing is ever new. When we think that something is new, *for us* it is new. For we are, at that moment, in a state of consciousness that the experience, or whatever it is that we judge is new, for that level of consciousness, it is new. But it is not new in the universe. There is nothing new under the sun, the light of eternal reason. The records, the Akashic records or whatever you may choose to call them—all experiences of everything is indelibly recorded. The principle of all law is contained within the records.

And when we truly accept, truly accept personal responsibility and the eighty-one levels of consciousness through which our eternal, infinite, eternal being is expressing, when we accept personal responsibility on the totality of the levels of consciousness, then we will know beyond a shadow of any doubt, for in those realms that's the light of reason. That's where wisdom expresses itself. And so, it is only the limit that we place in our consciousness upon what we can or cannot experience; that is the only way that we remain in the realms of ignorance. I hope that's helped with your question.

Yes, the gentleman here, please.

Yes, I have a question. How does one eliminate relatives that have passed beyond? How do you eliminate them from your life so that they lose an effect of people around you?

Yes. That's an excellent question. How does one no longer entertain the thought nor the experience of those who have left their life? Is that—that is basically the question, isn't it?

Yes.

You see, we have many people, they travel; they go back to New York. And they stay for fifty years or so or they go to Hawaii or they go to Australia, the Middle East, or someplace else. And we find these thoughts plaguing our consciousness, is that not correct?

I'm talking about dead ones.

Well, someone who goes to the Middle East in our consciousness could easily be dead, you know. So we are really talking about the thought of a person that we have had experience with, some way in our life, that is no longer physically in our life, is that not correct? I'm trying to help you and to relate that whether a person leaves their physical suit or they travel to the Middle East, there is no difference in reference to the consciousness of the individual who is having the experience or the plaguing. [It] doesn't matter where they go. It does matter that the intelligence and the experience exists within the consciousness and we must first make that step in personal responsibility in order to close the door. Now that happens when we eliminate, eliminate fear, for fear is the magnet that pulls the experience into our life. Fear is the magnet that keeps it in our life.

But then we must ask the question: What is fear? We understand simply, of course, that fear is the mind's control over the eternal consciousness or the eternal being or the soul.

Now how does one eliminate fear so they do not continue to experience someone that has left their life? Is that not a good question? Fine. Of course, there's a simple answer because truth is simple. But, then again, its application becomes more complicated. The teaching in the Living Light is redirect the energy, for the thought or the experience cannot exist within the consciousness without energy. Now energy follows attention. So the first step to make in freeing oneself of any experience that we find distasteful or not beneficial at any time in our life is to take control of our consciousness and choose wisely where we place our attention. I realize that it is—we make it difficult to redirect or put our attention on something else, something joyous and happy and beneficial. When a door keeps slamming in our face, it draws our attention, doesn't it?

But then we must ask our self, "What force or what power is slamming this door in my face? First, I cannot deny personal responsibility, for if I deny personal responsibility, I give something outside of my control power over my life." That is contrary to the very demonstrable law of the divine birthright of each individual of choice. So we cannot deny personal responsibility. We stop denying personal responsibility and we say, "Now this is my consciousness. These thoughts and experiences are entering my mind. They cannot enter my mind if I choose that they not enter my mind. For I have, by my divine right of evolution, I have what I know as the power of will." Now the power of will or the will power of man is the lord or the law of man's universe. So, we stop, we pause. The experience we find distasteful and not beneficial and we make a declaration within our consciousness that those experiences shall not recur, for we know the way. Through the redirection of attention, energy shall go to something of our conscious choice that we find more beneficial.

Now, what happens within the consciousness? The experiences are going on, but our attention and our consciousness is not on those realms. You see, when we understand that we are expressing through 81 levels of consciousness and these experiences may be happening on 1, 2, 5, or 10 realms of consciousness, we do not have to be there if we choose not to identify with those realms. Does that help with your question?

Yes, sir.

So, you see, you know, it's just like so many places and experiences in life of haunted houses, they call them, and all these different psychic experiences. The more attention that is placed upon them, why, of course, the stronger they get, for energy follows attention. And it takes energy, therefore, attention, for these things to move, to act, and to express themselves. Now when you take away the attention, you take away the energy. We must realize those who have passed out of our consciousness, they do not have this physical energy that we are using. We supply it to them in order for the experience to take place. Therefore, because we are the supplier—that is, the Divine source flowing through us by our conscious choice of direction is giving the energy to them.

It's like—remember, whatever in life bothers us, that is what is controlling us. So if we permit someone, here or there or anyplace else, to bother us, then we must accept we have some kind of a strange need within our self to be controlled by someone outside.

Now I've heard a lot of gentlemen say that their wives control them. I work with the husband and say, "Well, you must first find out what is your need to be controlled. Perhaps you never let go of your mother." Then I have a lot of women that come for counseling that say that their husband's controlling them. Because, you see, not to work with the individual who is being bothered is to deny the Law of Personal Responsibility and, therefore, not have the benefit nor the effect called freedom. So we must work with the person who is being bothered, for that is the person who has made the conscious choice to have the experience.

I know it sounds difficult. Personal responsibility is not a popular teaching in this world today. But personal responsibility is not a new teaching. Personal responsibility is the oldest teaching of the universes, for it is demonstrable truth. I hope that's helped with your question.

Thank you. I see our time is up.

FEBRUARY 5, 1984

Church Questions and Answers 46

This is your once-a-month opportunity to ask the questions, as our chairman has stated, that are of a general interest to all of us. And if you will be so kind as to raise your hand, I will come to as many as time will permit.

The gentleman on the aisle, please.

In the Living Light Philosophy, it states when you ask and you receive not, then you are truly receiving.

Yes.

Could you give a little bit more understanding of that statement?

Yes. Thank you very much. In reference to our study book, *The Living Light*, and when you ask and receive not, then you are truly receiving. That is in keeping with our teaching that ofttimes no is God's direction. And it is in life, it seems, that when we reach the hindsight years of the forties we seem to have a greater understanding in reference to what has passed, especially the many times that we were tempted to ask and seemingly not receive.

Now for a person to understand that teaching (when you ask and receive not, you are truly receiving) is to accept and to understand that there is an infinite, intelligent, eternal Power that is guiding our lives; that the thoughts of our mind have birth, and by the Law of Birth, they have death; that all form is created, therefore, all form returns to the source from whence it came. But the intelligent Energy, that which we truly are—not that which we think we are, but that which we truly are—it knows; it does not have to be told. So when we, in our own weaknesses, are tempted to ask and, in our weaknesses, experience the return of not receiving, that is the moment, the opportunity that we have to accept beyond a shadow of any doubt that the desire and temptation of the moment was not in our best interest. And it takes the illusion of time to pass to prove that to us beyond a shadow of any doubt.

Something cannot come out of nothing, and therefore, what we think we are has not come from nothing. It is formed by our experiences. By our own acceptances and rejections do we create these forms and these varying beliefs. If man was to accept that he is the thought of the moment, then man would have to face the demonstrable truth that he is, indeed, a most unreliable and undependable being in the universe. For the thoughts of one moment we find, through our own experiences, are in total contradiction to the thoughts of the next moment. Therefore, we pause and we clearly see we are not the thought; therefore, we are not the form, which is the effect of the thought. We are the intelligent, infinite Energy that moves the thought, that moves the form. I hope that's helped with your question.

The gentleman on the aisle, please.

What is it in human behavior and nature that puts the greater priority on authority than being—doing the right thing, being correct?

What is it in nature that places, within our consciousness, authority as a priority over right? Is that your question?

Yes, it is.

It has one answer and one word: it is denial. From denial grows need. From need grows demand, frustration. And from that denial of that which we are we establish the law known as our destiny, for man is a law unto himself. Life has revealed to us that which we have denied in our lives, time passes and we find our self marching on to it. The law reveals that we cannot grant unto another what we have not first granted unto our self, in keeping with the teaching, "O physician, heal thyself," because we are not qualified. We have not qualified our self to help another until we first help our self. That is contrary to the demonstrable law. And so, we look out, sometimes, and we see or think we see that someone has something or some things that we desire. We desire them for we have denied our right to them. We have permitted our limited minds to tell us that we do not have them. And we seek, our minds seek to have that which it declares it does not have. And so we find in our lives this great need. And we permit this need to be filled in our consciousness by what we believe is control or authority. And in so doing we sell out anything and everything to fill this need that has been caused from our own denials of the demonstrable truth which we are. And in so selling out, the priority of right or righteousness is ever subject to whatever needs we believe, from our own denials, we have established at any moment. I hope that's helped with your question.

The lady on the aisle, please.

Mr. Goodwin.

Yes.

Can you speak a little bit about death, the first days of death, like when a soul leaves the body?

In reference—yes—in reference to what is termed death or transition, as the soul is leaving the body the first few days? That, of course, is entirely dependent on preparation made by the individual prior to leaving the physical body. For example, many people are so filled with self-thought and fear that that consciousness, of course, that state of consciousness is what leaves the physical body. Ofttimes they are not even aware that they have left the physical body. That is one of the most difficult sufferings that I am aware of. Because they are consciously aware of a physical world and their surroundings and are unable to communicate physically, unable to move anything physically because they have left the physical, yet, in consciousness, are still attached to it. That is one of the effects of over-identification with self and what self has to offer.

Therefore, ancient philosophies for eons of time have taught a very simple preparation to prepare for the journey. There are so few people who prepare for the inevitable, which only reveals the phenomenal fear of it. And their fear of it prevents them from a reasonable, intelligent, sensible preparation. Now, therefore, there are untold millions of souls who leave the physical earth existence and find themselves in what is known in Spiritualism as an earth-bound state of consciousness. Fortunately, in keeping with the divine laws of evolution, they do not remain there, or anywhere, forever.

Now there are also those who have and who do make the conscious effort to prepare for their journey. Those preparations are made through an honesty with oneself. Because only in being honest with oneself can one truly perceive the obstructions in their consciousness that would be the instruments of magnetically holding them, through their emotions, to a physical or earth realm. Having made those preparations over a period of time, there are those, through an effect of that effort, who consciously leave the physical body, who are conscious through the entire process and enter the realm or the state of consciousness that they have earned in their evolution.

There are also those who are consciously aware of the various people who come from spiritual realms to help them with their journey. For it is the distractions, the lack of control of the human mind, that tempts the vehicle through which the soul is moving, in a mental world, that keeps them from the destination, immediately, that they have earned. For example, if a person, prior to transition and as a predominant pattern of their consciousness, is easily distracted from what they decide to do, then, of course, it reveals that they are easily tempted. And we all know that temptation is weakness.

Now in part of the preparations of transition that I have taught over these many years in various classes, it is critical and it is extremely important that we gain control over distraction, temptation, which is weakness, not by hiding from it—for to hide from anything is to weaken oneself further—but to face that weakness, to accept that it is in the consciousness of our own being, that we have created it in our days of ignorance, that that which we truly are is greater, of course, than that which we think we are. And it is those efforts and through that understanding that we are able to leave this physical world consciously and not have to spend so much time in what is known in some religions as the realms of purgatory or purification or in these realms of mental temptation, in these realms of the earthbound spirits.

One of the finest books, printed long ago, was and is, *The Tibetan Book of the Dead*, also *The Egyptian Book of the Dead*. When it is properly understood, with a little light from within our own consciousness, you will clearly see, they prepared, and still prepare, their people for a conscious transition to the inevitable journey that we're all on. I hope that's helped with your question.

The gentleman over here has a question, please.

Mr. Goodwin, I have a question on karma. It's a little bit twofold. My question is, Does a soul, as it has karma, as I know it, is there also karma on, say, the physical world? Like, for example, does physical property have karma? I know of a situation where there's been a piece of land that was for healing, and three or four healers failed. And I'm wondering, Is that entirely the healer or is that also karma on the land? And there's something to do— like fires and things like that—that comes about on a piece of property. Is there something that can be done to change karma on the land? I know, somewhat, about karma of a person, but I don't know if it's also of the land.

Thank you. Thank you very much. In reference to your question on the Law of Cause and Effect, commonly referred to as karma, as you stated in the beginning of your question that it is too full, I first want to clarify, in reference to this question of karma, that it is too full, did you mean to imply that your karmic laws are too full or what was.

No, no. I meant, is it two-fold, like does it apply to physical as well.

Oh, I see. Thank you very much. I'm glad you clarified that. In reference to this Law of Cause and Effect, called karma, let us understand, first, that cause and effect is a law that can only apply scientifically, sensibly, logically, reasonably to that which has limit. The Law of Cause and Effect cannot scientifically and does not scientifically apply to anything that is beyond limit, that is limitless and infinite. Therefore, that which we are is limitless, timeless, eternal, infinite, beyond the Law of Karma. The Law of Karma, demonstrably, is applicable to anything which has limit. And anything that has limit, we understand, is creation; it is form. So we find in form the Law of Cause and Effect applies. There are no exceptions to the Law of Cause and Effect, that Law of Duality, which creation or form or limit is bound by. When we permit our true being in its expression through a vehicle of limit, called our thought, which is form (our physical body, our mental body, our astral body), when we permit, through belief, that identification, we, in that moment, become subject to the Law of Belief, which is the Law of Limit, which is the Law of Karma. Does that help with your question?

Thank you.

Now I understand you had a second part to your question, in reference to a person trying to do something with a piece of property. Does the property have a karmic law? Indeed and of course it does. How does a person merit that particular piece of property with a karmic law? Why, in keeping with the law that like attracts like and becomes the Law of Attachment. Otherwise, it could not possibly work. You see, my friends, in Spiritualism and especially in the Living Light Philosophy, the laws of science are clear and demonstrable; they are the laws of the Living Light Philosophy. For a law is not a law unless it is demonstrable. Thank you.

Thank you.

The lady, the young lady there has a question.
What happens to animals when they die?
Excellent question. It's been asked before. And I'm sure there are many people interested. What happens to animals when they pass through this, this veil of transition, when they take their little journey? First of all, I think we should pause for a few moments and think what happens to our consciousness when we refer to this inevitable journey as *death, dying,* or *die* or *dead*. Within our consciousness we have created through belief, through our experiences, a form called death. It is a final thing. It is not a pleasant thing. It is something that our mind fears, for we have learned very early in life from those who have taught us that they fear it. And therefore, we fear it. We try to cover it up. We try to present our self as intelligent, adult beings. But there is, there is no reason in the realms of emotion. We all know that. And so whenever we refer to this inevitable journey of transition, moving from this place to that place, and we, in our mind, refer to it as dying, death, or dead, we support a form in our mental world and it becomes stronger and stronger and stronger as we grow older on earth, until our day comes and the light of reason does not shine, but the lesser light of emotion floods our consciousness. And it is the lesser light of emotion, flooding our consciousness, that is the chain that binds us to that which we are attached to. And transition, then, is indeed difficult.

Now what does that have to do with animals? If you love an animal and the time has come and your animal, your friend, goes on his or her journey, which someday you, too, shall go on, not knowing the day or hour, and you become an instrument through which the lesser light, the darkness, clouds your consciousness, that animal, now in another world, attached to you through its own emotional magnetic body, is pulled, magnetically, to an earth realm of consciousness. That is the greatest injustice that anyone could do to an animal, to a human, to anything. For it reveals and demonstrates not only the great error of ignorance, but it reveals, unfortunately, the great weakness of selfishness, self-love, over-identification with oneself.

And so it is that an animal evolves, is an evolving soul, that it comes into our life in keeping with laws established by the animal and by the one who cares for the animal. And the day comes, the animal has served its purpose, like we will someday, and the animal goes on. If you truly love the animal more than you love yourself, you will be joyous; you will flood your consciousness with the goodness of life that your friend, your pet, your animal got to take their journey into the happy lands where we're all going. And we'll get there sooner and not spend time on those realms close to this earth realm with discord and constant fighting and contradiction, realms of self-interest, not realms of God-interest, realms of darkness, not realms of light. We'll get there sooner if we make the effort today to remember the law that whatever happens to us is caused by us; that the journey is a journey that everyone takes; that the earth realm is a very short existence. Indeed a short time for the eternal, evolving awakening of our consciousness. That we came to this earth realm to serve a purpose, and that purpose, if not completely served, through transgression of the natural laws of evolution, we shall remain close to it until the job is done.

So we all know what we have to do in life. And if we permit our mind, in its temptations and weaknesses, not to do the job we know we must do, we may be rest assured we will be very close to this old earth realm for God only knows how many centuries. Until finally we accept personal responsibility and then we'll leave this earth realm. For there is no guarantee—absolutely, it is demonstrable—by leaving the physical body, we do not automatically enter a realm of consciousness where they're playing harps and eternal music. That is ridiculous superstition. For we leave our body many times during a night or a nap. The physical body is only necessary for physical existence. It has absolutely nothing whatsoever to do with being necessary for the mental existence. Our thoughts, our minds are not composed of physical substance. They are composed of electromagnetic energy that is not dependent on physical substance for its expression.

I see our time is up. I hope that's helped with your question. Thank you.

MARCH 4, 1984

Church Questions and Answers 47

As the chairman has just stated, this is your opportunity, once a month, to raise your hands and ask your questions on that which is of interest to you at this time. So I'll be happy to serve as the channel for an answer to your questions, if you'll be so kind as to raise your hands. And we'll get to as many questions as time allotted will allow.

Yes, the lady there, please.

In psychometry, what does the receiver see? It appears that you see all our past and, apparently, our future. Is that accurate?

Well, the possibility of such is, is truth, is accurate. That is not necessarily what takes place each time a psychometric, what you call, reading is done. The predominate vibration that is placed on any object, regardless of what the object is, is, of course, the strongest image that comes from the object. For everything we touch receives vibration, electromagnetic, from our own aura. Now thoughts, feelings, emotions emanate the strongest vibration from anyone and therefore that is the strongest image that can be psychometrized. However, without the guidance of what we call spiritual guides and teachers, the interpretation of the images is indeed most difficult, because the human mind is limited to its own interpretations based upon its own experiences. Does that help with your question?

Yes.

Yes. The gentleman there, please.

In the situation where, perhaps, you've lent someone a large sum of money or they breached a promise to you—that they've broken a promise that they've made, very seriously. In such a situation I find sometimes a desire to want to feel anger, a desire to want to get back, somehow. And I'm wondering in keeping with the idea of doing unto others as you would have they do unto you.

Yes—

What would be the best . . . [The remaining few words of the question are difficult to accurately transcribe.]

Well, of course, that philosophy, very ancient, do unto others as you would have others do unto you. Now, of course, in order to experience the truth that frees us, we cannot permit our minds to deny the Law of Personal Responsibility. Now if we, by our own conscious choice, choose to, as you say in your particular—or in this particular case, choose to loan someone a sizable amount of money, or whatever it may be, and on their promise that they will repay, then we have to understand if they do not repay what we have loaned them, then we are simply paying for a judgment that we made within our own consciousness. Now ofttimes we have a tendency, through denial of personal responsibility, to become emotionally upset with something that is outside. But to permit our self to think that there is something outside of our own consciousness that has the power or the potential to control our lives is a total denial of demonstrable truth.

So we must take a look at the cause. We made a conscious choice. Based upon our experiences, we followed a judgment of our mind. We did such and such and we do not appreciate, within our own consciousness, that we made an error in our thinking. And that is what upsets us. Then, rather than face that we have made a poor judgment, we tempt to project the cause of the problem that we are experiencing upon someone outside. Does that help with your question?

I do. If I may ask one more thing?

Certainly.

If the giving was done from a place of giving and then who promises each under those circumstances?

Yes, thank you. Well, in reference to giving, giving without the light of reason is not giving at all. Now ofttimes we think we're giving something because we make judgments within our consciousness: by doing such and such, such and such shall return unto us. Those are mental laws, governing by the Law of Creation, which is dual. It has so-called good and bad. It has positive and negative. It has so-called right and wrong. It has dark. It has the light. So if we, in our thinking, make the judgment that we are doing such and such and that is a givingness on our part and the demonstration in life, which is always the revelation for our own awakening, is not in keeping with what we thought the giving should receive, then we can be rest assured that that type of giving, mental giving, is not from the heart. It's from the mind and it must pay its just due of the dual Law of Creation. Does that help with your question?

Thank you.

You're welcome. The lady here, please.

My question is how best to channel, like, psychic or intuitive flashes, precognition, what-have-you, instead of having it scattered and just randomly happening to you. How you can best channel it, so it's something that can be very useful to you?

Thank you. In reference to your question, How can you best channel, which, of course, reveals or means control your experiences or experiences relating to psychic talent or intuitive impressions? Because we have a mind, a mental body, which is designed to be used to move material substance or the physical world, for there is no physical world without a mental world, which is the effect (the physical world) of a mental world, and etc., then, of course, we start with our efforts to discipline, which reveals control of the various thoughts, feelings, and emotions of our own mind. If that effort is not made, then no matter what the talent is that a person has, it cannot bring about continuous constructive good into their lives. For that which we are responsible for, that we do not make the effort to guide or control, sooner or later shall control us. And so, many people with psychic abilities and intuitive experiences instead of having them serve them for constructive good, it becomes a burden and a detriment to their peace and harmony. That is not the fault of the talent. It is not the fault of anything outside. It is the error of ignorance, the lack of controlling the mental vehicle that we are responsible for. Does that help with your question?

Yes.

You're welcome. The lady here, please.

Could you speak on the responsibilities of a step-parent and if there's a line between when you should stop and let the adult that has born the child take over?

Yes. I do feel that I follow your question in reference to the responsibilities of a step-parent. Well, of course, first off, we have to—the question must be asked: Is the person still the step-parent? One, through the process of marriage, becomes a step-parent. This is what you're speaking of. Now does one step down from that commitment or are they remaining in the commitment? That has to be first clarified.

Well, I'm saying to be in the commitment, where the child is among other children that are there in the home, so you are stepping up towards the responsibility of being the parent.

Yes, of course. If the step-child is in the home which the parent has the responsibility for, then, of course, the law reveals and demonstrates that we are responsible for all things that are within our charge. And that that is within our charge is what we're in. So in that respect, of course, the responsibility still remains with the step-parent. Until they step out or the step-child steps out.

OK.

Yes. Thank you. The gentleman here, please.

Earlier you said "positive" and "negative" and you said "dark" and "light," but you said "so-called right and wrong" and "so-called bad."

Yes.

Would you explain the differences?

Well, right or wrong is ever dependent upon a mental world of a thinking substance. For example, what you may think is right, the person next to you would swear on a stack of Bibles that it was wrong. So nothing is right or wrong, but thinking makes it so. Everything is good. For if we do not accept the demonstrable truth that everything contains within it goodness or God, then we must accept a belief in a pantheon of gods. Now this philosophy, the Living Light, accepts an intelligent, infinite, eternal Power, called, by man, God; that it is; by its very essence, [it] rejects nothing, accepts and sustains everything. The right and wrong processes are dependent upon creation, where the Law of Duality is governing and in control.

Now it is because for eons of time man has made the judgment—and all judgments, of course, are based upon a mental world—that this is right and that is wrong that he goes to war. And so, because he believes he is right, he fears the belief of another who believes they are right, and that is different than what he believes. And so it is fear that causes discord, disaster, and war. Because you cannot experience fear until you believe that you are threatened. For example, if the animal believes that its survival is threatened, it shall attack to defend itself. Truth does not have need, therefore, needs no defense. Truth just is. But it is our belief that has need.

Because, you see, we believe one thing one moment, and time passes and we believe something else. So our beliefs are not our security. We make them our security for a time. And as we continue to evolve and we continue to expand our consciousness, we find what we believed yesterday is not the same as what we believe today. We find that what we believed when we were little children, five and six years old, is certainly not what we believe today. So our beliefs are constantly changing. And our survival, if we permit our self to over-identify with our passing and temporal beliefs, if we permit ourselves to think that our beliefs and our thoughts are us, then we have a great struggle in life. Does that help with your question?

Thank you.

You're welcome. The gentleman on the aisle, please.

Do you have a practical method for not only striking up but maintaining a coherent conversation with somebody who has died?

Well, in reference, of course—when we understand within our consciousness that there is no separation in truth; that truth is what we are and we are changing our clothes, which we—at one time in our evolution we have this particular suit and then we move on in evolution and another suit and another and another. It's just like—the problem with communication is that we believe the appearance and, therefore, do not view the truth. So as we permit our self to *believe* that someone comes and *believe* that someone goes, as long as we *believe* in our own limit, then that's all we can offer to the universe. You see, we are, therefore, our own worst enemy. We are our own obstruction. We also are the way. So it is a matter of what we choose.

In reference to communicating with someone who is not present, the communication is within the power of your consciousness. It is totally dependent upon your effort in controlling your thoughts, which, in turn, control your emotions, which, in turn, finally still the activity of mental substance where you may view with that which you are, and then all obstructions are non-existent. Does that help with your question?

[Thank you.]

You're welcome. Yes, the lady here, please.

Mr. Goodwin?

Certainly.

OK. You're able to read people. Now—

Well, some people call it that. That is not my interpretation or understanding, but I do understand what you're referring to.

If you are to do that, to read people, what, what is your responsibility? OK, if you're telling me something, for instance, and I know that you're not telling me the truth.

Yes.

And I know how to read you, where—what is my responsibility in such? Because that scares people if they think that you know what they're thinking.

Well, in reference to your question, first of all, let us understand that truth is individually perceived. That doesn't mean that truth is individual. It certainly is demonstrable that truth is individually perceived. And we perceive at various times in varying degrees.

Now in reference to your question, What I think my responsibility is? My responsibility is to the Light that I, in my evolution, have earned and choose to serve. A wise man gives what he has to give in life and cares less what the receiver does with it. For otherwise, man is not giving anything; he is only loaning for a time. This is our problem in so-called giving. We give with ulterior motive. We give and ever wait, like panting dogs sometimes, what they're going to do with what we have given. That is not freedom. That is demonstrably not freedom. Therefore, that reveals clearly to everyone, that cannot be truth. For truth and freedom are one and the same.

Now if I should choose to go to a physician for something that I believe is a problem that the physician, possibly, may be instrumental in bringing about a cure, my responsibility in going to the physician is ever my personal responsibility. If I don't like the prescription they give me, then I choose not to take it. I do not choose, as hopefully an intelligent being, to stand there and argue with the physician after I have made the decision to go to a physician is what I choose to do. That is not intelligent, nor is it reasonable. Now if I go to a teacher to learn about music and I decide [to disagree] while the teacher is in the process of teaching me something about music (that I have voluntarily chosen to go for), then I am wasting my time. I am wasting my effort. I am wasting energy, and I am instrumental in wasting the time, energy, and effort of the music teacher. I do hope that has helped with your question.

We must not permit our self to deny the Law of Personal Responsibility. Thirteen years ago, when this church was opened, it was opened with one philosophy, its very foundation: those who come shall grow in keeping with their law and divine right of choice or they shall go. Therefore, we have no dogma. We have no creed in which members or friends or students of this association are required by any compulsory law or order to attend or not attend. To believe or not to believe is ever the right of each and every individual. We do not impose our belief. We do not believe, nor demonstrate, in going out to the world to impose our thinking upon others. But those who enter any temple, enter under the reasonable understanding that they shall be subjected to what teachings are offered in that particular school. I do hope that's helped with your question.

The lady back there, please.

Yes. I wanted to know what seems to be, to me, the confusion of helping refugees or people from other countries and, like, letting go of their own children at home . . . not helping them . . . [The remaining few words of this question are difficult to accurately transcribe.]

You're . . .

—trying to save others.

You—

To me, they're not saving their own . . .

Well, we cannot offer to anyone what we first have not offered to our self. You see, the law is very clear: we grant to others what we have first granted to our self, because if we have not first granted it to our self, we do not have it to grant to another. And so even the Bible teaches you, "O physician, heal thyself." You see? So if there's something we want to do, let us pause and see if we are qualified to do it. Then if we, in our own honesty, see that we are qualified to do it, then it is our conscious choice at any moment to grant it to another. But let us never forget that unsolicited help is ever to no avail and the Law of Presence is the Law of Solicitation. I hope that's helped with your question on refugees.

The gentleman here, please.

What do you mean when you say "so-called bad"?

Exactly. Because what is good to you may be so-called bad to someone else. Who's doing the calling? is the question. If you call it good and she calls it bad, then it is so-called by the individual who's doing the calling. Is that understandable?

Yes.

Yes, thank you.

I have another one.

That's fine. We still have a few minutes.

OK. Lately there's been a number of people that have said to me they really care about a friend or a relative. And they see that they're going the wrong way. As far as they're concerned they're not making the right decisions. And they want to help them somehow. Even though they are going to make a disastrous decision, they want to jump in there and help them. What do you feel responsibility—you know, as far as helping a loved one if you see that they're headed for disaster, what do you feel your responsibility is for that?

Quite simply, in keeping with the law that I understand and work to demonstrate, first of all, unsolicited help is to no avail. Presence is the Law of Solicitation. Now if the person that another person judges—remember, first they must make the judgment that that individual is going on the path of disaster—of course that, in turn, is based upon their own personal experiences. It may or may not be the path of disaster. It may be the best thing that ever happened to the individual because in all disaster there is Divinity; otherwise, God is not the sustainer of everything. Now it is up to the individual, once they make the conscious choice, in keeping with the Law of Solicitation and the Law of Presence, to give what they have to give, to care less what the relative or the individual does with it. For to care what they do with it is not giving at all. It is only a temporary loan and they're doing nothing but playing God. And in so doing they are going to suffer the effects of those types of laws. Does that help with your question?

Yes. Thank you. The lady here, please.

You twice mentioned the Law of Solicitation and the Law of Presence. And I'd like you to expand on that.

Why, certainly. You are here, present. Therefore, in keeping with that law, the Law of Solicitation is established. That means, under the Law of Presence you have established this Law of Solicitation; therefore, you are present and shall receive what is being offered. That means, clearly, we may or may not like it, but by your Law of Presence you have established the Law of Solicitation. Now, for example, if you go to a store, you have presented yourself. Therefore, you are under the Law of Solicitation; you have experiences that are what you judge are good or bad or etc. But you also have the Law of Personal Responsibility. You, by your own choice, placed yourself there at that time and exposed yourself to that person or persons. Does that help with your question?

Thank you very much.

You're welcome.

You see, law, the Law of Life reveals itself very clearly. If we pause in all our thoughts and activities and we permit our self to remind our self, "Just a moment. I feel good. Why do I feel good?" For one must ask themselves why they feel good, as well as why they feel bad. Because if they do not ask themselves why they feel good and do not come up with an intelligent answer within their own consciousness and they only ask themselves why they feel bad and they come up with a mountain of justifications—no! You ask yourself why you feel good just as often as you ask yourself why you feel bad and let's see if you get the same answer. Do you get the answer, "Well so-and-so did such and such. Therefore, I feel good." Then [when] you feel bad, "Well, he did such and such and I now feel bad." Because then, you see, truth is individually perceived. That reveals to you that you are dependent on something that is beyond your control. But in truth it is not beyond your control for that person exists within your consciousness. The thought is within your consciousness. You have the power. You have the responsibility to take care of your own backyard, and that's the backyard right here.

So in that respect, if you just ask yourself the question, "Now I don't like this particular image because I feel bad from this image. I see what this image is. I am responsible for it. I put it there in the first place. I now choose to change it." And you will feel good. Does that help with your question?

You see, to deny this power that flows through us by giving it so freely, in delusion, to something that is beyond our control is the path of suffering. Man is not designed to suffer, for man is not designed by self-interest and self-motivation. Self-interest and self-motivation offer to us a constant process of fear. We're constantly afraid that someone's going to take what we think we've got. But it is because we *think* we've got it and we don't really have it, that we're afraid so much. And then, sometimes, even get paranoid.

Thank you. I see our time is up. Thank you very much.

APRIL 1, 1984

Church Questions and Answers 48

[Give me just a] moment and I'll get this newfangled thing put in here. *[Mr. Goodwin secures his new microphone to his lapel.]* You know, it's like anything in life: you spend so much time with doing things a certain way, and if you don't move with the changes in life, then you soon find that the joy of life has passed you on by.

Now as our chairman has said, this is your opportunity, once a month, to speak forth the questions that are of interest to you and I will be more than happy to share with you the answers that I receive. So if you will be so kind as to raise your hand, I will be happy to reach as many as time will permit.

The lady on the aisle, please.

Thank you. Mr. Goodwin, I was wondering if you could speak to the issue of what's happening in the Middle East, specifically in the area of Lebanon and Syria.

Yes. Well—thank you. In reference to the situation in the Middle East, we spoke at one of our annual forecasts that peace would reign in the—begin to reign in the month of July. And that was speaking at that time in reference to the country of Lebanon. If you understand the human mind, then you will understand its great fear whenever it judges that it is threatened by anything close to it. And so what is taking place in the Middle East is what is taking place with all minds when they become over-identified with their little universe. The situation, there, will make a drastic change in the early part of December of this year. However, in speaking on that, I would rather speak more thoroughly at our forecast at that time. I hope that's helped with your question. Thank you.

The gentleman here, please.

Mr. Goodwin, can a person petition the powers of God on behalf of another who is ill?

No. In reference to petition, if you mean to tempt, if you mean to bargain, then, of course, that is absolutely contrary to demonstrable, natural law. If, however, by the word *petition* to goodness or God, to infinite, intelligent Energy, if by that you mean a request in reference for help or assistance to another person, whereas this philosophy teaches that God, an intelligent, infinite, eternal Energy, is not subject nor partial to the dictates or the pleas of the human mind, which are subject to the Light, which is known as God, and are not superior to the Light, which is known as God, then man will soon realize that all experiences in life are direct effects, in one's own evolution, of transgressions of natural and divine law.

Now everyone can look inside and they can see those areas of consciousness in which they excel in goodness. They can see those areas in their consciousness in which they are struggling to excel and to do better. And so, when we make a request of what we call God, then what we are doing, we are asking for the freedom or benefit for our self or another individual to pass the test of the lessons of life that we alone have established. Does that help you with your question?

Yes, sir.

Do you have a second one? *[After a short pause the teacher continues.]* Ofttimes, you know, a person, when asking a question, is not satisfied with the answer, but, then, that's not our purpose of being here.

The lady here, please.

[This entire question is very difficult to transcribe.]

What would you like to know about re—

Mr. Goodwin, I would like to know the doctrine of Spiritualism.

The doctrine of Spiritualism is stated in its Declaration of Principles. *[The teacher is referencing the Declaration of Principles of the National Spiritualist Association of Churches (NSAC), which was read aloud by the congregation as part of the devotional services.]* And in reference to Spiritualism, there are Spiritualists who believe in and, therefore, accept the doctrine of reincarnation. There are Spiritualists who do not believe in, nor do they accept, reincarnation or a return of the soul into form on the same planet of evolution. This particular church, Spiritualist church, has its philosophy, known as the Living Light Philosophy, which is a teaching of evolutionary incarnation in keeping with demonstrable truth that is revealed to us in nature. All things we view are in a process (their forms) of rising and falling. Through the ascent and the descent, form is changed and, therefore, refined. The evolution of that forms—the soul enters and experiences in the sense of its efforts to express through the limit of form and moves throughout the universes. And we do not limit life, intelligent life and its expression, to the planet Earth. Does that help with your question? Thank you.

The lady there, please.

I would like to know about the earthquakes in California.

What would you like to know about these wonderful experiences?

Is there a major earthquake coming in the near future?

Well, near future to one means weeks, days, or months; near futures to others may mean three, four years. If you mean by near future within the next six years, no. Earthquakes? Yes. If you mean by major, you mean the destruction or partial destruction of a city, no. I hope that's helped with your question for at least the next six years.

The gentleman here, please. Yes.

Thank you. There was a word used—reformation. [One of the principles of the Declaration of Principles of the NSAC uses the word *reformation*.] *When you say the word reformation . . .*

Yes, I'll be more than happy to. It is not the teaching of the Living Light Philosophy. However, it is the doctrine of the National Spiritualist Association of Churches of which we are a chartered member. That's the beauty and the freedom of

Spiritualism: it does not dictate and demand that its doctrine be accepted by its chartered membership.

Now in reference to reformation, our understanding—which means to reform—they are stating, in our understanding, that the possibility of anyone to free themselves from any transgression or error, which so-called sin is, is ever possible for all people; that it is ever present. We do not deny that. We have a bit of a different understanding of the word *reform*. Now to the human mind *reform* means, to most all people, to be free from what they have finally judged is no longer beneficial to them. Would you not agree?

Yes.

We find, at least this philosophy has experienced over these many, many years, that people who reform have not educated the weakness, which is the temptation, the limited desire that caused the particular pattern in the first place. They have simply suppressed it. In that sense, we find—may God, in his divine mercy, ever save us from the reformers. For if you have ever shared experiences with a reformer, you soon find out that either you are reformed or you're annihilated. Well, what that simply reveals is that a person who suppresses a pattern of mind, a person who suppresses the limits of their desires, a person who does not make the effort to educate them, is a person who is very insecure and constantly in fear of being tempted. Therefore, they must support their own security by forcing their particular reformation or their change upon everyone that comes within their zone of action. Does that help with your question?

[This response is difficult to transcribe.]

Thank you. The lady here, please.

In the Healing Prayer we say, "my heart is filled with gratitude for the Divine Law of Acceptance." Could you speak on the divine Law of Acceptance in that context? [The complete text of this prayer can be found in the appendix.]

Yes, thank you. In reference to speaking on "my heart is filled with gratitude for the Divine Law of Acceptance," we look about nature, creation, for that which is form, we see, is limited by the form; the Intelligence expressing through it is limited by the form through which it is expressing. And so, though there is no difference in the Infinite Intelligence expressing through the tree than there is through the bluebird, than there is through the human being, it is limited by the vehicle through which it expresses. Therefore, we clearly see there is intelligent Energy in the form of the tree. There is intelligent Energy in the human being. There is intelligent Energy in the bluebird. The Energy does not change; it is one and the same. Therefore, there is one God, one Intelligence, constantly expressing and demonstrating through the limits of the forms of creation. That, therefore, brings an awakening in the minds of all intelligent people that this Energy, this Intelligence accepts everything, denies nothing. All of life, which is intelligent Energy, is expressed through all forms. And in that awakening our heart is filled with gratitude for the living demonstration of an Intelligence that denies and deprives no one of the goodness which it is. Does that help with your question?

[Thank you.]

You're welcome. The lady here, please, has a question.

When one finds themselves caught up with judgments, what can they do to change their state of mind to the point where . . .

Thank you. In reference to the question, when one finds themselves caught up with judgments, I would like to clarify one thing in our understanding. It is true, we are "caught" whenever we have a judgment. But I would not consider that "up." I would rather consider that down. For I have yet to find a judgment which has risen the consciousness of anything, including a flea.

For judgment is a forming with mental substance and is based upon the limited experiences of the individual who makes it. And we find that judgments, no matter what they are, first, are limiting infinite intelligent Energy. They are dependent upon whatever has passed in a person's consciousness, not what is—for that would be truth; that which is, is truth—but that which has been, that which has passed. And so man, with his mind, gathers from mental substance all the shadows of the past experiences that he's already been through and he creates a limit to the divine, intelligent Energy. Now in creating that limit and in believing that he is the judgment that he has now created, man destines himself to the limit and the bondage of that particular judgment. Therefore, man, at those times, shuts himself off from the true Source, from his true being, which is total acceptance, which is freedom, which is truth. And man, denying his true being, man, denying his freedom, his truth, and the Light that he is, destines himself to the bondage that he has created by mental substance for the expression of his eternal being.

Now, you've asked how to be free when you become aware that you have caught yourself down there in limit. Man is freed from the limits of judgment when man stops believing that he is the judgment that he creates with his mind. As long as man believes that he is the thought of the moment, which is an effect of over-identification with what is known as the self, what is known as all of his experiences, when man pauses and stops believing he's the thought—he is responsible for the thought, but man cannot be the thought, for thought is form and form is limited. That's like saying that man is the hand or man is the toe. That's like saying that man is the form of the flesh, which has risen from earth and is destined by the Law of Rising to descend and return to it.

All things return unto their source. If you believe you are a thing, then you must accept total annihilation by the very law. For when you believe you are form and you witness the demonstrable law of all form returning to the source from whence it is composed, then you will have to accept and believe that the end is the end. I know that is not what you're asking, but it is very important in your effort to help yourself to be free from what you are asking: caught in these limits or judgments.

When a person has a judgment, they believe that's them. Would you not agree? They believe that's them. They don't believe that it's something that somebody sent to them; they believe that that is them at the moment they are expressing it. That is the great delusion. That *is* the karmic wheel. We believe many things, but we only believe them for a time. Sometimes we believe them for a minute, five minutes, five weeks, five months, five years, or fifty. Because belief is totally dependent upon form, which is judgment, by the very Law of Form, it cannot last. It cannot endure. It is not eternal. And it is not us. It never was us. It is what we have formed to serve us and we, in not making the effort to awaken, find someday that we are serving it.

We form a judgment. Totally contrary to demonstrable law, we form it. Totally contrary to the divine laws of goodness, we form limit. We form the limit because we fear. Because we fear, in our consciousness, survival, the animal instinct rises to defend and to protect us. Because, you see, we must defend and we must protect that which is falsehood. Truth, not having need, needs no defense. Truth is. That's what we are. As long as we believe we are falsehood, then we must fear, we must defend, we must judge, and we must suffer. Does that help with your question?

Thank you.

You're welcome. The gentleman there, please.

Mr. Goodwin, this question . . . but it was not. Personal responsibility implies choice. Now, if someone doesn't really understand the concept of choice as far as a significant issue in their life, like cancer or something like that, how—or alcoholism, for that matter—how can you show them or explain to them or make them see that they do have their personal responsibility? And by accepting that, they can deal with it in a more effective manner? ... [Parts of this question were difficult to accurately transcribe.]

Thank you. Well, in reference to helping another individual, first of all, a wise person does not transgress the Law of Solicitation. Now presence is the Law of Solicitation. We often find our self present in many places with many different kinds of people. And if we understand that presence is the Law of Solicitation, then we are following a law that will not bind us or transgress someone else's divine right.

Now, for example, in reference to this question of helping a person that may have cancer or a person that is alcoholic or etc., if they have solicited from you that help, then you can go as far, in your efforts, as the Law of Solicitation reveals that you should go. Now the light of reason clearly reveals a Law of Solicitation is that far, that far, or almost all the way. Usually it's a very short distance (the Law of Solicitation) because the first thing you come up against is the judgments and the dictates of the individual, who has a greater love for the attention they are receiving from the function of the pity of self than from the light of reason that is being shared with them.

Now if we understand that energy follows attention and that as children we often did many things, [like] felt sorry for our self, so we would receive energy from our parents. And if we look around our world about us and we see, ofttimes within our self, we do many different things that we wish we hadn't done. But we do them in order to get attention. In other words, we're low on energy and we need a charge. And that's why we do it.

Now a person, any person, over-identified with the negative within their consciousness is a person who is depleting themselves of life-giving energy. In other words, they're grounding themselves and the Divine Energy is not flowing unobstructed through them because they are the obstruction because their minds are limited and their minds are focused upon what they consider, what they judge is a serious injustice, that it is a great struggle, that it is a great difficulty.

Now whenever we judge that something is a struggle, we experience the wonderful opportunity to prove how right we are. We set our self up in order that we can prove how great we are. All we have to do is to make a judgment that something is very difficult. All we have to do is make a judgment of how much we give. All we have to do is make a judgment of how much we suffer, to make a judgment of how much we're doing without to try to help someone or do something, and because it's our judgment, because we believe our judgments are us, we work diligently beneath the conscious awareness to set ourselves up and prove how right we are. Because it is the very nature of the human mind to protect and to defend itself.

So [if] you want to help someone, be aware of the Law of Solicitation, be kind, understand their need, and share with them what your light of reason reveals you should share with them. Do not expect them to have the same understanding that you have, for you're an individualized being. And do not expect them to accept. If you go, in keeping with the Law of Solicitation, to help a person and you do all that you feel that you can and you are upset with what they do with your efforts, you may be rest assured you did not do it for them at all. The law is revealing unto you that you did it for yourself because you did it for your judgment. You judged how they would be benefited. You judged what they should do with what you have to give. That's not giving, but that is loaning. So if we go with that understanding (give what you have to give, care less what they do with it), we will remain free. Because whoever makes the effort to serve the Light shall remain free by the Light. Do you understand that?

Yes, sir.

I do hope so. Thank you. The lady here, please.

Could you speak for a moment on the symbology of the American eagle that's within all of us?

Well, in reference to the symbology of the eagle, because America's not the first one to use it in old creation. But, of course, the United States is known by its bald-headed eagle. You see, first of all, when you study any of these philosophies and things and you are interested in their various symbols, nature is revealing, in the various forms that are used for symbols, nature is clearly revealing to you the strengths and the characteristics of these different animals and birds and trees and flowers and etc. So if you want to understand the symbology of the bald-headed eagle, then the wisest path to follow is to study and to research the characteristics of that particular eagle. Do you understand? Then you will understand what our founding fathers here, in the United States, believed in. Not what is said they believed in, but what they believed in, in their wise choice of the symbols that are on your currency today. Thank you.

The gentleman back there, please.

In The Living Light, [The individual is referring to the first published textbook of the Serenity Association, the entire contents of which were later republished in *The Living Light Dialogue* Volume 1.] *it is stated that if a man is born without eyes to see, a mouth to speak, a tongue to taste, hands to feel, what would be the purpose of his being? Could you elaborate on that?* [This teaching is found in Discourse 45.]

Yes. If a man is born without some of the abilities of the vehicle in which his soul is temporarily imprisoned, then of what benefit would be the purpose of the incarnation? Now what that teaching is clearly revealing is that the human body, the house of clay, is designed by this great Intelligence, this Architect, to serve the eternal being. Now man's purpose in incarnating into form and forms is solely for the evolution, through refinement, through awakening, of the limits or the forms. As a person has and forms a thought, in reference to what is beneficial to them, and time passes and other thoughts are formed within his consciousness, slowly but surely the limit of the one thought is affected by the limits of the other thoughts that surround it. And so, man in his awakening is an instrument for the refinement of limit.

Man has a judgment one day. He has many other judgments that follow over a period of many years and his original judgment gradually, begrudgingly begins to change. Because the judgment formed by the human mind contains within it the intelligence of the human mind, as a drop of water contains within it all the constituents of the ocean from whence it came, so does a thought, so does a judgment. And because form, its very nature, is dependent upon its creator and because you are the creator of form, you have a responsibility to evolve or educate your creations. You have a responsibility to see that they are dutiful to your purpose of design and in that responsibility do you truly serve the purpose of your being. Does that help with your question?

Yes. Thank you.

You're welcome. Time is passing quickly. Do we have any other questions? Is that a question that I hear? Is that a question, Madame? Very well. *[It would appear that the woman who was considering asking a question chooses to remain silent.]*

Thank you.

JULY 1, 1984

Church Questions and Answers 49

As our chairman has already spoken here, this is your opportunity to ask questions which are of an interest to you at this time. So I will be happy to share with you our understanding, if you will be so kind as to raise your hand.

The lady here, please.

How can one increase their experience of self-worth and self-love?

The question is, How can one . . .

Experience more self—more of their self-love.

More of their self-love?

Yes.

The love of themselves?

Yes. I mean . . .

That is an area, if you're speaking of the over-identification with oneself, which is known as the love of self, that's the very thing that a wise person would want a decrease in, not an increase. For it is through the over-identification with oneself that we find our problems in life. For example, you see, as we identify more with the thought or the thought pattern which we feel or believe is our self, then we experience less and less of what we truly are, a part of the all. So by an increase in what is known as self-love, it is at the ever-increasing expense of a lack and a lessening of the universality which we truly are. Does that help with your question?

Well, ah, yes—no, I guess, then, I need to rephrase my question. How can one experience just a greater awareness of the abundance?

By a control of the mind, which spends over 98 percent of its activity in mental substance, over 98 percent of identification with the limited acceptance of what a person is. And the reason that that is done is from a lack of conscious effort to be aware of the thought in our mind at any given moment. And from a lack of that effort, we find our emotions are controlled by that which we do not consciously choose at any given moment. For example, we react to experiences, instead of acting to experiences. The reason that we react to the experiences we encounter is simply from a lack of effort to control our own mind. Does that help with your question? So, a wise man—as all philosophies have always taught: know thyself, ye shall know the truth. The truth shall set you free. One cannot know themselves without making the conscious, daily effort to be aware of the thoughts of their own mind. Thank you.

Yes.

What is the church's experience or understanding of the world mother?

Well, in reference to that term you're using, *world mother*, if you would be so kind as to share with us what you understand or accept is a world mother, then, perhaps, we could have some basis upon which to share with you.

OK. My understanding is that there is a world mother for every age, just like there's a world teacher. And that in different ages she's had different names or different forms. But it is the mother of the worlds. In our last age [she] would be known as Mary. In the age before that, would be Isis, has taken the form of Quan Yin. I was wondering what your understanding was.

I see. Thank you. In reference to the various religions of the present and past, which teach mothers of God, for, as you have already stated, Mary, the mother of God, and Isis, the mother of God, we find in our understanding that throughout the ages there has been these various so-called mothers of God and, therefore, they have been so stated as giving birth, virgin birth, to a son of God. Now the Living Light Philosophy and the church's understanding of that is the value man has placed, throughout the ages, upon purity, that which is pure. Virginity represents to the human mind that which is uncontaminated, pure, or virgin. For God, which we understand is an infinite, intelligent

Energy, formless and, by being formless therefore, free—unlimited, for it is not form—for God to have a mother would mean that God would be less than God, for there is something, therefore, greater than God and that would be the mother of God. So the Living Light Philosophy and the Serenity Church's understanding is these are various and different stories which are revealed throughout the ages in order to help man, limited by an over-identification with himself, to understand, to accept something besides himself. Man can only relate, when he is over-identified with self, man can only relate to the limits of his own past experiences. Does that help with your question?

Yes. Also, is there a work with the church with guides or ascended masters? And are there female ascended masters? And is there this great woman initiate, Mary, that is working over the earth right now with women and childbirth and with the moon?

Thank you. In reference to the question, Is there a Mary or mother of God working at the present age with the women and various things? the Serenity Church and the Living Light Philosophy understand and accept that there has never been, or shall there ever be, a time when man on the planet Earth is left without God's ministering angels. For the law reveals to all of us that no one exists alone. God has given his angels charge over us, lest we dash our feet against the stones of ignorance. It does not matter in truth what we call those guides, teachers, and helpers. They can be called masters or ascended this or that.

The process of ascending or evolving is not limited by the sex of the individual. Therefore, we understand that women evolve and ascend, if you wish to put it that way, as well as men, ever in keeping with their own personal effort. For from God we have come, wandered out, through an over-identification with creation, and to God we are in the process of returning. That returning process is not limited to what man understands as transition or death. We are all in the process of returning as we gain control over our mind. And [as] we spend less energy identifying with the limits known as creation, we ascend more harmoniously and more graciously. Does that help with your question?

Thank you.

You're welcome. The lady here, please.

Would you speak of the law of assumption and how a person who is transgressing it may be able to change that?

You are speaking in reference to assumption?

Yes.

And presumption?

Yes.

I see. We spend much of our time in our daily activities, as difficult as it is for us to accept the demonstrable truth, we spend much of our time expressing our prejudice, our prejudgment. That's what prejudice is: prejudice is to prejudge any experience that we encounter. So much of our time in the course of a day, unfortunately, is spent expressing our prejudice. We presume what is going to take place. We presume what a person is going to do or to say. We presume how a person will act under certain conditions ever in keeping with experiences that we have already had in reference to that person, place, or thing. Now to presume, which is to prejudge based upon past experience, is indeed a most detrimental expression for the human mind. For we grant unto others only what we grant unto our self and to presume, to prejudge, is to reveal to our self that we are prejudging each and every opportunity that's coming our way.

Now we are never left in life without a moment of opportunity. That opportunity goes through our computer mind and what comes back up is the presumption, the prejudgment, based on what has already been, what that opportunity shall really offer to us. Now we look at these possibilities in our life and that process goes on in our mind and we find when we go to make any changes, we find great struggle, great difficulty, and great emotional upheaval. We find that because we have prejudged the opportunity and if that prejudgment of that opportunity is not in keeping with what we have already experienced, then we blatantly refuse to accept the possibility of something better. So man in that respect is his own worst enemy. Does that help with your question?

Could you speak on assumption a little bit?

To assume?

Yes.

Well, to presume is based upon what we have already personally experienced. And to assume something is the lazy way of the human mind not to even bother to go through the process of presuming. *[Many in the congregation laugh.]* Does that help with your question? It doesn't even spend the energy to go down there and look at the judgments and the past experiences to come back up again.

Thank you. The gentleman there, please.

Individually, as you've taught, we're all responsible for our actions and their repercussions that come after our actions. And that's called by a lot of people, especially in Marin, karma. There's reactions for everything you do.

Thank you. I'd like to speak on that one word, *karma*, because it's such a convenient catchall to deny personal responsibility. So often a person says, "Oh, that was just my karma. Something I must have done ten eons ago." Thank you. Now continue on with that.

Correct. I know that's a loaded word. That's why I said—

It is indeed very full. Thank you.

Taking personal responsibility may be more accurate, that there are repercussions for our actions. And . . .

And we ofttimes don't like them. Go ahead.

Correct. There's also a world responsi—there's an overall karma or whatever you want to call it, there's an overall repercussion that comes as a whole, too, isn't it?

Yes indeed. Because like attracts like and becomes the Law of Attachment. So if you have two people or five people or a thousand people or ten million people in keeping with the law that like attracts like, that reveals that they're thinking in a certain way in their consciousness in reference to a certain subject or situation. Consequently, they create, in keeping with that law, a mass return. For example, we are not only known by the company that we keep, we are affected by the company we keep because the company that we keep is revealing to us, like mirrors we stand in front of, where we are, whether we like it or not. As they say, birds of a feather flock together, for like attracts like and becomes the Law of Attachment. Yes, go ahead with your question.

I agree with that totally. And I'm wondering, I kind of feel like I know this already, so it's almost not a question, but I feel that there must be a transition of the balance. I know overall we're all in agreement on some level to be all on this planet together. But there's also seems to be a difference with some people who are nowhere near the consciousness that we have, in this room let's say, aware of what they do at all, and causing war. And then there's people who are very conscious of evolving towards returning back to, you know, their divinity.

Thank you.

There must be a fluctuation or is there some kind of thing that's changing all the time with what's going to happen to this planet because of the state it's in?

Oh certainly. Certainly. Man shall never find anything more blinding or deafening than desire. Now let's take a look at what is happening with, as you speak, that there are people on various stages of evolution. A person in this room or any room at any moment could be awakened to a greater purpose in life than eating and sleeping and caring for the senses. They could, the moment they stop and are tempted and addicted by any particular desire, be so far from that consciousness you wouldn't recognize the same person. For the eternal soul of man is not only evolving through these various forms, but the eternal soul of man is expressing through various levels of consciousness. These various levels of consciousness are what the soul is expressing through here, now, in this moment on this planet.

If a person, through lack of effort, does not educate their desires, does not fulfill their desires, there's nothing left for them to do but to suppress their desires. And a person and a soul expressing through a vehicle which spends its life expressing its desires is in very dangerous and deep waters because it never knows (the human mind) the moment and the instant that its suppressed desire, clearly revealing a weakness in our own character, a lack of effort to educate or fulfill it—that weakness can be tempted at any moment. And we never know what moment that's going to be. You see, we could be walking down the street and all of a sudden we have this compelling, possessing desire in our mind, so strong, so forceful, that either we follow it or we end up in a total state of frustration.

Now let us look at the positive part of the human mind in that respect. We find our self ofttimes tempted. That reveals to us the areas of consciousness in which we need to awaken. For a temptation, that which tempts us, reveals to us where our weaknesses are. No human mind desires to be controlled by any other human mind. It's known as the Law of the Preservation of Self. And so, a person, if they will only pause in the moment they experience their weakness, known as temptation—they will look clearly at it and ask themselves the question, "Do I wish to strengthen this weakness in my character through a process of education and evolving? Or do I wish to fulfill it and be the victim of it? Or do I wish to, once again, suppress it, only to have it rise again, only to go through the same pain, struggle, and suffering from my own lack of effort and my own laziness?" Does that help with your question?

Yes.

You're welcome. The lady there, please.

Can you share with me or us a brief statement on soul mate or twin flame? What is the difference between them? Or what is the purpose of them?

Well, in speaking in reference to religions and philosophies of creation, for, for example, we have to understand that that which is form, such as mate and etc., refers demonstrably to that which is limited. And the infinite, divine, intelligent Energy, known to the Spiritualists as God, is not limited. Therefore, it is not form; it is formless. Therefore, it is free. Now when it expresses through form, it is limited by the form through which it is expressing. For example, God expresses through the leaf of a tree, through the branch, through the trunk. That is the same, the same infinite, divine, intelligent Energy that man calls God that is expressing through a human being. The same God that is expressing through the flower in the meadow. There is no difference. It is formless and free. It is infinite. It is intelligent. Fine.

Now when we come to that which is limit, that which is form, to the Living Light Philosophy, we are now speaking of creation. We are speaking of the infinite, intelligent Energy flowing through limit, form, or what man calls creation. Now the laws of creation clearly reveal to us that which is created is subject to the Law of Duality. In order for creation or form to exist there has to be the pair of opposites. We are now speaking of form or creation.

When the soul enters the earth realm, simultaneous [to that] what you call soul mate or twin flame is expressing in that instant in another realm of consciousness. Now man calls this a guardian angel. Some people call it a soul mate. Unfortunately, because of the thinking of the masses, the Serenity Church has refrained from public discussion on that particular matter because so many people use it as a grand cop-out for their domestic problems: that they didn't quite get their soul mate this time around and that foolishness, which totally denies the Law of Personal Responsibility.

Now this guardian angel is not limited by sex. Therefore, people who are thinking of soul mates as their eternal partner and etc., will awaken some day; they've got a real surprise for them. *[Some of the congregation laugh.]* It is simply a part, you understand—here your soul is expressing through physical matter; a part of it is expressing through spiritual matter. And if you wish to call that a twin flame or you wish to call that a soul mate, it doesn't matter, you see?

What does matter is that as you awaken within your consciousness, through a little daily effort of self-control, there's the amalgamation of the spiritual with the so-called material. There is an amalgamation, there is a unity, and therefore, the result or effect thereof is an awakening of the consciousness: that you are what you are. You have always been and therefore, you will always be. It is not dependent on form. It is not dependent on anything that is beyond you. Does that help with your question?

Thank you.

You're welcome. We have a few moments left, if there are any other questions. Yes, the lady here, please.

Being a god—we're all a part of God. And God is formless and free. Why would we ever go into—what, what was the cause of form, of going into form, expressing through form?

Yes. Well, the laws of evolution are applicable throughout all eternity. Everything is in a process of change or evolution. Man's problem is his refusal to accept that evolution is inevitable. He can fight it. He can buck it. He cannot stop it from happening. And so, man relies upon what he has already experienced for a false security. Now when man faces the opportunity, as we spoke earlier, to make these changes, then he goes through these emotional struggles because he has relied upon a shadowland, a twilight zone of past experiences for his own security. You see, we want to believe in God, but to believe—you see, we believe on that which we can control.

Oh, I believe in God. That wasn't my question. It was—

No, no, no. I, may I—I, I understand your question: Why have we entered limited form? But let us go to what we believe and the difference between belief and faith. Man says, "I believe in God." Well, man says, "I believe the electric bill's going up next month." And he's got a pretty good chance of being correct, being right. So man believes in that which *he* has the possibility of controlling. So when we believe, we believe in that which has form. So for man to believe in God, man must put God into form. And man has done a wonderful job of doing that in his consciousness. He's made him all kinds of forms. Now for man to have faith is where man shall be free. For as long as man believes, man is still identified with limit or mental substance. All mental substance is limited by the form that it takes. And so, we must move from belief to faith.

Now why don't you turn that over and we'll get to this question on why did we have to come to this lovely planet, known as creation—*[The teacher instructs the audio technician who is recording the class to change the cassette tape, and that results in a short gap in the recording.]*

How did form begin then? Because form is limit and God is limitless and we are part of that, then how did form begin?

We are that—

I know I'm—

Excuse me. We are that which sustains form.

All right.

You see, that which we are is the formless free Spirit, known as God. That *is* what we are. What we believe we are is not what we are. But as long as we believe we are, therefore, for us we are. But that is not what we are. That's the difference between faith and belief. This is why great philosophers of all time have tried to teach man, "You have the faith of a half a grain of mustard seed." Not the whole grain of mustard seed, a half a grain. That's very, very important. Because for man to have faith, the faith of a half a grain of mustard seed, instead of the whole grain of mustard seed, means that man must move from belief, for man believes that it is the Law of Duality in order to create. Therefore, a half a grain of mustard seed is where the faith is that moves man from creation to truth.

Now, why did we come here? Why are we in limited form? Nature reveals itself: that which sustains a thing is greater than the thing which it sustains. Therefore, that which sustains anything contains within it the power to change the thing which it is expressing through, to refine it and to evolve it. That is the purpose of the entrance of the infinite, intelligent Energy into so-called limit or form or creation. It is in keeping with the law of the evolution of form. God cannot evolve and still be God.

Therefore, God cannot have a mother because for God to have a mother, God would then be subject to the laws of duality. That is the false god, the idols with clay feet, of which all the prophets have taught to beware of. God cannot be form and still be God. But to man who finds it necessary to control life, to control experience, to that man, he must have a god of form, for that man is believing and is not accepting. You see, it takes total acceptance, the love of God, which is total acceptance, it takes that and total consideration for man to move along the path of faith. Go ahead with your question.

I understand that I am formless and free. That—

That is what you are, until you forget that.

That's right. I understand that. My question is, What caused form? I've also heard that life is illusion. And that we are—

I see.

—in fact, all formless and free. I'm not even questioning it. What I'm questioning is, What caused form, then?

The—in order—yes, you're asking a very deep question. *[Many in the congregation laugh.]* I'm trying to find the words that are deep enough to, to communicate with the question.

What caused form? If you look at infinite, intelligent Energy, formless and free—

But you can't look at it.

Yes. You, you must look at it—you must look at it from— look at infinite, intelligent Energy as you look at the air. What do you see? Nothing. No thing. Is that correct?

No thing.

Fine. You look at the air and you see no thing. However, you know the air is there. Now the question is, How do you know the air is there? How do you know that?

Probably from education. I mean, otherwise, you wouldn't have heard the word air.

Did you accept that it is there prior to your educating of the human mind that it was there?

I imagine my first breath—that must have done something.

Yes. There! The first breath revealed to you in consciousness, in physical consciousness, your awareness that you were, now, I. You had the first thought of the I. You see, when the soul, evolving, is in the womb in the nine-month process, you still are a part of something, even in creation. Therefore, you do not have at that moment the thought of I. You have the thought of I in the first breath you take in physical form. And in that moment that is when you identify with creation. That is the moment that you believe.

Now there are two schools of thought on when the soul entered: the moment of conception or the moment when the child takes its first breath. Well, the soul enters at the moment of conception, but it is the difference between the formless free Spirit, God, and the limited god of creation. One is faith and the other is belief, and that's the two schools of thought. So at the moment you take your first breath, at that moment, you believe. So you believe that without air, you will not be. Therefore, for you without air you will not be as you are in form. Does that help with your question?

Do we really know what caused form?

What caused a thing? What caused form?

What caused form? If we don't, it's OK. I—[Some in the congregation laugh.]

No. No, no, no.

We've explained it. We don't understand it.

Well, we best take a couple of moments longer on it.

No, no.

No, no, no.

OK. I'll listen to the tape.

Thank you. I'll listen to someone else too. Thank you. We will continue on. You want to know what caused form.

Yes. Just whenever it started.

What caused your thought?

Is that what caused it, then?

What caused your thought? Before there can be—Are you speaking of form as a material thing? Are you speaking of form, like the chair, that's a physical thing that your senses have an awareness of, that it exists? Is that what you're speaking of?

Form. I mean—

Like the chair?

—never anything formed.

Fine. Like the chair?

Yes.

Fine. All right. The chair exists as long as—think of this, now—as long as belief is.

So it's only in my own head.

It's in everyone's head.

Yes, I know, but I—it's all . . . [The remaining few words are difficult to transcribe.]

What is critically important—and many teachers have tried to reveal that and have been ridiculed throughout the ages: form exists in the realm of consciousness known as belief.

OK.

As you believeth, you becometh. Form only exists as an effect of belief, for a belief is the cement of the substance into form. All right. Now—and what's very important is that man, entering the planet, the soul's entering and the first breath, the awakening of the self, the dependence on the cement that creates that, known as belief. Man, therefore, is limited. So man is limited when he believes. Man is free when he moves in faith. And so that's what it is all about.

What is the cause? It's very simple. You have a spiritual consciousness, a mental consciousness, and a physical, material effect. Now the physical, material effect exists only as an effect of a mental world. Now when you no longer think of your self, in those moments you are free in faith. The instant you think of your self, you are controlled by, limited by, what is known as belief. And so man is in a constant process of believing many things and denying many things. But what man refuses to accept is that his denials are effects of his own beliefs. Therefore, man's destiny is subject to his own denials. For to deny a thing is to believe that it does not exist. Man, therefore, is still controlled by it. Does that help with your question on cause? Without belief, there is no cause. And without the love of belief—without belief, there is no cause. Without the love of belief, there is no effect. And it's totally dependent upon that.

But tell me, who in a moment is so great, through lack of effort, that can awaken to the instant before that first breath, which established the law of the thought of I and the bondage of the human mind? So, as man believes, so man is bound.

If you believe something is greener on the other side of the fence, if you believe something is brighter just down the way, then you shall follow your belief and pay the price of the bondage. You see, my friends, desires promise to man. Desire is the divine expression. But what man forms of that divine expression, man is bound by. And so, as man continues moving through his beliefs, he finds that these mountains of promises that his desires have to offer to him, they fall by the wayside, for they are servants of a god of clay feet, known as the god of creation.

I see our time has passed up. Thank you very much.

SEPTEMBER 2, 1984

Church Questions and Answers 50

[This is your opportunity,] once a month, to ask the questions which are of interest to you. And if you will be so kind as to raise your hand, we'll try to reach as many people as time will permit.

The lady here, please.

Besides taking personal responsibility for—my question is about forgiveness. And I'd like to know what helps, besides taking personal responsibility for what happens.

Well, in reference to taking personal responsibility for any experience in one's life and also in reference to our effort to forgive or to give forth, whatever we forgive or give forth, of course, no longer entertains our mind. It is no longer considered by us. Now we ofttimes find great difficulty in forgiving or giving forth and the difficulty that we encounter is dependent upon the judgment that we have made that we are blameless or innocent of the experience, that we had good intentions when entering the so-called situation, whatever it may be, and because of our good intentions we are, therefore, free from a return or an experience that we judge not to be in keeping with the good intentions we had when we established the Law of Involvement into the situation. Does that help with your question?

Somewhat.

Somewhat? Continue with your question, please.

I guess I would like more information on and more depth in how to forgive. Like, is there a, is there a . . . It's hard to . . .

Well, perhaps we could put it this way: we all understand that it is very human to forgive or to give forth. We also must realize that it is truly divine to forget. And so a person has, seemingly, great problems in forgetting anything which has made a sufficient impact upon their emotions. Now there is no automatic technique which a person can say that, "I forgive the experience that I have had, for I accept personal responsibility for it." In order to not have a continuation of the thought in mind of what we judge is an injustice to us, we must make the effort to take control of our mind. And when we take control of our mind, the judgment of the past experience, once it rises through the various laws of association, by making the effort to take control of our mind, then we will not have the continued experience of what we judge to be the problem. Does that help with your question?

Yes. Thank you.

You're welcome. The lady there, please.

I'm so concerned with the honest expression of dissatisfaction in order to supply comfort. Forgiveness is not like that. If you are not capable of this great gift of forgiveness, then are you supposed to be quiet until you do forgive or say, "I'm annoyed with you"?

Well, in reference to that question, we understand that honesty is not only the best policy but suppression of desire is one of the most detrimental experiences that a human being can encounter. For desire, the principle of desire, is the divine expression. To tempt to suppress that which is divine in principle creates many serious psychological problems for any human being. So our teaching is do not suppress desire; fulfill it or educate it.

Now in reference to what you stated, the gift of forgiveness, the Living Light Philosophy teaches that the Infinite Intelligence or God is not a giver nor a taker; that the Divine Spirit, called by man God, is an intelligent, infinite, eternal Energy. Therefore, we all have the potential to give forth or to forgive. Most of us in our efforts to forgive, we for-loan. We loan. The difference, you see, and the knowing between what is a giving and what is a loaning, if we give something, we no longer think about what we have given. If we loan something, we are constantly concerned about what the receiver of our loan is doing with what we have loaned to them.

Now the Living Light teaches the greatest gift that man can give to God, in order to be free, is the gift of self. It further states that self is the crown of the thoughts, feelings, and judgments of the human mind, once identified by the eternal being. For example, we cannot, in mental consciousness, recognize anything that we do not first, by the Law of Identity, identify with. The separation of truth (that which we are) from creation (that which we think we are) is the only path available to the evolution of the human species, the only path of freedom.

When we think we have been injured, we identify with what we have judged is right or wrong for us. In that process we deny that we and we alone have established laws of which the experience is a return of the law. Now because we all have the potential of forgiving or giving forth and because at various times in our life some of us find difficulty with forgiving, the question is, Should we be quiet about how we feel? Communication, honest communication, is certainly the wise path to take. If one believes at any moment that they are unable to forgive, they bear the personal responsibility to state their case honestly, without emotion, to the person or persons that they believe, temporarily, have done them an injustice. Through honest communication one frees themselves from the bondage of their own judgment.

We understand God, meaning good, could not possibly judge and, therefore, be good. So if we believe that we are greater in consciousness than God, the divine, infinite, intelligent Energy which sustains us, then we at those times must pay the price of the transgression of natural, demonstrable law. Does that help with your question?

Thank you.

You're welcome. The lady there, please.

I'm aware that the Living Light tapes should be played over and over in order to get the best out of them. I've discovered this to be true for myself. And I am also aware that hypnosis is used medically for overweight and for other problems. Since it is, since it is true of the philosophy—that it must be repeated to be effective—then would hypnosis be an effective tool for the reduction of weight?

Thank you. In reference to the law stated, the Law of Repetition, it is clear to all who investigate that repetition is the law through which change is made possible. In reference to your particular statement in playing the philosophy tapes, your experience in the repetition thereof, you have benefited, of course, more from them. It is the same with playing golf or basketball or baseball or anything else. What is the process when you place your attention upon anything? By placing your attention upon it, you not only identify with it, you become the instrument through which intelligent, infinite Energy and power is directed to it.

That which serves us best is that which we serve selflessly. And so it is in anything, the law reveals to us that we get out of a thing whatever we put into the thing. Now many people say they start off into a project or anything and they say, "I'm putting a lot of time and energy into this." And, not thinking, they judge how much they should get out of it. Consequently, they always come up on the short end. Because there is something about the human, uneducated ego: it believes [it does] more than it actually does. It looks at time and says, "I've been there a short time or a long time." And that judgment is based upon the desire of the individual at the time. It has nothing to do with sixty minutes or thirty minutes, but it has everything to do with where we are in consciousness.

Now if we believe that by giving our conscious mind, through which the soul faculty of reason flows, to a doctor, or anyone, in order that we may benefit, what we are doing in consciousness is establishing a dependence within our own mind. We have, within us, the power to control our mind. We have always had that power. We shall always have that power. For our mind is subject to the intelligent Energy that sustains it. Therefore, a person does not need to go to a hypnotist to gain control of their body, unless they believe that only in so doing can they gain control. Certainly, it is demonstrable many people have done that and many people have temporarily made changes in their life. The changes shall always be temporary for the Law of Dependence has been established: the dependence on another human mind for the benefit.

When the change in consciousness comes and a person realizes that they have that intelligent power within them, therefore, they are not dependent upon someone else for the benefit and the goodness of life, that it is within their power to gain control of what they choose to gain control of in the sphere and zone of their own action, in which they and they alone are responsible, that, indeed, is the demonstrable path of wisdom. For we are individualized souls. Our dependences are dependent upon our errors of ignorance at any given moment. And so it behooves an individual to remember, whatever one permits their mind to be dependent upon must serve as a temporary stepping-stone to the declaration of their own divinity: that goodness is not dependent upon the human mind; that goodness, the human mind is dependent upon; that it is when we pause and take control of the mind, we experience goodness or God in any and every thing we think or do. Does that help with your question?

Thank you.

You're welcome. The lady here, please. Yes.

He continually talked about getting control of your mind. And my problem is that I don't know when I am in control of my mind. How can you know that you are in control?

When the question no longer rises within the consciousness, you will know, for the question is from the mind.

You see, the nature of the human mind is to control everything that comes into its sphere of action. Man finds his problems in life through an over-identification with his own mind.

There he finds his suppressed desires. He finds his frustrations. He finds his so-called failures. He finds his few, so-called, successes ever in keeping with what the human mind dictates to us at any given moment.

The freedom from the human mind is when the mind is no longer in question. You see, a person says, "Well, I feel good at this moment. Everything is beautiful. Everything is running smoothly." Only in the next moment to feel and to experience the direct opposite. What has happened? The person's consciousness has identified with a different level of their mind and on that level the forms created by the thoughts and judgments of the mind—for the mind is the creator—are not happy. In fact, they are very unhappy. But if we pause and we make the effort and we move to this other level of consciousness, we say then—we experience—everything is beautiful. So it reveals to us, those demonstrations, throughout our entire lives, moment by moment, that we are not the human mind. For if we are the human mind, we are indeed more than one person. We are a combination of eighty-one, for that is the revelation of a person who believes they are the thought of their mind.

You see, we, we alone can choose the thought we wish to experience within our consciousness. That is the power that we are. Now when we do not make the effort to choose the thought or the level of consciousness, then we experience what is known as the shadows, the twilight zone of experiences of the past. You see, when we stand still, the light, the light of reason shines unobstructed. When we permit the mind to move and identify with the movement, then we experience the twilight zone, the shadows of past experiences. If we will pause and think that an experience or experiences that have passed cannot be changed—we can do nothing with a shadow. But a shadow does many things with us. For that which has passed, it has been created, it has been formed, is subject for its very movement in consciousness to the divine, intelligent Energy which we are.

Now when we identify with an experience that has passed, with a shadow, the shadow is activated and moves in our consciousness, for it receives from us the energy necessary for its movement. Consequently, if we want to experience anything that has passed, all we have to do is to think about it and in the thinking process we identify with it. And when we identify with it, we direct infinite, intelligent Energy to it; it is activated and the next step is we believe we are the experience, even though the experience has long passed. Does that help with your question?

Very much. Thank you.

You're welcome. The lady here, please.

Thank you. We've been taught that 72 hours is appropriate time for cremation, after the person passes over. We've been taught that if we have an important decision, to give it 72 hours. And I also find that in a traumatic situation, it has taken about 72 hours for my self to subside. What is there about the 72 that, that causes that?

Well, it is not the 72 that causes that. The 72 hours—as many philosophies prior to the Living Light's expression here on earth have always taught, it takes 72 hours for the consciousness to move through all of the various levels of the human mind. That's the time that it takes. Some people move in less time than that. However, the maximum time that it takes is 72 hours. So it is critically important, when a person has a decision to make in life, not to permit their weakness, known as temptation, to literally force them into making a decision without granting themselves the opportunity of going through these various levels of consciousness which they, of course, live with from that moment on.

You go out into the world and you have an experience and you must make a decision—you *believe* you must make a decision. You see, first of all, we must believe that we must make the decision. Then we must believe that the decision must be made in a certain length of time, because then we must believe that if we don't make the decision in a certain length of time, we are subject to or the victims of circumstances and conditions beyond our control. In that type of thinking, we have no control. No control whatsoever. Because we are not weighing it out in the light of reason and making an intelligent decision which ofttimes affects our life for years yet to come. I hope that's helped with your question.

We have time for one more, if there is one. The gentleman in the back, please.

What is the relationship between the soul faculty of humility and the healing process?

Yes, in reference to the soul faculty of humility, most of us, unfortunately, relate the word *humility* to humiliation, unfortunately. A person who expresses humility is a person who bows the dictates of their mind to a greater Authority within them; that is a humble person. First, they accept that there is a greater Authority in their life than the thought of their mind at any given moment. And because within them there is a greater Authority; being greater, it is reasonable to accept that it has access to knowledge, wisdom, that we do not have full access to.

Now the question the gentleman has asked is, "What is the relationship between the soul faculty of humility and the healing process?" Let us pause in consciousness a moment and think, and hopefully think more deeply. That which is discordant is known to man as that which is not at ease, which is known to man as disease. The opposite of disease, to man, is known as health. Health, in this philosophy, is the effect of harmony, the Law of Harmony, where all things flow united, serving the purpose of their design. And so we have before us, disease and health, harmony and discord, healing and humility.

When a person—and life has already taught us that—is not willing to bend like the willow, then the person must experience the breaking of the branch, for the storms and winds of creation are ever with us. And so, man, when he has a decision to make, accepts the possibility of change. The difference between making a decision, which frees us—for all decisions in truth are instruments through which we grow and, therefore, are freed—the difference between making a decision and making a judgment is self-evident. Decisions, as I stated, accept within their very formation the possibility of change. Judgments do not accept the possibility of change. Therefore, judgments bind and man becomes the victim of the bondage. Decisions free and man evolves through change, which is, of course, growth. For we are evolving beings. Without change, evolution is not possible.

And so, if you want, if you sincerely desire healing over anything in your life—for healing is the Law of Harmony. And so, a plant is receptive to healing, to the Law of Harmony, the same as a mechanical instrument, an automobile, or anything else, for they are subject to these laws of life. Man is, of course, subject to the same law, the Law of Harmony.

Many things in our life we find diseased at one time or another, not just our bodies nor our minds. We find our automobiles diseased. We find our jobs we work on diseased. We find our relationships in life diseased. We find many things discordant or diseased. And so by applying, through the soul faculty of humility, which is inseparable from faith and poise, man experiences the success, which is the unobstructed flow of intelligent Energy in anything he chooses to be involved with. Does that help with your question?

Thank you, sir.

You're welcome. I said we had time for one more question, but whereas the answer was rather short, we have time for one more. The lady here, please.

I've been reading in various publications about a scientific method of recording voices which are reportedly from the other side. I was wondering if you would comment on that.

Well, in reference to scientific method of recording voices supposedly from the other side, let us say that that process and that experimentation has been going on for many, many, many, many, many, many years. It is not something new. Ever since they've had a phonograph, that process has been going on.

Now the question must rise, Where do the voices come from? And if they are recorded, how do we know they're from the other side? What proof do we have? What demonstrable evidence is available? And let us think more deeply. I guess I'm known in many Spiritualists circles as the rebel in the cause, but I like to investigate everything. Considering I grew up, since I was born, with a medium and I have been in the work for forty-three years, I like to think about it as deeply as possible. I don't like to open my mouth and just accept that that is that and that is that, without thorough investigation.

First of all, for a spirit voice to become audible to our physical ears requires physical substance, which they no longer have. First, we must accept that scientific and demonstrable evidence. Therefore, the next step we must move to is, Where's this physical substance coming from? If—for sound to be audible to our ears, it requires physical substance, which we all know that it does, like it or not, if we want to hear it physically. Investigation throughout many, many years has revealed there is an energy, a substance within all human beings and within plants and animals, which the Spiritualists back in the last century called ectoplasm. In physical seances, which I grew up in—and I didn't even know the word at that time, I was so petrified and scared—this ectoplasm is taken from what is called the medium. It is used by decarnate spirits in keeping with the law that like attracts like and [they] use that energy, that physical substance to create various sounds and speak to those people present in physical, audible voice. Those voices have been and continue to be recorded.

Now the next question is, How evolved are those spirits? Are they from spiritual worlds of consciousness? Are they earth-bound spirits? Are they astral entities? And all of those questions must be answered. Then we move, after going through that great maze of investigation, and finally, hopefully, coming to some intelligent conclusion, we then move to the next step. And the next step is, Is this voice really from the other world or is it from the deep recesses of the human mind? So that question, then, must be investigated and must be answered to some satisfactory conclusion.

Then we move to the next step, where the so-called spirit, clothing themselves in the physical substance taken from the medium, taken from the attending sitters at a seance, taken from the plants, and whatever else has life force or prana in it, that is available. We see, with our physical eyes, the formation of a being, an intelligent being. And we look, in a state of, usually, emotional shock. The next thing you know, we touch them; they feel like a human being. They look like a human being. They even talk like a human being. They may choose to sit down and carry on an hour's conversation with us. Does that prove beyond a shadow of all doubt that that is a decarnate spirit? To millions of people, it does, especially if they tell them what they want to hear. To me, it does not. I grew up with it. It does not prove life eternal to me.

For the demonstration of communication with another world is for the purpose for which it is designed: to communicate, to awaken, to grow, and to evolve. Its purpose is not to make us cripples, dependent on someone else. That is not the purpose of good in life. You cannot prove, regardless of how many demonstrations of physical seances that you may experience, you cannot prove to a reasonable person, you cannot prove that that is, in truth, a decarnate spirit. Why can you not prove it? Science knows—some of the scientists know, beyond a shadow of any doubt, that deep within the recesses of the human mind is available to the individual the exact image, the replica, of those who have passed on. It is possible for that to form the ectoplasm and do what is done.

In this day and age in which communication is such a high priority of the consciousness of the masses, the barriers and barricades of superstition between this world and what is known as a spiritual world—which is in truth many worlds: earth-bound, astral, celestial, and on through the list, as it is here. We seem to not think. When so-called transition comes, we don't automatically get free from anything. We take *everything* with us. So many people think, "Oh, I'm going to lose this and I'm going to lose that. And I'm going to lose that. My house. My bank accounts. My money." You see, my friends, I've always taught everything goes with us. We lose nothing. Because you go with your mind and it all exists in your mind. So, you don't lose anything. It's like taking off your shoes. What have you lost? You haven't lost your mind because you've taken your shoes off. However, if somebody takes away your shoes, then, you say, "My shoes are gone!" But they're not gone in truth because they're still in your mind. If they weren't in your mind, you couldn't even think that they were gone. So, you see, you take everything with you, except a physical body, which is an obstruction to your flying around.

See, now you have to have a physical body and you move in an airplane to go where you want to go, to New York, London, Paris, etc. But when you shed this cumbersome, very heavy physical body—you, you won't believe how heavy your physical body is until you leave it. And when you leave your physical body, then you fly wherever you want to fly that you have in consciousness evolved to. Don't ask to fly to heaven, unless you're already heavenly. But if you are a heavenly person and you are demonstrating that goodness and heavenliness within you, then you may ask the divine law, "Yes. I want a ticket to heaven." And fly on there. But that's not how it works.

So, you see, don't search around for all of these different things. They cannot in truth reveal to you that law that you are eternal. You cannot take that which is infinite and eternal and confine it into the conception within your mind and say, "I have proof beyond a shadow of any doubt that I am eternal." You can't take the infinite and then try to define it by the finite and expect to have a satisfactory and intelligent answer.

I hope that's helped with your question. I see that our time is up. Thank you very much.

OCTOBER 7, 1984

Church Questions and Answers 51

Now, as our chairman has already said, this is the once-a-month time for you to ask your questions of particular interest to you. Once a year we set aside, in the last Sunday of December—and have for twenty-some years, [and even] before the actual opening of this church—a time for our annual forecast, which covers world events. Now I realize that whenever questions of a political interest are asked, not everyone can possibly be pleased or happy with the answers. But I do want you to know, before getting to your questions, that we contribute to the abundant good in life through the process, in a mental world in which we are moving, through the process of our own beliefs. For all of us identify with what is known as self, which in truth is a culmination of all of our experiences here on earth, [and we] work diligently, ofttimes unconsciously, to prove that we are right. It is difficult for any mind to accept that it repeats mistakes in its life. And so, in keeping with these mental laws that we all establish and follow, we find that we believe according to our own support and security of what we consider is our self.

What we find interesting in life is that, as we look back through the pages of our own history, personally, we can readily see that at one time in our life we believed that we were going to do certain things and accomplish certain things. And we believed at those times that it was absolutely necessary; in fact, it was essential for the good of our own life. Sometimes these things were accomplished and sometimes they were not. It simply reveals that we are constantly moving on a stream of consciousness through which many changes are taking place. We, however, are never left without choice. We can accept these changes with a good attitude of mind, looking for the good that is contained within them, regardless of our belief at the moment. For the law clearly reveals in nature that like attracts like and becomes the Law of Attachment. And so, a wise person, surely, wishes to be attached to that which they believe would be beneficial to them.

Ofttimes we look at little children and we see they will do things that they know they're going to be disciplined for. If they feel that they are not receiving the necessary attention that they believe at any moment that they need and require, then they're going to do whatever their mind will offer to them to receive the attention that they believe at any moment that they require. Now we can quickly see that in little children, but we have difficulty in seeing that when we become adults and [in] seeing it in other adults. For us to view that in another adult opens the door of possibility to accept that we are doing the same thing at different times in our own life. And none of us want to believe that we are childish in our thoughts, acts, and activities when we are adults, for we take that as an insult, an injury to what we believe is our own image. And so we find in life that most of our struggles and our difficulties, our frustrations and our upsets are the effects of our effort to protect and to defend the image that we believe we are at any moment.

This philosophy has taught for many years, truth needs no defense, for truth does not have contained within it what we know as need. For if it contained need, then it could not possibly be truth. So when man identifies with that which is truth, which is within him, he finds, as an effect of that identification, he finds a freedom from frustration, a freedom from discord and discontent, a freedom from the bombardments of mental desires; because he is what he is, he has no feeling and no need to defend whatever he really is. So our problem in life is finding within our self what we really are and not what we believe someone else thinks we are. Because by believing what someone else thinks we are, it places us in a very difficult position in consciousness to maintain, by defense, what we believe someone else thinks we are. Consequently, there are many people in the universe and they don't all think the same. And we find our self moving from one moment to the next moment trying to be what someone else thinks we are only because we want something because we believe we need something and we also believe that someone else has it. That's when man loses his true being and pays the price of the created one.

Now I can take some of your questions, if you will be so kind as to raise your hands. The lady there, please.

I have two questions, actually. I'm wondering if the leadership of the U.S.S.R. intends to force communism on the other peoples of the world. I'm also wondering if our country is building and maintaining a large military because it would deter them.

I see. Well, in reference to your first question, concerning the leaders of the Soviet Union, if we understand, when the lady spoke, do they intend to force their political views on the rest of us, and I accept that as the rest of the world, when we understand that force is an effect, not a cause, but an effect—force is an effect of fear. You see, when we fear anything—and, of course, fear is the effect of a judgment. And so, judgment is the effect of past experiences. Now when we fear anything, we go to work in our consciousness to protect and to defend what we believe is threatened. As long as a person—of which a country is but many people—as long as a person believes they are threatened they will do everything that is necessary to defend themselves. And so, the cause to the problem is a lack of understanding. In reference to the question, Will they force their views upon this particular country? I can assure you not in our lifetime, and we have a little ways to go.

Now, two people, fearing each other, do everything that their mind can offer them to protect themselves from what they judge is a threat to their way of life. Therefore, it requires the introduction—and it is essential to bringing about understanding and harmony—[of] a neutral third party. When you look at countries, you see the family feuds between them. But we fail to pause and see the similarity and the identical law taking place in a marriage. And so because countries are married to their survival, to their particular way, we can look with a little more understanding and see that they are married. They are married to the purpose of survival to what they believe at any given time. And it requires, and is absolutely necessary, a neutral, objective view in order to bring about peace and harmony. Does that help with your question?

Yes.

One country builds its defenses based upon its past experiences of what the track record of another country is. And I can assure you the thing to look for and to bring about some spiritual type of thinking is the population of outer space. Because you will not experience what you call a nuclear holocaust here on this Earth planet—No. It has been revealed for many, many years that shall not take place on this planet Earth. There are intelligences and powers far beyond the minds of men. It shall not be permitted on this planet. However, where the difficulties are, is the phenomenal scientific advancement and technology which will take Earth people to outer space to populate other planets and take with them the lack of understanding that establishes the Law of Fear and brings about these so-called wars. That help with your questions?

[Yes.]

You're welcome. The lady here, please.

I'd like you to speak on the nature of healing on the cellular level in relationship to . . . [The rest of the question is difficult to transcribe.]

Well, in reference to—you're referring to spiritual healing, for there are many types of healing—in reference to healing, we understand that it is not only the divine right of each individual but it is the divine responsibility to care for the vehicle through which we are expressing at any given moment. Now within our being are all the chemicals, everything necessary, that can be brought into harmonious balance that we may experience the abundant good which is the effect of balance and perfect health.

Now you cannot just say to the mind that you're having a difficulty with your health because of the lack of bringing about a harmonious balance. First of all, we can only have control over what we first accept, because in order to control anything you must accept its existence in order to investigate it and understand the laws by which it works. Once the acceptance is brought about, the next step is the understanding of the laws that govern the condition. Now from that, man has within him everything necessary to bring about the perfect healing that he is seeking.

Now stop and think. No honest doctor ever told a patient that they would heal them. No honest doctor in any medical profession ever made such a stupid statement. For they know beyond a shadow of any doubt they cannot heal. They can only be instruments through which the healing process already existing within the individual can be made manifest. They can prescribe based upon their various experiences and investigation. They can prescribe certain medication. They can prescribe certain chemicals, in hopes that a healing will take place. That healing process—you stop and think. If a person first believes that by doing a certain thing their health will improve, ever in keeping with the faith that prompts that belief shall the healing take place. Because it is not in the conscious mind; it is beyond the conscious mind.

We see, for example, people—especially in our country, there is such a great interest in the problem of weight control. I'm answering your question in the way that I think will be of the most benefit to all of you. So many people spend—there's billions of dollars being poured in yearly, annually, to bring about what the people judge is a weight in which they can feel happy and satisfied. So there're all kinds of pills on the market. There are all kinds of exercises—everything that the minds of men can possibly create to bring about the satisfactory results to each individual to bring a proper weight into their life. Yet we look the opposite way for the cause. Our experiences reveal to us repeatedly that weight problems are directly related to emotional starvation. And fortunate we are in this world that recently, recently, within these past few months only, medical doctors are beginning to accept that people who are emotionally starved have serious eating problems, the effect of which is a weight problem.

Now what is it that causes emotional starvation? When we make a judgment in our mind and dependent on how much we believe how valuable and how important the judgment we have just made is to our life, and those judgments, time passes and those judgments do not get filled, we experience in the depths of our subconscious trauma, emotional upheaval. No one wants to experience emotional trauma. No one consciously says, "I want to be emotionally upset today. Now let me see who I can talk to so I can have the experience." No intelligent being wakes up and makes that kind of a judgment. Yet we find millions of people in emotional trauma and upset. Because they believe the judgments they have made are essential to their well-being and those judgments are not being filled.

If we must make a judgment—and the mind has no problem in so doing. Wise is the one who makes decisions. Decisions contain within them the essential ingredient of the light of reason. Decisions contain the acceptance of the possibility of change. Judgments are very rigid. They do not contain the acceptance of the possibility of change. Consequently, we are bound by them, victims of their rigidity. So people make many judgments. The judgments do not get filled because we find that 90 percent of all the judgments are dependent on what somebody else does. And whoever depends on what someone else is going to do is going to have a problem in life. They're going to end up frustrated and it's not a very healthy way to experience life.

In reference to cellular healing, in reference to healing period, healing is dependent upon, number one: honesty. One cannot understand themselves until they're honest with themselves. When one is honest with themselves—so many people, you know, say, "Well, [if] you talk to yourself, they'll think you're going off the rocker." But do we understand our self? And how are we going to understand our self if we don't communicate with our self? You see, one moment we think we're this; another moment we think we're that. Well, these are different levels of consciousness. There are eighty-one, already, that have been revealed in the Living Light Philosophy.

Now, to suppress a desire is to guarantee frustration someday. Therefore, we have always taught you suppress not desire, for desire *is* the divine expression. You educate the desire or you fulfill the desire. The one thing you never do with desire is suppress it. People with suppressed desire have discord in their life. Discord is the opposite of harmony. Harmony is health and discord is disease. It lies within us to bring about that healing for the power is within us. The only obstruction to that, *the only obstruction* to that is the lack of controlling the human mind on deeper levels of consciousness where we can bring about the light of reason and permit that intelligent Power, that man calls God, to flow unobstructed.

No God that I have ever, ever accepted or believe in dictates that one person shall be healthy and another one shall be ill, that one person shall be wealthy and another shall be poor. That is not an intelligent, in my understanding, an intelligent God to accept. Because who would want to serve that type of fickleness in life?

Now in reference to healing, healing is in the moment of our own acceptance. When we take control of our mind, when we accept the possibility of that power (intelligent) flowing through us that causes us to speak, that is the power through which we're able to view whatever we view, hear whatever we hear; when we go beyond believing we are the form, we will be free to experience the divine healing which is available to all of us. I hope that's helped with your question.

The lady here, please.

Recently on television they've been showing studies of people who've passed to the other side and then been brought back. And invariably there is a tunnel through which they go and see the light at the other end. Can you tell us in the Living Light Philosophy what that tunnel represents?

I'll be more than happy to share with you the tunnel. First let us, in our understanding, bring about a little light upon what we, *we* believe a tunnel is. Is it a restricted area? Pardon?

Yes.

All right. So we accept that a tunnel is a restricted area. Do we accept that there is an opening on each end of the tunnel?

Yes.

Fine. As long as we first have some basis on which to share our understanding. Now let us look at the human mind. Do you see the human mind and its design similar to what you understand a tunnel is?

Yes.

Something enters it and passes through it. And you think it goes out the other end. Is that correct? You have a thought one minute and the next minute, you don't. It passed through the tunnel of your consciousness. Is that correct?

Yes.

All right. So when you hear that so many people have passed on—and it's not recent. My goodness, people have been passing on ever since there's been people. Ever since life. Life is! It just expresses through different forms at different times. So we believe that we have a feeling or a thought. It enters our consciousness like a person would enter a tunnel. And then, maybe an hour later, a minute later, a year later that thought no longer is there. It's gone! Yes, it's gone all right. It's gone so deep we can no longer see it. That's where it went. For nothing is ever lost. That's contrary to the very law of nature's demonstration. So man leaves this physical world and he experiences—and without exception, everyone passes through the tunnel of their own mental substance. Some tunnels are very short. Some tunnels are very long. It truly depends upon our own dependence upon our own mind. Does that help with your question?

Yes. Thank you.

But be rest assured, as all these people who have partially passed on—they haven't passed on, the Isle of Hist was never separated or they wouldn't come back and tell us. Not in the physical body, anyway. All of these people say one thing: there's a tunnel, but there's a light at the end. I hope that's helped with your question. And so it is with the minds of men, it's a tunnel all right, but there is a light at the other end. Depends on how long we want to make the journey. Some people make it long. Some people make it short. You see, the journey in consciousness is ever dependent upon us. You know, it's like falling in love. Some people fall in love, it's a short duration. Some people fall in love and it is a long duration. But let us understand that I never ever heard a person tell me in all my life that they ever rose to love. They all fall in love. Who wants to fall? You see, here, the Light is above us. So why do we want to fall to the ground? What law is here [that says] everyone falls in love? They fall in love. They fall out of love. The reason they fall in and out is because they fall in the first place. I hope that's helped with your question. *[Many in the congregation laugh.]* Let us rise to love because the Light is ever above us.

Are there any more questions before we conclude? If so, please raise your hand. *[After a short pause, the teacher continues.]* If not, I will take your silence as an endorsement of whatever I have to say. Because, you know, that's one thing that one should consider.

In your lives you meet many people. And many people say many things. When they say things that are not in accord with your own belief, they are not harmonious to your own understanding, and when they speak them forth in your presence, understanding that presence is the Law of Solicitation, when they speak them forth in your presence and you remain silent, you endorse within your consciousness whatever they had to say. That's a serious thing. That's a very serious thing. Because what happens with people, because they fail to be honest, what happens with people, the person goes away, here or there or whatever, and the person that stood there, demonstrating the Law of Solicitation, the person that stood there, demonstrating the Law of Endorsement, which is silence, that person goes home and they feel terrible. They're furious! They're furious from afterthought that they didn't speak up. They're very unhappy with themselves.

Hopefully, someday they'll become so unhappy with themselves they will fail not to speak what they believe is right for them to speak. They will no longer worry whether the person likes them or dislikes them. Because if we live for believing how much a person likes or dislikes us, then we must accept the demonstrable truth: the reason we live that way is because we want something out of those people! And by wanting something from man, we deny its avenue of flowing from God that is within us. And that's rather sad, that life becomes truly miserable because we do not speak up when we know deep in our heart that we should speak up.

It's not important whether or not someone likes you or loves you. What is important is that you like yourself. Because if you don't like yourself, you're not going to be happy with yourself. And not being happy with yourself, you are not going to be harmonious in your thoughts, acts, and activities. And not being harmonious, you can only be what is the opposite and that's discordant. And to be discordant within one's consciousness guarantees the disease and the illness of the being.

So man has a responsibility to himself. That responsibility is that he make the effort not to interfere within his own consciousness with the Divine Good that he truly is. And we interfere because we deny what we are and work, like a beaver, to become what we shall in truth never become. For man to work so diligently to become a certain way with the created form, not ever having the control nor the power to dictate how long it shall remain on Earth—it takes a foolish man to identify with effort to control form, for form is beyond the control of man.

Man cannot dictate, nor can he wish, nor can he judge how many minutes, hours, days, or years he will remain on the planet Earth. Man does not have that power to do that. But man can accept what he truly is. And when his suit wears out, throw it where all worn out things belong: thrown below in the garbage can. A foolish person, after wearing out their shoes, would put them in a glass case to look at them and remember they used to be good shoes to serve a purpose. Well, friends, when something no longer serves the purpose for which it has been designed, reason reveals that you remove it from your universe.

Now many people demonstrate that in the many love affairs they fall in and out of. When it no longer serves the purpose, through which your mind designed in your consciousness, that that man or that girl would serve for you, that's why we have divorces. They finally came to the awakening (someone does) that "This person is not serving in the way that I originally designed and believed that they would." Now if you make the effort to change your original design, if your original design for entering into the love affair or the marriage contained within it decision, if you made a decision and not a judgment, then you won't have to worry about a divorce. You won't have to worry about falling out of love, because you made a decision which contains within it that essential ingredient to make changes and to grow. If you made a judgment when you got married, then you've got a serious problem. Because your judgment was based upon limited experiences at the time.

Many people say, "I never knew he was like that." Ten years pass, a man says, "I didn't realize she was that type of a person." You see, that experience was based upon a judgment. It didn't contain a decision, where the person could say, "I see that they're growing. But they're growing in a different direction than I'm growing. Therefore, we must come to some understanding, first to accept that we are growing, in truth, in different directions. And by growing in different directions we will meet again—or do we desire to do so?"

You see, you can't have harmony when there is emotion, which is the defense mechanism of any judgment that you make at any time. You can tell when a person is bound by judgments: when they're threatened, the emotions will be unbelievable.

Thank you very much. I see our time has passed. Thank you.

NOVEMBER 4, 1984

Church Questions and Answers 52

As our chairman has already stated, this is the once-a-month opportunity that you have to ask your questions of a general interest. And before speaking to your questions, I would like to say just a few words. This, as we all know, is a time of year that has traditionally been set aside for our experiencing of the spirit of joy. We understand that joy is the effect of the expression of gratitude. And so the opportunity of experiencing joy is ever available to us. For when we know where we're going, by remembering where we have been, we are then qualified to make an intelligent choice and, by so doing, experiencing the effect of the expression of gratitude, which is known as joy.

Now it's your time to raise your hands, if you have a question that is of interest to you, which I'm sure will be of interest to all of us. The lady there, please.

What purpose is served by knowing what past lives were?

In reference to past lives, the Living Light Philosophy teaches that we have always been, therefore, we will always be. The always being is not the limit, which we, at times, identify with as the personality, the physical, or mental form. It is the divine Spirit, the intelligent movement of energy, which we are in truth.

What is the benefit by knowing of past lives? The question implies what is commonly known as reincarnation, which is not the teaching of the Living Light, which is evolutionary incarnation. One has a full-time job in looking at past experiences, which in truth are lessons, in the short earth life. The benefit of looking at a shadow is only beneficial to a person who is ready, who is willing, and who is able to choose intelligently a path of abundant good and joy. And so, as we look at the shadows, the events, the experiences, the lessons that have passed, as we view those shadows, we are then able to choose whether or not we wish to continue to serve that which our intelligence reveals to us is not beneficial for our life. Does that help with your question?

[Yes.]

You're welcome. The lady here, please.

I am wondering, sometimes people say that there are healers. And so I'm just wondering what does that mean? Does that mean people have an ability to heal another? Or is that—I guess that's what my question's about.

Well, in reference to your statement that people say they are healers, people say they are many things. The demonstration in life, of course, is the revelation. If one demonstrates the ability to restore their health, then one is demonstrating the possibility that they may offer that talent, that understanding to someone else. The only thing in reference to healing or any other profession, a so-called healer is one, through the continuity of effort to gain control of the fickleness of the human mind, in such a way, through control, to be an unobstructed vehicle through which the harmonious vibrations of the Divine Spirit may flow through them unobstructed to the recipient to the degree that the recipient, through their own effort, becomes receptive to the vibrations that are flowing unobstructed at any given moment. Does that help with your question?

Yes.

You're welcome. The lady there, please.

Could you share with us some of your own personal history in being born into the world and at what point you realized that you were a medium and how you dealt with it and some of your experiences?

Thank you. Well, I wouldn't want to take up too much of your time with any of my personal history, but I will share with you how I dealt with the realization that I was different, because that's the first thing that I judged it was: different. And, of course, no one at any age in their life consciously desires to be different. Oh, we ofttimes *think* we want to be different. And we move from one particular set [of] patterns of one group of people in society only on into another group. So in that respect, for a short time, we think we're being different, but we find security and support in familiarity with those who believe, act, think, and do as we do. So in reference to becoming aware of what is termed mediumship, I didn't take it very well at all because I had no friends of mine at the age of fourteen, that I was aware of, that had those kind of experiences.

It only goes to show that the ability and the willingness to make changes in our life is ever dependent upon the degree of control that we have of our own mind. And so we find that so often in our life we are not willing to make any changes because we believe that what we think and how we think and what we are doing, even though ofttimes the experiences are miserable, we have no willingness to change, for to change would mean that we would have to make effort and cast the light of reason within us on the beliefs of our mind and their dependence upon the way things have been in our lives.

So here we are on this Earth planet, the great planet of faith, here we are with that one lesson to learn, to learn and to discern, moment by moment, between faith and belief. Though life has already, through the many experiences that we have encountered, life has already shown to us clearly, beyond a shadow of any doubt, that our beliefs are in a constant process of change. Therefore, our beliefs are not reliable. They are not dependable. They are not security for our emotional needs and hunger.

And so, as we slowly, but surely, awaken to that simple truth: that faith in an intelligent Energy, Power, known to man as God, is ever present. It is not partial. It does not respond to your begging, to your pleading. It does not respond to the mental threats and dictates of mental substance, for it is an intelligent Power that sustains mental substance. And no matter what mental substance (the human minds) may decide to do or not to do, has no effect upon the intelligent Energy known as God.

Sooner or later in our lives, we gradually move from belief, which is dependent upon the shadows of past experiences, which offers to us constantly the prejudices that we express, for we prejudge ever in keeping with our dependence upon the limited experiences or shadows of our past. To prejudge does not bring harmony into one's life; it is the pea-shooter view of the universe. And so, until the day dawns in our consciousness that belief is a device of the human mind to keep us from making intelligent effort that we may finally accept that we are not the thought that passes through our mind, that we are in truth the Power that moves the thought, that we are not the judgment that binds us to discord and disharmony. But we are the power used by mental substance to create that bondage, that victimization, and that slavery.

Emotional starvation puts us into many difficult experiences in life. Feeling good is not a luxury. Feeling good is the experience of good or God. Nothing lives without feeling good. Survive, it does, but it does not live. Survive, for a time. And so man does what his mind offers to him to feel good or experience God, for the drive to feel good is something that we cannot with our minds control. We cannot go day after day and decide we wish to feel bad today and tomorrow and every day thereafter, for to feel bad creates within our consciousness an experience of pity of our self. Misery not only loves company, without company it does not exist. No human being will sit by themselves day after day, week after week, year after year, and permit themselves to feel miserable. They will seek out whatever ear they can find, for they know deep inside themselves that they are but surviving.

Now this emotional starvation that many people satisfy momentarily by whatever they permit their senses to express—in our society it's usually, we can see clearly, it's eating. And we all know that Americans eat more than any country in the whole, wide world. Well, there's nothing wrong with the senses until we make something wrong with them. Overindulgence in anything is contrary to the Law of Balance. Balance is necessary for the expression of the Law of Harmony, and without harmony, health does not exist. So balance in all things is what a wise man seeks, for a wise man knows that in a balanced mind the faculty of reason [flows], through which intelligent energy transforms our life, that we may enjoy our purpose of being.

A wise man knows that whatever comes into the mind, by the Law of Coming, is destined to go. Therefore, no one, awakened within, permits themselves to depend upon an image in mental substance, for to do so is to place a deep, thick fog between their true being and the very Source thereof. Year after year, day after day, our minds tell us that our God, we may experience in this or that different way. That is not an experience of truth, the effect of which, of course, is freedom. It is, however, a bondage that we alone have created. When our goodness and our God is dependent upon what our mind and physical body can do at any given moment, then our God is demonstrably the false gods, the golden calves that someday in our consciousness are destined to crumble. Thank you for your question.

We have a few minutes left. The gentleman here, please.

You mentioned the Earth planet of faith. And I'm wondering, Are there other such Earth planets where the spirit can learn in the physical form throughout the universes or are we all alone in that regard?

Thank you very much for your question. The planet Earth is not the only planet in universes that is inhabited by physical, intelligent beings. If we understand that environmental conditions of each planet are responsible for dictating—and the composition of the planet—are responsible for dictating the physical forms that may inhabit the planet and if we are willing to broaden our horizons and to accept that Intelligence—intelligent Energy is expressing through many forms, whether or not those forms are similar to our own has absolutely nothing to do with the divine law—that a form, the effect of a negative and positive pole of nature, that the intelligent Energy, known as God, shall enter.

Fortunately for us, here, at this time on earth, we are in a state of scientific development through which, under the guidance of reasonable people, with a bit of inner awakening, can be of great benefit to ourselves and to the universe. We are quickly passing the days when the forms known as the human form can only be created a certain way. We are in a day and age through which the so-called science fiction novels of the past are no longer fiction, but an awakening of the scientific facts of the day. The cloning of various forms on this planet has been in process for some time. Therefore, it reveals to us that man's dependence and his bondage upon the past in that area is slowly and gradually breaking down. That is our freedom, if it is used in the light of reason for the benefit of the whole.

There are other planets—many planets—that are inhabited by intelligent beings long before this planet was ever born in the universe. All planets, like all people, like all form, they have a birth, a growth, an age, and a death. They all return to the source from whence they have come. As spiritual substance returns to the source of its origin, so all physical substance returns to the source of its origin. And so it is with humans and animals on that planet, and so it is with the planets themselves. They have come from a source, a physical source, in this particular solar system. And to that source they are in process—ever in keeping with their age—they are in process of returning to the physical source from whence they have sprung. And so the planet Earth, prophesied by our prophets in this world so many centuries ago, shall be consumed by fire. Well, of course, it shall be consumed by fire. From fire it sprang forth; to fire it is destined to return. And so each moment, each second the planet Earth is slowly, but surely, returning to the Sun from whence it came.

So man, his physical form, having come from the planet Earth, returns to the planet Earth. No man can change the laws that he is subject to. His mental body, created from mental substance, returns and disintegrates into the mental substance from whence it sprang forth. His spirit, clothed in what man calls an individualized soul, is the effect of, that clothing, of the evolution of the soul throughout the universes. Spirit knows beyond a shadow of all doubt; therefore, all wisdom is spiritual, as all knowledge, based on fact, is mental. And so man's individualized soul, springing forth from what other philosophers have taught for eons, the Allsoul, returns unto its source.

Now think how man—and what is it that man experiences when he believes that he is such and such? And the day comes when he awakens and no longer believes what he used to believe. Now many people get married and they believe that that is paradise revealed. And for them, for a time, that is paradise revealed. As long as they direct intelligent energy to their belief that that is paradise revealed, for them it shall be paradise revealed. When they no longer direct intelligent energy to that particular belief, the world is filled with sadness and divorce, would you not agree?

And so, is man his belief? He cannot be his belief. He can only *believe* that he is his belief, for the intelligent Power that sustains that belief, once redirected by the Law of Identification, the belief disintegrates before his eyes. And so, we have marriage; we have divorce. We have one job, then another. We believe that it is an abundant life; we believe it is a limited life. And we believe many things. Man first realizes that is not him; that is what, through his over-identification, he has chosen, for a time, to be satisfied and to believe. That passes. But that which he is, intelligent Energy, that doesn't start and that doesn't stop. That's something that has always been. It always is. It always shall be.

So man will evolve harmoniously, graciously, with all of the goodness he could possibly seek, if he will always remember, "This thought, this feeling, this judgment is not me. However, because *I* have permitted the creation of it, it is my child. It exists within my consciousness. It is what I have created and because I have created it, I can change it at any time I choose to do so." And so, that is the power, that is the great power ever available to us. But in order to exercise that power, and in order to experience that good, we have one requirement. There's no pill to take for that to happen. It takes the conscious effort to work with the vehicle known as our mind to put it where it justly, rightfully belongs to be: a servant through which we may experience the good that is our divine birthright. Does that help with your question?

I see our time has passed. Thank you very much.

DECEMBER 2, 1984

Church Questions and Answers 53

Now our chairman has stated that this is your time and your opportunity to ask the questions that you have that interest you. As is stated, we ask that they be of a general interest that all of us may benefit. And so if you will be so kind as to raise your hand with your question, I will answer as many as time will permit.

The gentleman there, please.

In your messages sometimes you refer to, like, parts of the body, [the] anatomy. And I think in particular you mentioned to me about keeping your feet warm. Would you explain that a little bit, please?

Well, there is, in the science of the Living Light Philosophy, there is a clear, definite explanation of the various parts of the temple of God, which is known to man as the human body. In reference to the feet, and because it is of interest to you, it should and does reveal, of course, spiritually, they are representative of the soul faculty of understanding. And ofttimes we find, from thorough investigation and analysis, that difficulties ofttimes associated with that part of the human anatomy are directly related to a struggle within the consciousness in reference to their understanding of anything. Does that help with your question?

Thank you.

You're welcome. The gentleman there, please.

Sylvia Browne made a prediction recently that this year would see a great interest taken in Spiritualism. And I'm wondering if you have any comments on that.

Thank you. In reference to the prophets and prophetesses that make their predictions, I am not at liberty to publicly comment. However, in reference to a question in speaking of the growth of Spiritualism, are you referring to the growth of numbers or the growth and evolution of the movement in its own progressive awakening and understanding?

The latter.

The latter. In that respect, like all organizations, all religions, all philosophies, they are composed of human beings. Because they are organized, by the Law of Organizing, we limit. It is the payment that we all must pay in life for the limit or organizing of anything. We organize in life at the expense and exclusion of other interests in other areas within our consciousness. Hopefully, a person in respect to their individual, divine right of expression organizes or limits with an understanding of what they are doing and does not base the stability and security of their organization upon the shifting sands and fickle principle of fear.

Now if it is strictly composed and built upon the foundation of mental substance, then it is destined to the experience of fear. For fear is demonstrably revealed to be nothing but the power of faith directed to a mental world. Because a mental world is composed of a dual principle, and anything that is composed of a dual principle is destined to experience both ends of that principle. So whenever we organize anything upon the principle of mental substance, we are not only destined to fear but we are destined to prejudgment or prejudice, which is the effect of the fear of what we are attached to.

Now in reference to Spiritualism per se, Spiritualism, founded as broad a horizon as any modern religion known to man, is still composed of people. As the people within any religious organization, or any organization, grow within consciousness, broaden their horizon, expand their tolerance, they grow spiritually. For the divine and infinite, intelligent Spirit, known as God, cares for the daisies of the field as well as the roses of the rose garden. So man, viewing those divine principles within nature, taking an example from them, is then freed from the bondage, the limit, and the frustration and struggle of fear, or faith directed to the limits of their mind. I hope that's helped with your question.

The lady here, please.

Is caffeine detrimental to the body, like to any of the vital organs of the body?

Well, in reference to the question on, Is caffeine detrimental to the organs of the human body? The air that man breathes can be detrimental to the human body. Without it, there is no human body as we know it, of course. It *can* be detrimental. To many people the air that we breathe is more detrimental to their body than it is to other bodies. We must first understand that we are not only composed of physical, material substance. Our body is the effect of the composition of mental substance, which in truth (our mental body) is the effect of the composition of and the growth and expansion of our own spiritual body. Therefore, what the mind judges, the mind limits. As the mind judges and the mind limits, it restricts itself from the abundant flow of the only power there is in the universe for the restoration, the restoring to balance, the effect of which is known as peace or perfect health. So if man first permits his mind to judge that by breathing certain air he is being affected in a detrimental way by that air, man establishes a judgment or limit within his consciousness. That judgment or limit is solidified by man's belief in the judgment that he has made.

Therefore, all great religions—and this religion and philosophy—teach and have always taught God is not a judge. Judgment does not exist in the Principle of Peace. Judgment only exists in the duality of creation. So as man believes in his own creation or form [or] limit, man, therefore, is affected by his own judgment and belief thereof.

So in reference to caffeine or any other chemical, when man awakens within consciousness that to varying degrees his human, physical body is composed of all elements of the planet

Earth, which include caffeine, that wisdom clearly reveals to all mankind that all things in balance serve the Principle of Peace, that peace is the power, that man's health, which is the effect of harmony, which is the unobstructed flow of peace, is totally dependent upon man's own willingness to free himself from limit. I do hope that's helped with your question.

The lady here, please.

Mr. Goodwin, you mentioned that judgment only exists in duality. Would you explain where principle exists and, also, sometimes when one is trying to do what they call "stand on principle" how they can be sure it isn't casting judgment?

Thank you very much. In reference to the duality of creation and the principle, which is the essence of anything, first of all, principle cannot be principle and be dual. Principle is a neutral law. Principle is not restricted by nor limited by a mental world, which has the Law of Duality to see the bad in all good and to see the good in all bad. For it is only the human mind that sees difference. The spiritual principle, which is the essence of life itself, as I have just stated, is not limited nor restricted by the thought of man. For God sustains, being a divine, neutral Infinite Intelligence, God sustains the so-called good thought of man as well as God, this great power, sustains the so-called bad thought of man.

Now where is justice? Justice is ever in keeping with the Law of Personal Responsibility. We have experiences in life and we question why these experiences have entered into our universe. Personal responsibility clearly reveals that whatever comes into our life must first be sent out for the Law of Attraction is infallible. It is a divine law. And so, as man sends out thoughts of good—that is, form of good, for all thought is form—and as man sends out thoughts of good, man experiences thoughts of good as a return of what he sends.

The reason that we have such difficulty in accepting our experiences in life is because our memories are so short when we choose them to be. We seem to quickly forget the thoughts of envy, the thoughts of jealousy, the thoughts of hurt feelings. We seem to quickly forget the judgments that rise in our consciousness, the prejudgments, which we know as prejudice, we forget them. But if we pause and we first accept that we are not perfect because we are thinking the word *perfection. We know* we are not perfect for perfection is not limited, nor can it be expressed through limit. Therefore, when we are honest with our self, we, facing an experience that we have encountered, accepting that nothing happens to us in truth that is not caused by us, there is no one to blame and there isn't even our self to blame for we are a part of the evolution of form, and, therefore, when we pause in our consciousness and we say to our self, "I blame nothing outside, for I blame nothing inside."

You see, to blame another for our frailties in life, to blame another for our struggles and our difficulties reveals to us, in the law that we cannot grant to another what we have not first granted unto our self, it simply reveals to us that we are blaming our self. Therefore, by establishing the law of blaming our self, we are able to offer that to others. We are then able to offer to others, "Because of you I have a miserable day. Because of you, I have struggles in my life because of what you did do or didn't do."

So in awakening to what we are doing, almost unconsciously, we gradually begin to awaken inside. Knowing that like attracts like and becomes the Law of Attachment, we can then say to our self, "I'm grateful to God. I'm getting closer to this wonderful freedom which is the effect of my efforts to demonstrate personal responsibility, the ability to respond to my own thoughts, acts, and deeds." Now that's the benefit of growing up. That is the benefit. Now we must accept the demonstrable truth, sooner or later, that in blaming others we first must blame our self in keeping with the law that we grant to others what we first grant to our self, then we must accept the demonstrable truth: we are a house divided. For there's a part of us that says, "Oh, no, it's not my fault at all. I don't blame myself at all. I blame another." We totally disregard that law and in so doing we suffer the consequences.

The mental world, being a world of duality, knows much. Wisdom, being on a higher evolution, wisdom, being of the spiritual principle, has no concern. Having no concern, it has no need. Therefore, having no need, it does not have to prove to itself what principle is and what principle is not. For it has no need. Need is the effect of denial. We deny many things in life and we experience many needs. When man stops denying the demonstrable truth that God *is*, truth *is*, there is no need for defense for it just *is*. All of life reveals to us this Infinite Intelligence *is*. It is not concerned, for it doesn't say, "I will give this much intelligent energy to the dog. And I will give this much more to the human. And I will give this much less to the blade of grass." The divine Infinite Intelligence, not having concern, not having fear, is not composed of mental substance. That which is composed of mental substance is that which fell from grace by its own divine right of choice. I hope that's helped with your question.

Yes, the lady here, please.

Could you please discuss so-called crib death and reveal its true cause?

Thank you. In reference to so-called crib death, which there has been more publicity about here in the past ten years than ever before, it is like all transitions. We come to this planet Earth. We come here not by some fancy, fickle choice that we make. We come here as an effect of laws established in our evolution. We look around at creation and we see that every form is in a process of evolving. Nature reveals a constant refining process of all form. The Divine Principle, flowing through the limits of form, is expanding form. The more form expands, the freer form is. For the form that can walk and fly and swim is certainly freer than the form that can only walk. It is freer in its expression.

And so it is in the entrance of the souls on this particular planet. This planet is the fifth planet in this particular solar system. It is governed by—and we're here to learn—the lesson of the soul faculty of faith. Everyone has faith. What everyone does with it at any moment is their choice, *their* choice, their right. If they infringe upon another with their right, then their right shall be infringed upon; that is the demonstrable Law of Life.

Now so-called crib death—when we—and I can only say so much in reference to that very important question—when we permit ourselves to be the very authority in our consciousness, that life is totally dependent upon us, we establish, for life, the Law of Limit. Now I know that that seems to be evasive of your question of crib death, but it is striking at the very cause of crib death. Thorough investigation shall someday reveal that crib death is through a limit of the soul faculty of consideration, that in the evolution of the human species, they base their care upon the limits of past experiences. Each case, of course, is individual.

We are not instruments through which birth or death is decided. We only think we are, but we are not. The soul to enter Earth enters Earth in keeping with laws far superior to the thoughts of man. The leaving of this planet is in keeping with laws that supersede the judgments, desires, and thoughts of man. But in that understanding let us not forget that we, in a world of creation, establish laws that have effects upon life, but they have effects upon life in keeping with the higher law of the evolution of the eternal spirit and the soul. I hope that's helped with your question.

The gentleman here, please.

That sort of ties in with the question of abortion.

Yes.

Could you talk about the ramifications of abortion for the unborn souls?

Well, in the evolution of the soul—or souls, if you wish, because there's millions, trillions, zillions; they're beyond man's ability to count in the universes. Prior to our soul, any soul's, entrance into the form of the planet—for the soul is limited in its expression by the elements of which any particular planet is composed at any particular time in any particular universe. This particular planet offers to us this particular form at this particular time in its own evolution, for planets evolve, as man, animals, and all things, of course, do evolve. The soul is well aware, prior to its entrance into any form at any time and including, of course, the human, so-called human form, the soul is fully aware of the experiences that they shall encounter prior to entering the limit of form. It is not only aware of these many experiences, it is aware of the cause of those experiences. Therefore, in that, of course, awakening, the soul, in keeping with its evolution (that awareness), it enters into the mist known as creation.

You see, creation is the mystery. The light and the purpose of the Living Light Philosophy is to take that "mist" out of the mystery. The mystery exists in mental substance. Truth does not exist in mental-substance expression. Only the mystery lies in that domain. For that which is a mystery, man becomes quickly a victim of. For man becomes dependent on what man believes he cannot control. Man's mind becomes dependent on what it judges is superior to it. Man's mind does not become dependent on someone who it believes is weaker than it, or inferior.

So we see that this mystery, this creation, this mist, the soul enters. As the soul enters that, this awakening, this knowing of what lessons are to come—whether it is to come for only a few seconds into form when the negative and positive pole comes together, the soul enters at that instant, or it's to stay for a month or two months, three months, thirty years, fifty years—as it enters and becomes identified with the limit of form, which is the mist, the intensity of the density is in keeping with the solidification of the mental substance. So as the mind becomes more active, the light of the soul becomes dimmer. And so all philosophies have always taught: still the mind, take control of the mind, for in so doing you shall not only experience the peace that passeth all understanding but you shall awaken within. You shall enter that consciousness which you truly are and no longer be deceived by what you believe you are, for belief is the domain of the mist, which is mental substance.

So in reference to so-called abortion, you have many, many factors at stake. If you want to look at the principle of aborting, many souls are aborted by many chemicals that permeate the atmosphere. So we have taken *aborting* and *abortion* to mean the physical removal of an embryo from a human being. Is that correct? And we are losing the principle of the word *abortion*. For our minds have restricted the word *abortion* and *aborting* to a particular procedure. Would you not agree?

But we must broaden our horizons. And when we look at a word we must not limit our self and be prejudiced in our expression of a word designed to express a principle. So we look at the word *aborting*, derived from the word *abortion*, and we see experiences where grown men are aborted, their souls, from the poisonous gases in the depths of the Earth known as a coal mine. We see the blatant disregard for human life on the planet Earth in countries known as Ethiopia.

So we must ask our self the question, "Where is my personal responsibility? Because if I cannot face my personal responsibility, how can I possibly face my spiritual responsibility?" The word *aborting* [or] *abortion* has become, here, obviously, a political bombshell for politicians who choose to use any particular stand, for organizations who choose to impose from fear their own particular judgments and prejudices upon others.

I do not stand for aborting or not aborting. I do not stand for abortion or not abortion. The Living Light Philosophy simply reveals its understanding of the word *aborting* and what man chooses to do with it. I hope that's helped with your question.

I do see our time is up. Thank you.

JANUARY 6, 1985

Church Questions and Answers 54

As our chairman has already stated, this is the once-a-month opportunity that you all have to ask questions of a general interest. And so, I will be more than happy to be the channel through which your answers come. If you will be so kind as to raise your hand, [I will] get to as many as time will allow.

The gentleman there, please.

I asked once before about the substance of thought and I don't think that I clarified my meaning. By substance, I mean physical substance is differentiated, like from, say, the essence of thought, or from a—in learning we sometimes use what we call allegorical, you know, we relate what we can understand to something that we can't understand. And I can understand the interdimensional nature of physical substance, that is, a liquid substance can become a solid substance. A solid can become a liquid. A liquid can become a gas. A gas can become a radiant. And a radiant travels throughout the universe. And I have the notion that our thoughts are something like physical substances that travel throughout, for billions of years, throughout the universe. Would you care to respond to that?

Well, thank you for your understanding in reference to the question on the substance of thought. Whereas pure, infinite, intelligent Energy is the source of all manifestation of which we are aware and unaware, therefore, it follows that from the infinite, intelligent Energy, known to man as Light, all things spring forth, including what we call the substance of thought.

For example, what is the obstruction to intelligent Energy when intelligent Energy is the very essence of all form? Therefore, being the essence of the seeming obstruction, the seeming obstruction cannot be that, an obstruction, in truth, to what is its own essence. So, therefore, with the form of mental substance, if we in our thinking believe that thought is formed from a substance of water, then for us we make it true. And in a sense it is true, for those who are aware and who have made the effort in their own evolution to go beyond the belief of the obstruction of the vehicle of a tree, to those who have grown beyond the belief in the obstruction, they are able to communicate intelligently with the intelligence within them and the intelligence within the tree. Therefore, we find that some people are able to readily communicate, intelligently, with the intelligence that is flowing through an animal. Some people are even able to communicate intelligently and gain understanding through communication with another human being, for they are not obstructed by the belief in their judgment that the person they are tempting to communicate with does not understand. And, therefore, they justify the reason why they don't understand and consequently clear, intelligent communication is not possible for them.

And so, we alone make life the way we find life. This is the great beauty of the reminder of what man calls experiences. Experiences are not in and of themselves teachers; they are reminders, intelligent reminders of the changes necessary within our own thinking process in order to bring about changes in our experiences in life. The teacher is the faculty of reason that is ever available to us to cast the light of reason, intelligent energy, upon our will power which is necessary to bring about the changes in our own thinking in order that we may experience a greater understanding and, therefore, be the living demonstration of the power that we truly are, not the obstructions in life that we believe that we are. I do hope that's helped with your question.

Thank you.

The lady here, please.

Recently on the news there was a report of some UFO sightings and I'd like to know if it was substantial.

Well, in reference to your question on sightings of unidentified flying objects, to many people in many parts of the world certain species of birds are unidentified flying objects. However, through the laws of association within the consciousness of man, they make the judgment it's just another type of bird that they haven't already seen. I know that what you are speaking of is not the understanding of the observer, but your question in reference to the existence of what you believe is an unidentified flying object, something that is alien to you in keeping with your present understanding. Is that correct?

There is no just reason for any mind to think, nor to believe, that intelligent beings exist only on the planet Earth. Just because man, over the eons of time, relates only and accepts only what is in harmony to what he has already conceived in his life and man readily rejects what is not harmonious, through the laws of association, [with] what he has already experienced, man finds struggle and difficulty in his own evolution and refinement. The question in reference to flying objects, it is not something new. It is not something old. It's something that *is*. And it is something that mankind gradually, spasmodically, periodically is awakening to. I hope that's helped with your question.

The lady there, please.

This is related a little to that question. They've discovered some images on Mars. And the scientists say that it's chance configurations. My question is, Is it a message that those who are receptive are receiving on Earth or is it just chance formations of the planet? Thank you.

Thank you. In reference to that question, the law demonstrably reveals to us, moment by moment, daily, there is no such thing in the universe known as chance. It is a superstitious deception of the human mind. Nothing exists outside of demonstrable, natural law. Because man is yet to understand the law governing many of his observations, the laws governing his own experiences, he prefers to call things accidents. He prefers to call things chance. For by so doing he believes that he frees himself from responsibility to further investigate the cause for the experience or observation. Therefore, in reference to your question about that planet and those formations, they are not there by chance. They are there, have been there—they are not something that has just been created. They are effects of demonstrable law. Now I'm sure that your question, further, is, Have they been placed there by intelligent Energy expressing through the individualization of some particular form or forms? In that respect their patterns distinctly reveal that intelligent Energy has first designed them and placed them there. And I hope that's helped with your question.

Thank you.

You're welcome. Yes, the lady here, please.

For what purpose was that monkey skull there?

For what purpose to our life, this moment?

That would be helpful. But [for] what purpose was it constructed?

What purpose was it constructed for? Well, publicly I can say this: there has not been a time when intelligent forms did not exist in the planet of which you are referring. Because man has yet to awaken, and therefore to accept, that intelligence is not limited to a particular type of form, known as mankind, that intelligence expresses itself in all forms and because a form is not familiar to us, we fear it. And by fearing it, we reject it. Throughout the universes there has been, there are, and there shall continue to be various things, such as the one of which you spoke, to remind future generations that intelligence has been there, and there, and there, no matter where man goes. So if you find within that answer a reasonable, sensible purpose for your question, then you have found the answer for you.

Was it for navigational purposes, too?

Navigational purposes are not limited to travel through the element air. And therefore, there are navigational purposes and there are charts that man follows within his own being. It is few people who take charge of their ship of destiny, chart their course intelligently, and then follow the course they have charted. For example, you think of charting a course only to move a physical, material body. But however, the charting of a course and the intelligence for its purpose is not limited to moving a physical body when there are mental bodies that we are serving, until we awaken and we chart our own course. And then they serve the purpose of their design and they follow the course (our minds) that we, using our faculty of reason, have charted for them. I hope that's helped with your question.

Thank you very much.

You're welcome. Yes, the lady there, please.

It is my understanding, from having read something like The Blue Island, *that when man passes to the other side if he is not in a spiritual body, that he has a body that looks like our physical body in the astral realms. If that is the truth, why would he be so attached to his physical body and hover over the Earth?*

Thank you. In reference to your question of one's attachment to their physical body, when it is demonstrable that we have a mental and an astral body and many other bodies. However, we all accept that we have a mental body. We all accept that we are capable of forming, from mental substance, a thought. And we use it, usually, without much consideration. So the question is, Why, in man's awareness that he is more than a physical body, should he, after leaving a physical body, attach himself to an Earth planet where the physical body is the vehicle of movement? Is that not the question?

Yes.

That which moves a physical body is a mental body. Now ofttimes in our life we have so many experiences. We find our self attached, we believe, to a physical person. Due to seeming circumstances beyond our control at the time, the physical person leaves our universe. Now the question must arise, Does the mental person leave our universe? Are they no longer in our thought?

No. There they are.

Ever in keeping with our attachment to our belief through the Law of Identification that we are the limit known as a physical body, that we are the limit to that known as a mental body, an astral body, ever in keeping with the demonstrable Law of Personal Responsibility, we shall find our self in the realm of consciousness that we have, through over-identification with the vehicle, become bound to. And so when man becomes bound to the belief that he is the limit of his own mind, then man must live in the limit that he alone has created for himself. And so we find many people hovering close to earth, where a mental world moves physical bodies. Though man may have his hand amputated, man still has the sensation of the leg or the limb that has been amputated. For unless the amputation takes place within the mental consciousness, that limb still exists in a mental consciousness, although physically it has been removed. Does that help with your question?

Thank you.

You're welcome. Yes, the gentleman there, please.

It appears to me that Marin County is sitting astride what we call the San Andreas Fault. And half of the county is moving in one direction and half in the other. And that, like San Francisco and Point Reyes and Bodega Head are kind of comparable to ice hummocks that are being pushed up. Is this true?

Well, in reference to this particular county split in half, one part moving one way and another part moving another way, I think we would all agree that that which separates in consciousness is destined to separate in its effect known as physical substance. And so in reference to a question of that type, we must first awaken to our responsibility that we are not only responsible for the vehicle that we are presently using on this planet but we are directly responsible to everything on this planet. We are responsible for the elements for the intelligence flowing through us reveals to us clearly that that which is in accord, that which is harmonious, that which is united, is healthy. And, therefore, abundant good manifests itself.

And so, in reference to this split and division of which you speak, yes, that is in keeping with the laws firmly established. We, however, must never forget that we are only vehicles through which this infinite, intelligent Energy flows. We are not the intelligent Energy itself as long as we believe, through over-identification with limit, that we can control that which is limitless. Yes, your answer is affirmative.

The gentleman here, please.

Could you speak on life's greatest responsibility and how to fulfill the purpose of our being?

In speaking on life's greatest responsibility and how to fulfill our being—is that your question?

Yes, please.

All right. What does life reveal to us as our greatest responsibility? We look at life and we pause to think. Is good limited? Does the flower in its growth experience good? Does a man, sailing upon the sea, experience good? Does the blade of grass experience good? Does a human being, doing what they believe they must do based upon experience through the laws of association, do[ing] what they believe they must do, experience good, if they have judged that's how they will receive good? Is that not correct?

Yes.

Fine. Therefore, we look at life and we see there are many different types of flowers. There are many different types of animals. There are many different types of insects. And surely, many varieties of trees and shrubs. And yet, we cannot deny, as reasonable, intelligent beings, we cannot deny that there is an Energy flowing through them, that there is an intelligent Energy, for they have their cycles. They grow. They mature. They age and move on. To be replaced in kind by another generation of flowers and trees and etc. So if we only look at the forms, we see there is a refinement of that flower; it's now called a hybrid. There is a refinement of that tree. Man, we look only at the form and we see this change over the eons of time on our planet. We see what we judge: there's a greater refinement. Man is more capable of doing more complex things than before. Man, now, is no longer dependent on striking flint together to start a fire. Man has gone far beyond that, we say, when we look at form and we see what has been accomplished in a physical world.

And yet, even with great scientific advancement and with this phenomenal speed for accomplishment and advancements of technology, we see that they contain within them what we know as good. That they do contain good, would you not agree? And we must then ask our self, What is this that denies nothing, that no form is denied of its very essence to exist? What is this that does not deny us thinking badly or our thinking in what we call good? What is this intelligent Energy? How does it work? For there is no place that we can look and say it is denied, the dandelion in the field. There is no place in the universe that we can look and say some form has been denied this intelligent Energy. So what does this intelligent Energy demonstrate to any intelligent being? It demonstrates total acceptance. It demonstrates that the will or the movement of this infinite, intelligent Energy, this principle of demonstrable goodness that denies nothing, is a total acceptance of everything that it sustains. And there's nothing it does not sustain.

So what is man's greatest responsibility? To awaken within his consciousness; to free himself from the bondage of prejudice, which clearly reveals prejudgment based upon ignorance, the lack of effort to thoroughly investigate. Our greatest responsibility to life is to permit our self, by control of our own vehicle called our own mind, to accept the possibility and divine right of all expression throughout the universes. Because we accept the divine right of anything does not mean that we become a part of it. If you accept the divine right of one person to drink a cup of coffee and another to drink a glass of milk, if you accept the divine right of those two people to do that, then you are free from the bondage of prejudgment. And whoever frees themselves from the bondage of prejudice shall awaken within their own consciousness that God or good is everywhere; when *we* make the effort to see God or good in all things within our self, we will then qualify our self to see it without. And whoever sees the good within, experiences the good or God without and is freed from the bondage of his own ignorance and therefore, truly fulfilling his responsibilities to life. Does that help with your question?

Thank you.

You're welcome. The lady here, please.

Healing physical ailments through spiritual understanding.

Yes. In reference to that question—Is that a question?

Yes.

Yes.

How to go about it.

First of all, we must begin, in our acceptance of the demonstrable truth, [to accept] that our physical body is an effect of what is taking place in our mental body. Now we have accepted, some of us, to varying degrees, such a thing called psychosomatic medicine. None of us readily accept that our physical bodies are completely effects of our mental bodies. When there is discord, there is disease. When we have disturbances within our mental bodies, they reveal to us the discord, the disease in our physical bodies. To bring about corrective measures with this discord in our mental body—one cannot control what one believes they are a part of. One must disassociate from that belief. Therefore, the healing of the mental body and its effect upon the physical body must take place with a body that is not a part of a mental body. But a mental body is subject to the body which is doing the work.

Now when a person enters a state of consciousness where the movement of mental substance, known by man as thought, does not exist—and to accomplish that, one must free themselves from the belief that they are the thought that they identify with and, therefore, believe they are. Now life reveals clearly to each and every one of us that we had certain thoughts at a certain time in our lives, that we had certain judgments at a certain time in our lives and we no longer believe those judgments. We no longer believe those particular thoughts. Would you not agree? Hmm?

For all of us there are some thoughts that we can look in our hindsight and some judgments and say, "Now I no longer believe that way." However, when we have the thought and when we have the judgment and when we are over-identified with it, we believe that we are it.

All right. So we have an experience in reference to our health, which reveals there is discord within our being. It is manifesting, through our identification, in a physical body. It is the effect of a mental body. Now I don't mean to imply that we sit down and we say, "Now let me see, I want to be sick today. Which disease shall I choose?" It doesn't work like that. It can; it is in keeping with the law that is demonstrable. And it can make the physical, chemical changes necessary. No, we're more like children in that respect. When a child wants attention and it has tried many things and not received its attention, which is energy, the child will do many different things, including being sick. Now it is not the adult being within us that does that. It's what is known as the child. Most people refer to that little child as the emotions. And the emotions, we understand in the Living Light Philosophy, are instruments through which our judgments, that we believe we are, may express themselves. And so we find that at times in our lives we believe that we are ill, that we are sick.

Healing of the discord or disease is dependent upon the awakened consciousness. And the awakened consciousness is dependent upon our own effort to control our own mind, which, at the time, is discordant and our bodies are reaping the effect. It is most encouraging to anyone to pause and think, "It is within my power to make this change within my consciousness and experience the abundant good that is my divine right." When the consciousness is awakened, it will find other ways, more reasonable, to receive the energy that it needs for its own good.

You see, energy—we are as receptive to infinite, intelligent Energy as we control our mind and remove the obstructions. And so, spiritual healing is an effect of the harmonious flow cast over our mental body. For reason exists only in perfect harmony. And it is reason that will transfigure and transform us, for all judgments are effects of denials. All justifications are servants of those denials. All excuses, accidents, and seeming mere chance are effects of the denial of wisdom and truth. We are as good, as happy, as wealthy, as healthy as we will permit ourselves to be through our own effort to awaken. Does that help with your question?

Thank you. Yes.

You're welcome. We have time for . . .

One more. [The technician recording the class made this recommendation.]

One more question. Yes, the gentleman there, please.

Is there some truth in the saying that the one insult no man can tolerate is that he doesn't have any trouble?

Well, in reference to tolerance, I'm sure we cannot help but agree, what we cannot tolerate in another is waiting to be educated within our self. For the moment we educate these limits that we believe that we are, tolerance is no longer a problem for us. We only experience intolerance because we've yet to educate those judgments inside of our self.

Now many people—you can pick anything in the universe you'd like to pick. Well, let's pick the Russians. They seem to be popular again today. We cannot tolerate them for this and that. And do we know them all? Well, let's pick the French. Some of us can't even tolerate the Frenchmen. Or perhaps we can pick on the Spaniards. Some of us can't tolerate them. Some of us can't tolerate the Mexicans. Some of us can't tolerate the Germans. Some of us can't tolerate the Finn, the Swedish, the Swiss. Go down the list of our intolerances and we will get a much broader perspective on our prejudice. We'll leave Spiritualism out of it because that intolerance is a living demonstration; every knock is a boost. However, let's stop and think about these things. Let's awaken to the demonstrable truth of how intolerant we really are!

And yet, we seek and we search for success. Without tolerance, there is no success. What would have happened to the F. W. Woolworth Company and the founders if they decided and they made the judgment they would only permit certain races to enter their stores? I'm sure we would all agree they would not be as abundantly wealthy as they have demonstrated already. Or let's pick on Sears, Roebuck. And let us say that those founders decided that only certain colored people could enter their particular stores or could purchase from them.

We do it to our self. However, in doing it to our self, let us never forget, the weight of responsibility to a wise man never exceeds his love of God. For a wise man knows that the weight of responsibility is the judgment of his own mind. That's where weights are. And that the judgment is as heavy as his own belief that he is the judgment that he has made. So if you want the health, wealth, and happiness that is your divine birthright, don't give power to something beyond your own being to get it, for all that you desire reveals that's what you judge that you need. And that which you judge that you need is your payment for denying the truth of the good that you already are.

Thank you very much. And let us remember, our life is ever the way we make it and, of course, it's always the way we take it. Thank you.

FEBRUARY 3, 1985

Church Questions and Answers 55

As our chairman has already stated, this is your opportunity, once a month, to ask the questions that are of interest to you.

And, I think, before getting to those questions, if we will pause for a few moments and consider the exposure that all of us have earned in our present incarnation to the mass media communications of negativity, disaster, which instill within our consciousness even more fear of what tomorrow may bring. So often we think that it does not have any effect upon us. And it is ofttimes much later in our lives that we realize whatever we expose our self to has [an] effect upon us. How much affect that has upon us, of course, is in keeping with the laws of association within our own consciousness.

For example, we find that we go along in life and we hear so much negative news in reference to the financial condition of the United States and other countries. We hear so often about the ever-increasing cost of things. We go to the stores and we experience what the news has been speaking about, and we hear so often [about] so much illness and sickness in the universe. It has an effect upon us. We consciously do not like to think that it has an effect upon us because we are not personally relating to it. And we soon find that later on in our lives that it does, and has had, indeed, a deep effect upon us.

We are programmed from the time that we enter this Earth planet, as similar to the programming of a computer, with which we are all a bit, at least, familiar. And so, we are programmed to think in certain ways from early childhood. We establish certain types of thought patterns. We believe we are the effect of those thought patterns, known as judgments. And in keeping with, of course, our belief that we are those things, we indeed are affected by them.

So it is important for us to understand the process of our mind, considering it is the vehicle with which we are the most familiar. We are all aware of our feelings. We are less aware of the cause of our feelings. We are even less aware of the initial programming in our minds, very early in our lives, that have established, firmly, those judgments, which we believe, unfortunately, that we are.

When we leave this Earth planet, we only leave a physical body. We don't leave our thoughts. We don't leave our feelings. We don't leave what we believe that we are. And so, anyone who states that we leave a physical body to rise in a glorious hereafter, where angels with wings are playing harps and beautiful music—it indeed is a very fine dream established to escape reality.

But let us pause for a moment and let us be a bit more honest and realistic with our self. When the foot is amputated, in consciousness in our mind, we still have a foot. We only lost the physical foot. We cannot lose the foot of our mental body until we make changes within our consciousness. So the sensation of an amputated foot or a leg or an arm still remains within our consciousness, for we still have a mind and contained within that mind, like a computer, is a foot, an arm, a leg, and all the other things that we have programmed into that mind.

And so it is when we leave this physical world, we still have our hopes, our fears, our hates, our loves, our adversities, and our attachments. That's a mental world. That's the world we are familiar with. That's the world we leave the physical body with. However, that, of course, is not the only world that we have. For if it was the only world that we have, then what we know as suicide would instantaneously became a mass experience, for there are times when we wish to escape from this so-called mind of ours. When we believe that experiences are not in keeping with what we should have in life, that's the first thing we want to do, is deny personal responsibility and try to escape from it.

And there is something far greater than a mind. But the only way to experience that which is greater than the thought of man is to go beyond the thought of man. So we cannot go beyond our own thought until we first make that step to go beyond our belief. Now if we look honestly at our life's experiences, we readily and quickly see that we have believed many things. We have believed that we were going to be this in our early lives. We have believed that we were going to be that in our later lives. Only to grow and move along life's path to find that belief didn't quite hold up. That other belief didn't turn out the way that we believed that it would. We have fallen into love and we have believed that we were in love. If that were true, we wouldn't have fallen. And so, we've gone through many, many, many beliefs. And when we're honest with our self, we cannot help but see clearly that we are not what we believe. We only believe that we are what we believe, for our beliefs are in a constant process of changing. Therefore, that which is in a constant process of changing has no stability. It has no security.

No one in their right mind would rely upon that which experience has revealed to them is fickle and may change at any moment it chooses to change. Therefore, a wise man does not rely upon his mind for stability, for security, for happiness, for wealth, or for health. A wise man uses his mind in an effort to accomplish that which he desires. A wise man does not dictate that what he desires shall be filled in keeping with the judgments of his mind. A wise person does that which they know for them, in their evolution, is right for them to do. A wise person does not concern themselves with the fruits of action, knowing that the joy of life is in the effort, never in the reward. A person knows beyond a shadow of any doubt if they do not move their legs over a long period of time, their legs will no longer serve the purpose of their original design. And so a person does not seek permanency of satisfaction, knowing that permanency of satisfaction is the opposite of evolution, change, growth, and awakening.

No wise person chooses to sleep twenty-four hours out of twenty-four hours. No person consciously chooses to lose conscious awareness by an increase in their so-called satisfaction of sleep. What can a person consciously do with a mind and a body that is incapable of conscious thinking during a state of satisfaction known as sleep? No, one does not choose so foolishly to destroy themselves. Yet, we find in life that we spend much of our time, ignorantly, through our own error of ignorance, destroying our self. How are we able to accomplish that? It's truly quite simple. Look at someone that you don't like and you will be able to see more clearly how much they pity themselves, called self-pity, and that's why they're in the state of affairs that they're in. Do not look at someone that you like, for that reveals a degree of attachment, and you lose objectivity. You cannot see objectively, impartially, when you look at a person that there's any degree of attachment with, for you are in truth, through the blindness of the attachment, of course, looking in the mirror at our self. If you do not think that is true, then correct a child of another parent. You will soon see how quickly that law reveals itself.

And so, we look at that which we consider adverse to us and in so doing we quickly find the cause of the many faults of the individual. We can clearly see that they constantly think of themselves and in so doing they entertain within their consciousness the most destructive force known to the human mind. There is nothing more destructive to the human mind than the pity of self. It is the direction of intelligent energy to the absolute obstruction to the true purpose and design of the human mind. And so, each moment that we think of our self—it doesn't take many moments before we begin to experience, "What a terrible world this is! I haven't been feeling quite well lately. Now I think I'm feeling worse." And whatever it is, when you begin to think of your self, you can be rest assured there will be nothing but obstructions for you to view. For by looking only at our self, we shut our self off from that which we are.

We are infinite, intelligent, free, abundant good. That is what we are. We do not experience that when, through errors of ignorance, we limit our view. And therefore, the greatest healing we shall ever know is in following the demonstrable law that does not fail: God helps those who help themselves by helping others. When we work in life by a broadening of our horizon, each and every time that we work to lift another soul, without consciously thinking of lifting our own, the law fulfills itself. That's how God, the Principle of Good, truly works. Because we can only grant to another what we first grant unto our self. And so when we are the instruments through which another is assisted in awakening to help themselves—because each and every person, surely we realize, helps themselves.

We help our self to just about everything we can get our hands on to. But our hands are controlled by our minds. And so, when we pause and think, we see our minds indeed are very full, for our minds are helping themselves to everything they hear, everything they see, everything they sense, feel, touch, and can hold.

Now in keeping with that beautiful, demonstrable law of truth, remember, that which we hold destroys us; that which we free unfolds us. Many a parent over these forty-four years has come for counseling in reference to their children, in reference to their lives slowly—the lives of the parents—slowly but surely deteriorating and their goodness and peace and harmony and happiness being destroyed. And the instrument of the destruction, oh, is not the child: it is the thought of the child in the parent's consciousness. That is what destroys us. It's what we hold in our mind. It's not what we free in our mind that destroys us.

Love is love. If we permit our self to deceive our self and permit our minds to tell us that love is what we can hold, control, manipulate, and have serve us as a tool for selfish desire, we soon learn in life, someday, that's not love. That is lust. The lust of the human mind.

And so, we must pay for the error of ignorance, for ignorance is no escape from law. Law is impartial. Law has no feeling. Law has no emotion. Law has no personality. Law is blind to the fickleness of creation. Law has no form. Law has no special interest. And that, known as Law, Divine Law, the Principle of Good, known by man as God, is the only thing we shall ever find—if you can call it a thing—it is the only thing that is reliable. It is the only thing that will not fail. You cannot manipulate it. There's no possible way to control it. It's a total waste of energy to even tempt one's mind to do so.

So often we find a person saying, "I have fallen in love." And how true it is. Fallen, not risen. I've yet to hear a voice speak in this world of creation that they have risen in love. No, that would mean the Principle of Good. We seem to fall in love. And fall, indeed, we do, if the controlling of another being is what we call love. We find so many marriages, we find so many divorces, we find so much so-called happiness only to guarantee the opposite, known as sadness. And why do we find that? Why is the honeymoon so short-lived? What makes it so short-lived? Is it because we, in truth, are growing much faster than we realize? And that the average honeymoon in the world today is a seeming miracle if it goes beyond six months? Is it quite possible that we are growing at such a rapid speed in this great nuclear, atomic age in which we live? Then, indeed, it is encouraging that we can awaken in six short months that we may gain a new perspective on what love truly is.

Whoever loves, truly loves, has no want, no need, and no desire. God is love. The Principle of Good is its expression. Love contains, as an indispensable ingredient to its own expression, it contains the soul faculty of respect. If we do not respect the goodness within our self, and in keeping with the law that we can only grant to another what we first grant unto our self, then it is not possible for us, under the guise of love, to respect the rights of an individualized soul. If it is true—and it is demonstrably true—that the honeymoon is a limited view, limited by our own selfish desire, and that desire does not evolve and expand itself and grow up and educate itself to respect, then no relationship can possibly endure, whether it is the relationship with another human being or the relationship between a person and a flower, a person and a cat or a dog.

Our needs in life are the effects of our own denials. We did not consciously in our very early formative years deny the goodness of life. We were programmed by those who were in charge of our upbringing. So is it our parents' fault that we experience so much need, the effect of our own denials? No, it's not our parents' fault. Our soul came to earth in keeping with its own evolutionary path. There were no other parents that we could experience this earth experience through. They were the ones that we alone have earned. And we should be indeed grateful that they were on earth so we could get here. Because if they weren't here, we would have to wait until the right combination got here for us to learn the lessons that we have to learn.

Now because all things take place within our own mind, that all experiences and all thoughts, all feelings, all needs, all denials take place within our own mind, and because that mind is a subject and a servant of the Intelligence that we are, we can do something about everything in our life. There is no thing that we cannot do something about. Because it's our mind. It's our thought. It is our judgment. Now a person says, "My daughter is doing things that are most detrimental to my life. What can I do about my daughter? What can I do about my son?" Well, our daughters and our sons are forms that we have created within our own consciousness. Our consciousness is our ship of destiny. Now we can once again be the captain of our ship. And we can tell the ship exactly what port it's going to or no port at all. It's our ship. It's our mind. It's our thought. It is our judgment.

Now a person may say, "Well, now my son is under my own roof. How can I make these changes to get him to do what I want him to do?" Well, it's quite simple. Birds of a feather flock together. Like attracts like and becomes the Law of Attachment. If we make the changes within our consciousness, that which is not similar to us shall very soon go of its own accord. If we are married and we do not appreciate what our wife is doing—or if the wife does not appreciate what the husband is doing, she can state clearly her case, without emotion, for that will reveal her freedom from attachment. Without emotion is the light of reason. She or he may state their case clearly, honestly with themselves. If that is not in harmony with the other, there is no problem at all. Whoever is being disturbed by the problem is the one who has the problem, for that which disturbs us is that which controls us. And so, if the wife is disturbed by what the husband is doing, she is the one that has the problem. She is the one that must make the changes within her consciousness. And if it's the other way around, then he is the one, being the one disturbed, who must make the changes.

So from that awakening we go to work with our own mind, where we can do something. We make the necessary changes and we soon find out in life that he or she grows or goes. Now, being adults, we know that babies don't always grow with laughter and a smile on their face. We know there are times when they scream, when they have tantrums. And so, prepare yourself when you start to grow, for that that is around you will either grow with you or, kicking and screaming, be dragged up some hilltop somewhere, but not in your life. Thank you.

Now it's time for any questions that you may have. I hope I haven't spoken too long. If you will be so kind as to raise your hands. The gentleman there, please.

There is something that's been going on recently in the news that I've been wondering about for a long time that has to do with restrictions on imports and exports with the various countries. I've always felt, ideally, that we were trying to evolve into a state of borderless nations and equal monetary systems, things along those lines. And yet, right now I observe our government establishing restrictions or when they let up restrictions, as they have over the last couple of days regarding the Japanese car imports, everybody is up in arms and screaming about how it's going to destroy our economy. Can you offer me some sort of awareness or solution regarding that whole situation?

Well, I'll be most happy to share with you our understanding. And it's a very, very important question to all people throughout the world, and it is not something that is new. It is—at this time, we are discussing trade embargoes, trade exchanges. As far back as human history records on the planet Earth there has always been the various tribes working diligently to protect their people, their society, from contamination of alien ways of life, of foreign and alien false gods or things of worship.

Now specifically today we're speaking in your question of the United States and its open-door policy and then its closing door policy, and its open-door policies and closing door policies. We first must consider and respect the various civilizations on our planet, the various customs of the different countries, the multi-varied priorities of the peoples and their cultures of different countries. Now, the United States spent most of the years of its history in a state of isolationism. It is only in recent times that the United States of America opened its doors to become the Santa Claus of the planet Earth. You hear? Now, has it been or is it in the best interests of any country to, number one: be a complete isolationist; to, number two: to be a wide open-door policy of trade? The light of reason must be used.

And so it's like an individual, for a country is nothing more than a combination of many individuals. We move ofttimes in life from total restriction in our experiences to the direct opposite of total license. At the present state of the evolution of the United States of America, it is in a process of balance between the isolationism of the past and the wide open-door policy of these latter years. That balance is coming about. It is difficult. It is difficult even for an individual to move from total restrictions in their life to total license and then come to some degree of reason and sensibility, would you not agree?

And so, here we have this fluctuating situation and our economic reports reveal clearly, if the United States of America continues with a wide open-door policy, its culture and its own prosperity, based upon material wealth, will come into a drastic change that the people of the country will not accept. Therefore, balance is in the process of being brought about from an open-door policy to a—from a closed-door policy to an open-door policy to a reasonable, sensible import-export [policy]. Does that help with your question?

Thank you, sir.

And I accept by your question you were interested in the position of the United States, is that correct?

Yes.

Thank you. The lady behind you, please.

When you talked about that our parents had to be in the right place at the right time for us to come, and then people talk about people that they've known in previous lives.

Oh?

It would seem to me that the design is pretty set. That they had to also enter with their parents being in the right place at the right time. And is there such a thing as what they call soul mates, people that we lived [with] before on this planet or another planet?

The only time that we have an awakening that we have always been, therefore, by that law, shall always be, is when we're in the sunlight of reason. That's when we know. When we leave the shadows and enter the light, we know beyond a shadow of any doubt, for there are no doubts in the light. Doubts are the effects of shadows, which are nothing more than what obstructions cast upon the light of reason. That's all that doubts are. That's all that shadows are: the effects of obstructions. So when we enter the light within our own consciousness we go beyond question, we go beyond doubt. There is nothing new under the sun. Does that help with your question? *[After a short pause, the teacher continues.]*

Not quite. You want something to satisfy the judgment. Well, you know, I'm very outspoken, perhaps that's why so few people come sometimes. But it's not for numbers that we speak. You see, we are prompted to ask a question—now let us think and let us grow in the process—we are prompted by a judgment of our mind that has not been satisfied. Would you not agree?

Yes.

Now that's very human. That's what prompts questions in our mind. You see, we are also censored by our pride. And therefore, sometimes we find great difficulty in questions being asked and sometimes we have no problem. It depends on whether or not the judgment has been dissatisfied long enough to prompt us to override the censorship of our pride that tells us we should know the answer to that anyway. Does that help with your question? Now we'll move on to the rest of it.

And so, you want to really know if you have a soul mate.

Yes.

Well, yes, I understand. Well, if you are looking at creation, you see clearly that all things appear to be half. Nothing appears whole. Is that correct? Isn't that a way it appears? For the manifestation of life, there takes two halves. Would you not agree?

Yes.

It takes the negative and the positive. That's creation. Indeed, it is. And in order to have the manifestation in creation, you must have a mate. Would you not agree?

Yes.

Why, even a dog and a cat has to have a mate. All things in creation must mate in order to manifest. Does that view of creation limit us to being whole, complete, and perfect? Would it not depend on what we identify with? Fine. Now, we are Spirit formless and free. Being formless, being free, being truth, for that's what we are, we can only be limited by identifying with limit or form. Correct? So when we are identified with limit, we're only half there and, therefore, we are not fulfilled. Would you not agree?

Yes.

When we no longer identify with limit, we are whole, complete, and perfect. Therefore, we do not experience need. We only experience need, we only experience the need of unfulfillment by denial of what we are and believing what we are not. So as long as we identify with the limits of our mind, we can only be half there. Does that help with the question?

Yes.

Thank you. Are there any other questions?

Now I know that none of us like to think we're only half there, but it's not anyone else's fault if we choose to believe we are unfulfilled and only half there because we don't have the other half to control. Would that not help, you see? And so, in keeping with that, we can clearly see that our beliefs are effects of our own denials.

This is why this philosophy teaches and demonstrates that acceptance is the divine will. The Divine Will, God, is the Principle of Goodness. So man experiences through his own acceptances, and if he chooses to accept to deny what he is by believing what he is not, then he must pay the price of the transgression of that demonstrable law and feel, think, and be only half there.

Now sometimes I say to my students, "Are you out to lunch? Or are you out to breakfast? Or are you out to breakfast, lunch, dinner, and snack?" *[Some members of the congregation laugh.]*

You see. Our physical bodies are ofttimes someplace we are not. Then we wonder, "What was it they said? What happened there? I can't remember. Isn't that strange?" Well, how can you remember what went on when your body was there—it's like leaving your shoes and you're walking down the street; your body's there, your mind is someplace else.

You see, we have many bodies, but because we so over-identify with the flesh, we don't even pause to think that there's another body someplace else doing something. There's an astral body. There's a mental body. There's an emotional body. There's all kinds of bodies and that it's our vital energy that is flowing to them and we are the directors of that intelligent energy.

We are all extremely successful. I know many, many, many successful people. Many. Ex-students and present students. We are successful at failing at whatever we choose to fail at. We are successful of experiencing what we call accomplishment at whatever we choose to accomplish. We succeed at whatever we really want to do. The problem is we can't remember, it seems, from moment to moment what it is we really want to do. We want to do something on Tuesday. By Saturday, it's totally changed. We experience what we say is failure on Saturday because we forgot what we desired on Tuesday. Now I find that a most interesting thing. I'm sure you all do.

And if there are any more questions—our time is really just about up on this. The lady here, please.

Mr. Goodwin, will you please explain why 10 percent free will? Why not 5 or 6 or 8 percent?

Well, in reference to the teachings of the Living Light Philosophy that man has 10 percent free will to change whatever laws he has set into motion—and you want to know why it isn't 5 percent, 1 percent or hopefully, maybe a hundred percent. We don't have a hundred percent. Once you establish a law, once you first have a thought you entertain in consciousness, the thought you permit to flood your consciousness until it becomes an established thought pattern, the effect or expression of the thought pattern, known to be—which it is—a judgment, and through over-identification with the mental body, known as the human mind, you believe, through over-identification, that you are the judgment, you have established the Law of Cause, and you are destined to pay the effect of the law, known as experience.

Now you have established the law known as the law of the totality of form or creation. Now totality, and I'm sure we will all agree, totality, the number of totality, the highest number there is, is the number nine. It is the line of infinity. It is the circle of old eternity. And so, having established the totality of that Law of Creation, you have left only the light of reason, known as God or the Principle of Good, available to you to bring about the changes in that law by establishing new laws to neutralize the forthcoming experience.

Now how much energy, how much identification, how much belief will that take to neutralize a negative law established by our minds in our own errors of ignorance? It will take [an] equal amount of energy that it took to establish the original law. Equal. Now first of all, a person knows how much they think about something that they believe that they need, that they believe that they desire. We know how much energy we direct to it through identification with it. It will take an equal amount of energy to establish an opposite law in the world of creation in order to neutralize the negative law established in ignorance so that we do not have the experience coming our way. Now if you want to have an opposite experience, then you must put more energy into a new law after the other negative law has been neutralized. Yes. Did you have another question?

Yes, sir. Can you please explain, you said something about thought and judgment—Is thought judgment?

It is—judgment is the effect of thought. I'll take a few moments and then—

We're out of tape. [The vice president informs the teacher that the audio cassette recording the class is almost full.]

We're out of tape.

On this side.

Well, then, you just have to turn it over. *[The conversation continues as the tape is being turned over. Once changed, the class resumes.]*

Now, you have a question in reference to thought and judgment. Judgment is the effect of thought. It's the final end of it, you see. You have a thought. You think that you need something in life. You think that you need, perhaps, happiness. This seems to be a very common need with people. You *think* you need happiness. The reason we think we need happiness is because we believe that we don't have it. The reason that we believe we don't have it is because a judgment rises in our consciousness and tells us it's not having its own way. You see, we have within our subconscious, we have a whole package that says "Happiness." Now happiness is dependent upon that, that, that, that, and that. Now when we permit our mind to over-identify with form (self), with self, we push the button and up comes the judgments that say, "I don't have what I need." Now we *believe* that we are those feelings that rise within us.

A few people, through—you know, every philosopher has taught know thyself and you shall know the truth and the truth shall set you free. But we're not making the effort to know our self. We have a feeling. We think and we believe we are the feeling and we don't pause to know ourselves, to understand that is a judgment, which is the effect of a thought pattern, which was created by the over-identification with a thought within our mind way back when. And so, we go through our life and all of a sudden we say, "I'm unhappy." And when you—you see, it's a question that comes into the mind. And we keep our self so distracted, so tempted with creation, we're not even aware anymore, rarely aware, "Why do I think I'm unhappy?" If we were truly making the effort to know our self, we would hear this judgment-form come up within the subconscious and tell us, "I am unhappy. I represent happiness and I don't have that, that, that, that, and that. Therefore, I am unhappy. This is what you do."

You see, that which we do not make the effort to control controls us. If we do not make the effort to control what we are responsible for, we very quickly learn in life we are controlled by it. More than one parent will tell you, later in their life, "I thought I made the effort, but I did not make the effort. And now I am controlled by that which I was responsible for and I am helpless." That is what's happening to us. You see, we have a feeling. We have a thought. We *think* we have a thought. We believe we are the thought. And it's a judgment from who knows when and from where. Have we in that moment—and there are several laws involved. Is it our own personal experiences? Or have we over-identified with another person and, through the Law of Personal Responsibility, over-identifying with another person, begun to experience the judgments that another person believes that they are? Did that help with your question?

Very much. Thank you.

You're welcome. Now that he's turned the tape over, we might go to another question. Yes, thank you.

The question I have has to deal with semantics. We, we—

Semantics?

Semantics.

Oh, semantics. Yes.

Oh, sorry. There's a legal definition of what is an act of God. And then there's—

A legal [definition.] I see.

Kind of a philosophical question. What's the difference between an act of God and a phenomenon of nature?

Well, not being a lawyer, though some of my students are attorneys at law, I do not feel qualified to answer the legal aspect of your question. However, in reference to our understanding of what God is and the expression of God, I would be happy to share with you.

Thank you.

Would you like us to share that?

Yes, please.

I see. And the question appears to be, What is the difference between an act of God and the phenomena of nature?

Yes.

What do you understand the "phenomena of nature"—what do you mean the "phenomena of nature"? Do you mean the forms of creation? Do you mean the winds and the tides of the ocean? Do you mean the variety? Or do you mean the expression of that variety, by the "phenomena of nature"? Do you mean the design of the various forms? Or do you mean that Intelligence which causes them to activate? Hmm?

Yes.

Which is it would you like to discuss?

Ah . . .

The purpose of their design? The Intelligence that causes them to be active instead of inactive? Or the purpose of being? What purpose do they serve? You see, there are several questions that must be asked in reference to a statement of an active God and the phenomena of nature.

First of all, an active God—we understand that God is the Principle of Good. That's what God is. Spiritualists call it Infinite Intelligence. However, an active God implies and suggests that there is such a thing as an inactive God. Therefore, we cannot discuss with you an active God, for we do not find such a thing as an inactive God. So for us to discuss an active God would necessitate our accepting the delusion of an inactive God. The Principle of Good is the Principle of Good. It's not active or inactive, only to a person who chooses—it's like the air. If you choose not to breathe, does that demonstrate there is no air available? If you choose not to breathe it? No, no. If man chooses not to see God, the Principle of Good, does that prove that God does not exist? Does that prove that God—if man has very poor business relationships with people, does that prove there is no good in the world? No. So, you see, our God is as active for us as we will make it so.

The good in our life is subject to and dependent upon our willingness to grow up. Now if we're not willing to grow up, then we must not expect the abundant good which is waiting for us. You see, goodness waits for us only in the sense it's ever available. It's up to us to grow up and accept it.

And so, the phenomena of nature is served by the greatest servant any universe could ever know. God is not a creator. God is not a judge. God is the Divine Principle of Good, denying to nothing and to no thing its sustaining power. And that which sustains the thoughts of the minds of men is far superior than that thought that it sustains. So if a person wants to experience the good of life, they must go to the Source of the good of life. The only thing that keeps us from going to the Source of the good of life is believing that the good in our life is ever subject to and dependent upon our own control.

We can control everything within our mind. We waste all our energy and our efforts to control that which is uncontrollable. God, being a servant, is not subject to the thoughts of man, for God sustains the thoughts of man. Man has the right to choose the thoughts that are constructive or the ones that are destructive. I do hope that's helped with your questions.

Thank you.

Thank you very much.

MARCH 3, 1985

Church Questions and Answers 56

As our chairman has already stated, this is the once-a-month opportunity for you to ask your questions that you have found of interest to you. So if you will be so kind as to raise your hands, I will be more than happy to share with you that which I receive.

The gentleman on the aisle, back there, please.

Thank you. I'd like to clarify some difference of opinion. In some religious doctrines they teach that we're born in sin. And then there's others that say—which I interpret that to mean, you know, we're born in ignorance. Some say that ignorance is bliss and what a man doesn't know won't hurt him. Would you care to comment on that, please? Thank you.

Well, if, in reference to your question of the various teachings of different religions and philosophies, that some teach that man is born in sin and ignorance and [people] have many different understandings of that statement, if we understand that, as you have stated, that ignorance is bliss, what we don't know won't hurt us, and, of course, what we don't know, what we are ignorant of, if we're ignorant of the laws of the land, we are blissful until our debt comes due and we must pay for our own transgressions of laws that we, through lack of effort, chose to be ignorant of. Therefore, in reference to ignorance being blissful, I think the divorce courts of our land will prove that the bliss is a very temporary state and many other things in this world of creation prove to us daily that the blissfulness of ignorance is very short-term, for none of us sleep forever.

We sleep at times, in what is known in the Living Light Philosophy, as satisfaction. We are satisfied, only to awaken to be tempted to be satisfied again, to awaken and to gradually, slowly but surely, to evolve to that state in consciousness known as personal responsibility. And once we evolve to that state of consciousness, we are no longer controlled by what we believe is beyond our ability to control.

Now everyone—that is, if you're speaking of our minds, of our physical form—[merits a form that] is in keeping with the laws that we alone have set into motion in the evolution of our eternal being. Our eternal being cannot, by the living demonstration, be our physical body, for we already experience its constant process and change. It cannot, by our own demonstration, be our mind and the thoughts thereof, for we see, moment by moment, the constant process of changing. We have a thought for a time, only to replace it with another. Some thoughts we hold to tenaciously, year after year. We hold to them only because we believe for a time that we are the thought and the judgment of our mind.

And so in reference to being born in ignorance, in keeping with the Law of Form, we are a part, that is, in form, of our parents, and therefore we are born into a mental body that is composed of what our parents had to offer us. We are affected and, therefore, controlled in keeping with that mental program. We are controlled by circumstances and conditions that we expose our self to, for we believe that we are them. Therefore, belief is limited to and dependent upon a mental world and the minds of men. We demonstrate that truth each day. We believe this, only to change and believe something else. But that is not what we are; that is what we believe we are. Because we are not those ever-changing judgments and belief does not free us from our responsibility that we have to them. For we are responsible for all that we create and, of course, including the thoughts of our own mind. We are responsible for entering into certain circumstances and conditions at the moment of conception. We bear with us in our evolution that responsibility.

The longer we choose to make no effort to awaken, the longer we believe in the so-called bliss or absence of personal responsibility in our life does not keep us free from it. We are only ignorant of the laws and especially ignorant of our responsibility for them. We are responsible for the air we breathe. To say to ourselves, "What can I do about it when everyone is polluting it?" we deny our personal responsibility of being a part of the whole. We can do everything about anything that is within our domain of responsibility. We can change the air we breathe. We can change the thoughts we think. We can and are changing the world we live in. Because through our own choice not to face that responsibility does not exempt us from being a part of the effect that we experience in our life. Does that help with your question?

Thank you.

You're welcome. The lady here, please.

Can you please speak to us on the situation in South Africa and how we can best serve to help that?

Well, are you referring, in reference to South Africa, are you referring to the political situation in South Africa? Are you referring to our awareness of the conditions in South Africa? As I just spoke to the gentleman here a moment ago, we are responsible for the world in which we live. Now if in the world in which we live, we recognize—and by recognition we, of course, must accept. You cannot see what you do not accept exists. This is the great difficulty we have with our minds. We look at the flowers. We accept that they're flowers in keeping with what is already programmed in our mind and therefore we recognize them as flowers. And so we find that our world is subject to and is dependent upon what we accept and what we reject.

We find in life that which we deny or reject we are destined to experience. This is how, in our life, we find that our adversities are guaranteed to become our attachments. And so, if we're unhappy with something, all we have to do is to continue to think about it, all we have to do is to continue to put our attention upon it, known as the Law of Identification, and if we thought we were unhappy yesterday, we have yet to face tomorrow. Because whoever sees the obstructions in life never finds the way.

What does that have to do South Africa? It has everything to do with South Africa. We can look at any situation in the world and we can do something about it within our own domain. Few people, outside of the American Indian tribes of long ago and some of the various primitive tribes, accept the power that flows through them is directed by their own mind. That power, known as God, the Principle of Goodness, is constantly available to us. We can use that as we use the thoughts of our mind. We can use that in a constructive, beneficial way. When we take a look at our world and we see how receptive we are to what we call mass advertising, mass programming, when we see how truly receptive we are, then we can awaken to what is within us, what we can really do.

We accept moment by moment what is negative and detrimental to our life. We can accept moment by moment what is good and beneficial to our life. Now we cannot grant to another what we do not first grant unto our self. We cannot grant abundant good, we cannot grant the joy of life, we cannot grant the happiness and health that is our birthright to another if we blatantly refuse to grant it to our self. We cannot grant control over our mind unless we make the conscious effort to do so.

We can do everything in our world about South Africa or anyplace else or anything else because we have the ability to create. We are creators. We create our thoughts. And the masses in their seeming blissful ignorance are receptive to whatever the predominant thoughts are in the atmosphere. If you choose to become a part of discord, then you must pay the price of what discord offers, for discord is a lack of harmony. It's known by the minds of men as disease, the opposite of ease and peace and goodness. So if you want to do something about the suffering masses, do something about the suffering self, for we cannot grant to the suffering masses the goodness that we do not first grant unto our self. We have and we bear that responsibility to our self, to the world in which we live and breathe.

If we cannot awaken with a thought of good and we cannot experience that goodness which flows through the vehicle known as the thought of our own mind, if we insist on denying our right to abundant good, then we do not have that to grant to others. If we insist on believing that our God is a stingy God, if we insist on believing that our God, the Principle of Goodness, grants to others, by some partial choice, and refuses to grant to us, if we insist on believing that way, that's all we can offer to the world. That's all we can offer to Ethiopia. That's all we can offer to South Africa. So as many philosophies and religions have taught, "O physician, heal thyself," for in the healing of thyself are we qualified to be instruments through which others may be healed through an awakening to, "It is possible for one, therefore, by demonstration of the law, it is possible for me." I do hope that's helped with your question.

Thank you.

The gentlemen there, please.

I'm both confused and concerned about all the coverage and the tragedy of AIDS. And I can't help but wonder whether it's a great misfortune—and I find it hard to believe that it could be the wrath of God. And wondered what the church thought about it.

Well, I will speak as the minister and founder of the church. And I know that many, of course, will agree with me and I know that many will disagree. And that's the type of church that Serenity has and has always had. You speak of a specific disease, known to our minds as AIDS. And the question is, or the statement is, Is it the wrath of God? Then what kind of a God would do such a thing to so many people? Well, I can assure you, first of all, I am not one of those believers in the wrath of God. I am not one of those believers in the fear of God. I am not one of those believers in the partiality or "Santa Claus" God.

I do, however, accept what has, and is, demonstrable for me. God is an intelligent Energy, infinite, has always been and, by the law of always being, shall always be. Therefore, that is beyond question and no one can prove or disprove the Principle of Goodness. They can agree or disagree with the Principle of Goodness. They can say it does exist for them or it doesn't, or it is subject upon their begging and their pleading, their rabbit's foot, and all their superstitious foolishness. That we can do.

However, we all get to that point of growing up someday. And we take a look at life with a little different view and we see clearly that what we experience in life, though we may have been ignorant of, is an effect, only an effect, as all experiences are effects, effects of, through our own ignorance, of establishing laws that bring various things into our life.

I accept that there's good in all things. It doesn't matter what the mind calls it. There is the potential of good in all things. Sometimes we look at something and say, "I can see no good or God in that." Then we deny that God, the Principle of Goodness, the Infinite Intelligence, sustains all life. Just because we disagree with one person's lifestyle or another person's lifestyle, because we do not agree with what they want or don't want, does in no way deny the demonstrable law that without Infinite Intelligence to sustain it, it could not exist.

Now what is the good in disease? Would that not be your question?

Somewhat. The whole tragedy, I mean, the innocent victims, babies, and people who have nothing to do with—

Who is to say who is innocent and who is guilty? This is the question we must address. All philosophers have taught judge not that ye be not judged. So when we become the judge of what is good and what is bad, when we become the judge of how Infinite Intelligence shall be permitted to express itself, then perhaps we'll mow down all the dandelions. Perhaps all the weeds will no longer exist on the planet. Perhaps some of the trees that we don't agree with, that we don't see the usefulness of them, perhaps those, too, shall be chopped down. My good friend, listen to what your light of reason says within you. The moment that we rise to judge what God is and God isn't, in that moment do we deny the very Principle of Goodness in our life.

And so, we find what we believe—it's what *we* believe. We believe if such and such happened to us, it would be a great tragedy. That's our right to that belief. We do not know, for we are not having the experience, whether or not that so-called seeming tragedy is permitting a soul to be freed from this tired, old world of creation. We do not know, for we are not having the experience yet. We do not know if we shall have the experience. We do not know that the way we live is not a great tragedy to other people. We can go only next door—we don't even have to go to Russia or China or anyplace else to ask them if they think our life is a tragedy, for I can guarantee you in keeping with their programming they're absolutely convinced that our life is a tragedy. And so, tragedy and suffering is a very individual perspective and it is totally dependent on whether or not we would want or choose or [have] the desire for that seeming tragedy in our own personal lives. Now if you have a cold, is it a tragedy? Can you so-called die from that step of having a cold? Is it not possible? It could become pneumonia, couldn't it?

I guess.

You never heard of any one passing on from pneumonia?

Well, I have, not in—

Then it's possible, right? And so, having a common cold establishes the law and the potential of leaving this physical world, would you not agree? However, because we have accepted that having a common cold is a very common thing, it's no longer a tragedy, is it? Would you not consider it a tragedy to the person when it moves from a common cold to pneumonia and to passing from this world? Then would it be a tragedy? *[After a short pause, the teacher continues.]* Pardon? Would it be a tragedy or would it be the wrath of God?

It would be a tragedy.

I see. Well, my friends, when we accept personal responsibility, we will take a look at life not from a point of judging what is good or bad, not from a point of judging what is right or wrong for another, not of a point of judging that we do not have what we should have because of what someone else is doing or not doing. When we all grow, we will take a look at the world [and] we will see the beauty of the world and we will know beyond a shadow of any doubt that God and goodness is everywhere. The only thing that puts the light out for us is what we know as our own thought, our own judgments. It is only when we rise superior to the Divine Spirit that sustains our very thoughts, it is only when *we* become greater than the Principle of Good that we see a wrath of God. Does that help with your question?

Yes, you've made it somewhat—a lot clearer. Thank you.

Thank you. Are there any more questions? The lady there, please.

How does somebody recognize that they have healing powers?

All things, whether it is the flower in the meadow, the human animal, or the four-legged animal, all life contains within its very being what is known as healing or restoration. Now, you see, healing, what we call and understand healing in the Living Light Philosophy is the unobstructed flow of the Law of Harmony. We have many people over these thirteen years go into our healing chapel. *[As is the custom in many Spiritualist churches, a portion of the devotional services of the Serenity Spiritualist Church was dedicated to healing.]* Our healers are there in their meditation as instruments through which this Law of Harmony may flow unobstructed. If they think of themselves, they're not a good instrument, for it is the nature of the human mind, being created under the laws of creation, which is duality, for each good thought, to contain its opposite. Therefore, a healer that *is* a healer has control over their mind, control over their emotion, and through a daily effort of meditation—it doesn't guarantee it—it only offers the potential, the possibility to make some effort to control one's own judgments, one's own thoughts for a time. Now each person has that ability.

When we pause that we may experience the harmony, the joy of life, when we begin to make that effort, there's always something rising up to rob us of the serenity of the moment. That something is ever the shadows of what has been. We know beyond a shadow of any doubt that we can do everything with the moment of which we are conscious. We can do everything now, this moment. All things to the Principle of Good are possible in this moment. Therefore, only this moment, moment by moment, does a wise man direct his energy, through the avenue of identification. That takes control of one's mind.

We are plagued by what has been, for we *believe* we are the thoughts of our mind. And yet, when we are honest with our self and we view how many thoughts are in our mind and how many millions of thoughts we have already experienced, we do not agree in believing that we are the thoughts of our mind. We demonstrate that belief, that bondage when we permit our self to identify with what has passed. When we permit our minds to identify with what has passed in our life, even though it's a moment ago, and we believe we are that which has been, we lose the goodness of life in that moment.

The restoration of harmony in our life, the freedom from discord and disease is dependent on our conscious choice moment by moment. If we cut our hand, its time for healing is dependent upon our belief that we are our hand. The stronger our belief that we are the physical hand, the longer it takes to heal, for it is the identification of the discord of our own mind that interferes with the natural restoration of harmony. And so, we can heal our self of any discord of any disease at any moment that we choose. And we can, in so doing, once again experience our divine right to health, wealth, and happiness.

Now some people with seeming healthy bodies have very unhealthy minds. And some people with very healthy minds seemingly have unhealthy physical bodies. What is healthy and what is unhealthy? Peace is the power, the unobstructed flow of the divine Law of Harmony. It does not benefit man to have a perfect physical body at the expense of losing peace of mind. If the foot must be removed that we may once again experience that which we are, the perfect peace, the harmony and goodness, then it is beneficial, of course. Remove the foot, for we are not the foot. It is our belief that is our bondage. It is our own belief that is the obstruction to the goodness that we are.

Life is a mirror; she reflects our life of where we are at any moment. If we are confused, the reflection is cloudy. If we are still in our minds, the reflection is very clear. And so, when we find those moments when we stumble and we seek the restoration of the goodness in our life, that which we truly are, it's available to us if we truly are willing and we have made our self ready, for we are all able to restore that goodness in our life. Whoever believes they are their experience is destined, on the wheel of karma, to the bondage of old creation. Does that help with your question?

Yes, thank you.

The lady, here, has a question.

Yes. I'm interested in the Old Man and how he—he's in this—he works through you. Ah . . .

Well, you're interested in the father of our philosophy, is that it?

Yes.

I see. Well, then the only thing I could suggest for you: we have available almost 600 direct-taped sessions. And it would be in your best interests, if you're interested in any subject, to check and find that which you're interested in, that you may study what you are interested in. And that would be the best way [to accomplish] something of that nature. For of what benefit is a person or their history unless it is the only avenue through which we will permit our self to awaken, to grow, to learn the laws that are demonstrable and to apply them? Would you not agree?

People come and people go. What lives on that can benefit us in life? Only the law that we know beyond a shadow of any doubt does not fail. There's one thing we can all be assured of: the law doesn't fail us. Not the laws that the minds of men have made. The laws that are; they do not fail us. If we want to believe in poverty, if we want to believe disaster, if we want to believe in tragedy and horror, if we want to believe in the suffering, if we want to believe we have no money, the law does not fail us. The law guarantees that we can prove how right we are. You see, we make great effort with our minds to prove how right we are. And so, when we believe we have no happiness, we are the living demonstrations of misery, the opposite of happiness.

And so, looking at it from a positive view, "I have a right to choose my thought. This thought has proven in my life to bring me the experiences of goodness. I choose this thought, this thought pattern." If we must judge—and judge we must as long as we identify with what we believe is self—then let's at least direct it to something that is good in our life. Let's believe in the abundant good. We have proven what our beliefs have already offered us. We have proven how the economy has almost gone into a total disaster. However, it didn't. And then we had to work on our minds to say, "Well, I wasn't right that time." We have listened to the prophets of doom that the state of California was going to go by an earthquake, now, for years. It hasn't happened yet. We listen to the weather man who says we're going to have a drought this summer because months ago it wasn't supposed to rain anymore. So, you see, life is what you choose to make it. And we're all in a process, in our mind, of believing this and believing that. Why not believe something that you already know brings good into your life?

Believe, so that you are not dependent on something you can't control, for woe to the man or woman who believes in something they can't control. If that was not true, then our divorce courts would not be filled. When we believe in something we can't control, then we have problems. When we believe in that which is our right (something that we can control) we have no problems. So when we believe that we don't have the goodness of life because of something out there or someone out there—many people believe that they don't have the goodness of life because their wife is doing this or that, or, perhaps, she's not working on three jobs. Many men believe that the problem is the woman that they've married. Many women believe that the husband should be doing more than what they are doing. But, you see, they can control themselves, but they can't control their husband. They can't because that's another human being. That's contrary to the law of the individual right, you see. And many people choose to believe that had they not made the mistake and married the person they did that they would have all of the money in the world and be so happy, etc. That kind of thinking is the thinking of the bliss of ignorance, as one of the people spoke earlier. It is blissful until you no longer care to suffer the bliss of the experience.

Now, so before we conclude, let us think for a moment. All of life, our life—and it's our life we must take care of, for by taking care of our life we will qualify our self to be the instrument through which others may be inspired. Not guaranteed. No way possible. But we may be the instruments from our living demonstration that there is something better in life. When we permit our self to believe that our God, our goodness, our happiness, our joy is what someone else does, what someone else doesn't do, then we have opened the doors to slavery and become one of the willing workers. That's our choice each moment. If we want to believe that we have so little money in our life because we've gotten a president in for the country that we didn't vote for and that's the whole problem, then we're going to have to suffer through those four years, or possibly eight, with no guarantee of any change after that, only a hope, but no guarantee.

And so, you see, it's the same way with everything in life. We can always find someone to blame, for by finding something outside to blame, we can say to our self, "What can I do? I'm a helpless [victim.] It's her fault. There's nothing—I've tried, I've tried to get her to change, but she wouldn't change." [Or] "No, it's my religion's fault. It didn't give to me what I expected it should give to me." It's always someone's fault outside of our control while we are in the sleep of satisfaction, known as the bliss of ignorance. I do hope that's helped with your question.

I see that our time is up. Thank you.

APRIL 7, 1985

Church Questions and Answers 57
[Fourteenth Anniversary Service]

We begin with our address this morning on the Fourteenth Anniversary. What we are celebrating, of course, is fourteen years of the continuity of service, specifically in the Serenity Church. And in our discussion this morning we would like to take that fourteen-year continuity into perspective and application in the endeavor of anything that we decide is worthwhile.

We find in our lives many, many beginnings. And we find so many beginnings with the energy and the enthusiasm necessary for what we term or judge is success. And often we find that the beginnings that we involve our self in are of very short term. We seem, that is our minds, to have great difficulty in sustaining the effort necessary for the fulfillment of endeavors that we involve our self in. This, we can clearly see, is an effect of an uncontrolled mind, a mind that is readily and easily tempted to distraction.

And so, as we look at our lives, we see that we have gone to many things, had many beginnings and few, if any, completions. The distraction of an uncontrolled mind is in truth the destruction of the faculty of reason. For one, in their efforts to begin anything, begins it with an interest and an effort, an endeavor to accomplish something that they alone have decided is the wisest thing for them to do. And so, as we go on in life and we find ourselves with many beginnings and few, in any, completions or fulfillments, we see that when we find those difficulties in our endeavors that we are distracted, distracted and tempted to what we judge at the moment is an easier path. We begin things in our life with many judgments of what we will get out of what we choose to begin with. So we go into business with a set package of judgments of what the business is going to give back to us. And when the business doesn't give back to us what we judged it should give back to us when we began it, most of us find we set it aside only to try something else. And we go on in life and end up in what we understand as a state of frustration and disappointment and failure and the pity of self.

Those types of experiences are directly contrary to demonstrable law: that whatever we involve our self in, we get out of anything what we put into the thing. We don't get any more out and we certainly do not get any less out. And so, in our life and our experiences and in our efforts, we find, as we get older, the absolute necessity of growing up. And growing up is known in the Living Light Philosophy as personal responsibility: the acceptance of demonstrable truth that whatever we do in life, our experiences reflect back to us what we're really doing.

We don't appreciate, ofttimes in our life, the experiences that we encounter. But not appreciating something, by acceptance of the law that we set that into motion and it has returned to us, is vastly different than not appreciating an experience by the blatant denial that someone else is the cause of that experience in our life. To permit our minds to think that something beyond our control, beyond our control is the cause of our struggles or our difficulties is not only foolhardy but it is a childish attitude of mind. For whoever permits their mind to tell them that their experiences in life, they have no control over is a person who has yet to grow up, a person who has yet to experience the demonstrable truth of personal responsibility.

For whenever we believe that someone else has caused the condition that we find our self in, when we permit our minds to tell us those things, first, we have created within our mind a false god that is destined to crumble. We have created, by that type of thinking, a false god that is destined to crumble by first denying the truth that we are and the God that truly is our only sustenance in life. We are tempted so often to create these clay-footed gods by believing that something we cannot control is the cause of our experience, for by believing that way we do not have to emotionally mature. There's always someone that we can do nothing about that is causing our experience. That is not only a childish attitude of mind, a very immature attitude of mind, but it is in truth a destructive attitude of mind.

When we look at life and we see that the law is clearly revealed—that like attracts like and becomes the Law of Attachment—we not only, once again, through that ability to personally respond to life, we once again become the captain of our ship. We once again become the master of our destiny. And as this beautiful hymn, that we just sang, clearly states, "Destiny at my command." Destiny is at our command when we grow up mentally and emotionally and accept what is justly and divinely ours.

If we find difficulties in life, they are only effects of our attitude, but we have the ability to change our attitude. And through a change of our attitude we change the Law of Vibration and through that change, we attract unto us, in keeping with the law that like attracts like and becomes the Law of Attachment, we attract unto us the things that we truly want: the goodness of life. And that's the benefit of growing up. And when one compares the benefit of growing up emotionally to the detriment of the denial of our right to grow up, the blatant denial of personal responsibility, the temptation to look outside for the cause and to experience a life of struggle and tribulation, when we make that effort and we begin to awaken and we begin to grow, we will clearly experience what we choose to do in life is not dependent on something outside. It was never dependent upon something outside. That is the grand delusion of the human mind.

Everything for an abundant, happy and joyous life, we already are. It is a denial of that truth that causes us to seek outside and become the dependent victims of so-called circumstances beyond our control. It is that denial that makes us the victim of uncontrollable circumstances. For whatever we, in our mind, permit to disturb us demonstrates that which disturbs us is that which controls us. And so we find our self in life ofttimes controlled by many things. For many things, we find, disturb us. And yet, many things do not have to disturb us when we, once again, accept the truth that we are and stop believing the falsehood that we are not and can never in truth ever be.

Now because it is our tradition and because it has proven to be beneficial to those in attendance, I'm going to take the remaining time and permit you to raise your hands with any questions that you might have. *[After a short pause, the teacher continues.]* No questions? Then I won't have to work. Yes, the lady here, please.

I would like to know, if, when one hurts somebody, by thought or deed, intentionally or unintentionally, how can you right that hurt?

Yes. In reference to that question, as you have stated, when one hurts someone, intentionally or unintentionally, and I would like to speak on that part and take your question in the three parts that it truly is.

First of all, intentional or unintentional is ever subject to the awareness of the human mind. For there are, demonstrably, eighty-one levels of consciousness of the human mind and what is unintentional on one level of consciousness is definitely intentional on another. Therefore, all thoughts, all acts, and all deeds done by and entertained by the human mind are intentional on some level of consciousness.

Now how does one correct or right what they judge has been a wrong? Now if we understand these many levels of consciousness and that we as eternal beings are identifying with one, two, three, or thirty or more of these levels and that some levels of our mind judge we have done a wrong, while other levels of our mind judge that it was justified and, therefore, right. And so we have these divisions in consciousness until we bring, through the faculty of reason, an awakening to all our levels of consciousness. For example, we do something in our life and after we have done it, we may feel good about it for a time. And then, at another time we move in consciousness to another level and we feel that we have done a great wrong and a great disservice to someone. Does that not help explain your question?

Yes, it does.

All right. So it only reveals that on one level of consciousness something is done by our mind, and on another level it is absolutely, definitely adverse to what that level would do or choose to do. Now, first of all, to right a wrong, we have to come to terms with all of these levels of consciousness. And to come to terms with all these varied levels of consciousness, we must cast the light of reason, which is a soul faculty, upon the human mind. In so doing the judgment that we have done right or have done wrong will no longer disturb us. For in that awakening we will realize beyond a shadow of any doubt that the law is just and the law is fair. That whatever we have sent out in our life, by the very Law of Sending, returns unto us. And so, divine justice is not dependent upon fickle, mental experiences. Divine justice *is*. It balances the scales in our life and we do not need to concern our self with it.

Now a person may say, "Well, you can do a wrong and then be free from it?" No one does anything and is freed from any thought, act, or deed. A sparrow does not fall that divine justice is not aware of it. So there is no thought, there is no act, there is no deed that does not return unto the sender.

The wisest path in this awakening, of course, is to place one's consciousness in the eternal moment, for only in the eternal moment is truth, only in the eternal moment is freedom. Everything that has passed is a shadow and, therefore, a limit. Everything yet to come has not yet manifested and, therefore, is not truth and is not freedom. For that that has passed is limit; that which is yet to come is limit, for that which is to be or has been is governed by the Law of Limit. We are not limit. Therefore, to place our attention and, therefore, our identification on what has been or on what is yet to be is to place ourselves in bondage, for limit is bondage. That is the *maya* of the mental world. Therefore, a person, having done what they have done while tempted on one of the many levels of consciousness, has a responsibility unto themselves to accept experiences in their life, and if they are not happy with them, to accept the responsibility that they are only effects. They are not causes; they are only effects. And to move on in the eternal moment, the eternal moment, for what has been, has been. What is to be, has not yet [become]. Does that help with your question?

Thank you so much.

Because, you see, only in truth, the eternal moment, is there freedom. So one is only freed in the moment in which they are consciously aware, the moment of now.

Yes. The lady over here had a question. Thank you.

Oh, I would like to ask you a question about the spirit realms. I hope this isn't—how do they differ, when we crossover, from the mental realms? Can you elaborate on the realms? Is this a proper time, Mr. Goodwin?

That's fine. We can take, certainly, a few moments in reference to sharing our understanding on the difference between a mental realm and a spiritual realm. Is that the basic question?

Well, I was interested, if I may interject this, more in a description. I think I know well the mental realms.

I see.

OK.

I see. All right.

The spiritual realms.

Yes, all right. For example, the lady would like a little description of the difference between a mental realm and a spiritual realm. Well, we are very familiar with a mental world. I'm sure we will all agree—because we spend so much of our life thinking and so much of our life judging and so much of our life experiencing what we call need—that we are well qualified in what is known as a mental world.

Now, perhaps, this will help you. Say that you have a desire to have a bouquet of red roses. Now you have that desire in a mental world with which you are familiar. The moment that registers in your consciousness, with its registration comes many judgments of how to attain them. Would you not agree?

I'm not sure I understand.

Well, let's put it this way, [if] you desire a bouquet of red roses, you've got to do something to get them. Is that not correct?

Yes.

I mean, they just do not materialize before your eyes.

Correct.

Fine. Well, the basic demonstration of the spiritual realm and a mental world is because—a spiritual realm is not governed by the laws of duality, which are the laws of creation and limit. [In] a spiritual realm, if there is a registration within the consciousness for a bouquet of red roses, in the registration in consciousness the bouquet of red roses appears.

I understand.

Now in a mental world, when it registers in the human mind, [what] comes with that desire [is] a mountain of judgments of how to attain them. The difference being that in a mental world we *believe* that we must take certain steps in order to attain what we desire. Belief is the Law of Bondage subject only to a mental world where denial of God, known as need, exists.

Yes.

Denial of God does not exist in a spiritual realm. Therefore, belief and bondage does not exist. And so when the desire, which is a divine expression—that's what desire (the principle of it) is—registers within the consciousness for a bouquet of roses, the bouquet of roses appear. Does that help with your question?

Beautiful. Yes.

And so, that law, of course, applies to everything in the realms of light, for that's what man *is*. However, as long as man insists on *believing* what he is not, then man, from the insistence on believing what he is not, denies God, the truth that he is, and experiences need and chases throughout the universes to get what he already has. He cannot experience what he already has because he believes he is not it. Does that help with your question?

May I ask—

Yes.

A further elaboration of that? In particular then, what I wanted to ask you was if we're in a spiritual consciousness on this earth, can we then—in other words, spirituality is, is in, is our consciousness—

That is correct.

So can we manifest like that, once attaining that level, while we're still in form?

Yes. In reference to a manifestation of it, it is very fleeting, very momentary, because for us to, as you say, manifest the full spirituality that we are, it is at the sacrifice of identification with limit. And to no longer identify with limit, we will not have a mental body and, therefore, would not have a physical body and, therefore, would not be in a physical, mental world. You see, in order for our being to manifest physically and mentally we must have and entertain a denial of the truth in order to have a belief in the limit and experience what we call creation. Our problem is that we have so over-identified with creation that we have finally saturated our consciousness to believe that we are creation. And in that belief is our bondage, our denial, and our suffering and our great need. Yes.

You mean to say, sir, then we cannot—I understand exactly what you meant about we would disappear then—

That is correct.

We would leave the physical realm.

We would no longer be in the realms of limit.

Yes. Now—

That is correct.

My next question is, So, therefore, if we do desire things of this world, do we have to apply the mental laws to get them? Do we have to go through the—

Your question is, indeed, most interesting. And that is, If you desire things of creation, of the mental world, do you have to go through those laws in order to get them? We don't have to. We do, because we believe we are the need. And because we believe we are the need, then we must pay the price of the mental laws to fill our needs.

Yes, but how would we get the things that we think we—suppose we desire something. We don't need it, but we desire it. Well, if we desire, if we achieve it through the spiritual realms and we attain that high consciousness, we would disappear, like Christ rose.

Yes.

So if we, if we desire those things while still in form and we have things to do on this earth—

Thank you. I understand your question; it's most important. For example, say that you desire to have a Hawaiian vacation. Now a Hawaiian vacation is possible for you without any limit, without any limit within your consciousness. But a person will not be still and experience a Hawaiian vacation for they do not yet make the effort to have that much control of their mind. The mind, therefore, judges, "I must have so much money. I must go on an airplane or a boat. I must physically move my physical body. I must do this. I must do that." And all of the laws of limit are firmly established within the consciousness and a person believes that they are those limits and, therefore, denies that which they are and does not experience their Hawaiian vacation without fulfilling all of the judgments that their mind has to offer in reference to that particular desire. Does that help with your question?

Indeed.

That does not change the law that a Hawaiian vacation is possible for all people within their consciousness, for that's demonstrable truth. But then the mind further goes, the mind of limit, and says, "Well, that's just a daydream!" Well, we are the ones who are living the dream, whether it's a daydream or a nightmare. To those—you see, life is a dream and we are the dreamer. So that is demonstrable to all of us. So being the dreamer, a wise person chooses to dream a life of beauty rather than to experience a nightmare of living hell. But that is entirely up to us. This moment is our moment of joy if we choose to make it so.

Now if we choose not to make the effort to control our mind, then this moment is a miserable moment for us. We all have available to us—and surely, must admit how well qualified we are. We all have experiences that we can thrill on misery. Some people, it seems in life, they get a great thrill out of disaster. They experience a great sensation from the disasters of life. Now we all have experiences that we can identify with at any moment and say, "Oh, what a miserable life this is. What a terrible struggle I have. I don't have enough this. I don't have enough that. I never have enough money. Nothing's ever right." Now we all have that available to us. Then there are some of us who take another look and say, "I have a pair of shoes. How fortunate. I remember the day when I didn't have. And think of all the people that don't have any. I have a coat for when it's chilly. I have a roof over my head. I have food in my stomach. How fortunate I am." So, you see, if we must insist on living in the shadows of what has been, we all have available to us the joy of life. Does that help with your question?

Thank you.

You're welcome. We have time for one more. Yes, the lady here, please.

In your reference to the eighty-one states of consciousness, levels of consciousness—

Yes.

Is the goal to unite those eighty-one levels?

Yes! You see, harmony is the demonstrable Law of Health. Now, unfortunately, we limit health to just the—usually—the physical body. We rarely consider the mental body. And even rarer to do we consider the health of an abundant life in all experiences in our life. In unity, of course, there is strength. In harmony, there is health. So our birthright is strength and health and abundant good. That is our right.

Now if we pause each day for a few moments and we become consciously aware of the thoughts and feelings that we are experiencing in our mind, we will very quickly see beyond a shadow of any doubt very few of them are in accord or agreement, would you not agree? I mean, just without even, seemingly without thinking about anything, this thought rises up and with that thought—it may be a good thought and you feel good from having that thought—comes another one that's totally doubtful and adverse. Is that not true?

Yes.

That cannot be considered a house united. That is a house divided. Now a house divided is a house of discord. A house of discord is a house that is not at ease and therefore man calls that disease. Disease is not something that the Principle of Good, known as God, hands out to people that he feels have done him wrong. That's ridiculous and superstitious foolishness. Disease is a lack of ease and a lack of ease is a lack of harmony and a lack of harmony is readily demonstrated in discord, the opposite of unity.

So man's responsibility is, first, to become aware that his house is divided. Therefore, it cannot long stand. And in that awareness to see his responsibility clearly to bring harmony into his consciousness by taking control of a discordant and diseased mind, because that *is* man's responsibility.

Now none of us want to entertain the possibility that we have a diseased mind, but all we have to do is to be honest. If our mind is not at ease and we are not experiencing peace, health, wealth, and happiness, then we have to face the demonstrable truth that we have a diseased mind. Now we seem to be willing to accept that we have a diseased body, that is, physical, but woe to the one who tells another, "You are in need of great help for you have a diseased mind." No one wants to hear that they have a diseased mind. They seem to have no problem in sharing the diseased mind. They just don't want anyone to know what it really is *[Many in the congregation laugh.]* because they don't want to accept the truth themselves. So let's—except a few of my students who have managed to survive these many years. There are a few left—not many—but it only takes one.

Anyway, if we will only be honest with our self and we say, "All right. These experiences are not harmonious in my life. These experiences don't seem to have any good for me. They are discordant. I am not happy. I am frustrated. I must face the truth. My mind, temporarily, there's a possibility that it's diseased." Just accept the *possibility* that temporarily you have a diseased mind, possibly you have a diseased mind. And by accepting the *possibility* that your mind's got a little disease, depending on how discordant you feel, you have an opportunity. There's then that great potential to say, "That's it. These thoughts are not all harmonious. Therefore, I am divided in my consciousness and I am not experiencing my right to the Principle of Good, known as God. And I have a right to that experience." You will be amazed. If you will accept that demonstrable truth each day—because it'll take each day because there's a part of our mind [that] says, "Oh, no. That person I can see they're mentally diseased. There's no question about it. But not me!"

But accept the possibility that your mind is not at ease and in accepting that possibility, you establish the Law of Possibility to take control over it and put it where it belongs: your servant and you, the master. For that is your—not only your right in life, that is our responsibility in life.

Now a person says, "Well, I don't want to experience this disease and my body's not well. And my life isn't well. And I haven't been successful," and on down the list. No one consciously chooses to experience that. No one does that. But we must face the truth: that it is an effect of our not telling our own mind, "I don't like this thought. I've had this thought before. It has brought me no good. I choose not to permit this thought to control me." Now when we take charge of these thoughts in our own mind and we tell those thoughts, "Out! This is my house. You are not going to get in here again. I have already paid a dear price for this experience. I know exactly what you offer. You have offered it to me before. You have brought me no good. I accept the truth that I am responsible. You got back into my house, but now I'm kicking you out." Now when you do that, you see, and that is done, as I teach my students, that is done through a process of re-identification.

You see, first of all, you declare the truth: it is not you. That is the separation of truth from creation. And until that's done, you cannot experience freedom. First you must declare the truth: the thought in your mind is a created form. You are definitely responsible for it. You don't have to leave it in your house. So first you declare the truth, "This is a thought in my mind. I'm responsible for my mind, but this thought is not me. I created it in my days of ignorance. I root it out." Then you take your consciousness, that which you are, and you direct it to something that you enjoy in your consciousness, and that thing that you don't want to experience, you will have no awareness of.

You see, a thought, a thought in the mind is a created form in mental substance. Now many philosophies call them thought forms. You call them whatever you want to. They are created by energy; energy that we direct into a mental substance and form it or limit it. And so, all thoughts, all judgments are created by our identification in a mental substance—we create that form. Now that thought form—in other words, we give it birth. Therefore, by being the mother or father of it, we are responsible for it. Now that form exists as a limit form in mental substance as long as energy is directed to it. When energy is removed from it, through re-identification, the thought form, in time, disintegrates back into a mental substance.

What happens with the human mind is we have created many thought forms. Now those thought forms have all of the intelligence of our own mind because they are created by our mind. Therefore, when they need energy, they rise in our consciousness and they demand their feeding, for their survival, their existence is dependent upon energy, the food for their very livelihood. They have no soul. They are created by mental substance. They are soulless creatures. Many philosophies have called them the demons of the deep, go down the list. They exist and that's just the way that it is. Now when we permit ourselves to believe that we are those soulless creatures that we have created in our ignorance, when we permit our self to believe that we are them, that's when our vital life energy is absorbed by them. They grow and become stronger. So it's a great responsibility that we have.

It's just like going into a business. Well, you go into a business with certain beliefs, judgments, and thought forms, all right? Now if you believe that you are those forms that you have created, if you believe that you are those thoughts that your mind alone has created, if you really believe you are them and they do not have *their* way in the business, through you they will destroy the business that you are working for.

Now many a person has had the experience of failure. And you see, failure is a great success; it is a success of the forms we alone have created. You see, when you create these thought forms and these judgments, you do not change them. They are solidified in the atmosphere. They will disintegrate when you no longer direct energy, through attention, to them. But they don't become something else, you see. No, no, no, no.

You must create new forms. And in your efforts to create new thoughts, new attitudes, you have a battle between the new ones you are creating and the old ones that are already created. And the old dog—we'll pause a moment in just a moment. The old dog gets all the feeding, do you understand? And the new one gets pushed away. And so, that's the way it is in a mental world. That is not what we are, but that is definitely, demonstrably what we are responsible for. And so, a person finds great difficulty in change.

Without change, there is no evolution. And we can do many things, but we cannot stop evolving. In spite of our self, we do grow up. Now we can grow up harmoniously, joyously or we can grow up miserably. But no matter what we do and no matter what we do not do, we are not going to stop the Law of Evolution, for we are not greater than that law. Turn it over, please.

[There is a break in the recording as the audio cassette tape is turned over in order to continue recording the class.]

As I have ofttimes spoken to some of my students, the value of Serenity Church, the true and only value is the philosophy that it brings to the world. And ofttimes in the bringing of any philosophy to a world, it is usually centuries before its true value is perceived. For when we understand what we are and no longer believe what we are not, then this so-called heaven that man seeks, he will experience at any moment that he chooses to experience it.

It is not some great struggle to pause several times a day to be aware of what thoughts are in one's mind that they may consciously choose in those moments, "This is not beneficial. No. I don't want these thoughts. I refuse to identify with these thoughts." That is not only man's responsibility but that is man's freedom. That is the goodness that is ours. We can do that at any moment.

But you must understand creation. If you try to understand what it is like to be a created form, totally dependent on something for your survival and if you will try to understand that, then you will understand the tenacity of the thought forms we have created. Their very survival, their very existence is dependent upon us directing energy to them through attention. So when you understand that, then you will understand a little more about possession. You'll understand a little more about obsession. You see, you hear in some religions things about possession and obsession, but you rarely ever hear anything about man's responsibility and that how man alone opens the door for the entrance of these things and man alone can close the door at any moment he chooses.

You know, I have heard at times where a person will say, "Well, I just cast a great, white light, a circle around them." It protects them from all of those things. Well, now if you were a form totally dependent on someone for your survival, do you think the thought of a white light around him would keep you from eating, would keep you from survival? It doesn't work like that at all. It takes more than a thought of a white light because the thought of a white light—those forms got a lot more energy than one is directing to the thought of a white light. So that superstitious foolishness, just like a rabbit's foot, doesn't protect anyone. In fact, if anything, it helps them to laugh at that kind of foolishness. Because don't ever forget, they are created by our own intelligence. That's what created them. And so, they have, they contain within their forms, those thought forms, all of the intelligence that our mind has because it is our mind that created them.

Now I don't see anything sad or discouraging about the awakening to the thought forms that are the workers for what we desire in a mental world. I mean, after all, they're not all bad. Not all people have thoughts that are terrible. A person has a thought they want to go into business and they think, "Well now, let's see, if I do this and I do that, then that will work out like that and etc." And you create those forms in the consciousness. They go out into the universe. They're your children. They are responsible to you. They know that you're their parent. And they go out there to do their job, you see? And so, when they come back, they want their feeding. But the sadness in life is that you created those forms thirty years ago. They've served their purpose. You tell them you're finished with them now and they don't leave you alone. How many people have been married and divorced and they still think about their last husband? Or the fifth one or the sixth one or the twelfth one? Whatever. And they keep comparing the latest one to the one before. So, you see, the truth is revealed that those forms, created, didn't go away at all. Would you not agree?

Yes. Thank you.

So remember, they don't go away because you tell them to. Just be hungry and have the restaurant tell you, "Go away." And then you'll understand more about them.

Thank you very much.

MAY 5, 1985

APPENDIX

The Divine Healing Prayer

I accept that the Divine Healing Power
Is removing all obstructions
From my mind and body
And is restoring me
To perfect health, wealth, and happiness.
My heart is filled with gratitude
For the Divine Law of Acceptance
That is healing both present and absent ones
Who are in need of help.
Peace, the power that healeth,
Is guiding my thoughts, acts, and deeds
As God and I go hand in hand
Living a life of joyful abundance.

The Total Consideration Affirmation

I am the manifestation of Divine Intelligence. Formless and free. Whole and complete. Peace, Poise, and Power are my birthright.

The Law of Harmony is my thought and guarantees Unity in all my acts and activities, expressing perfect Rhythm and limitless flow throughout my entire being.

Without beginning or ending, eternity is my true awareness and sees the tides of creation, as a captain sees his ship.

As the Light of Truth is sustained by the faculty of Reason, I pause to think and claim my Divine right.

  Right Thought. Right Action. Total Consideration.

    Amen. Amen. Amen.

Divine Abundance

Thank
(Gratitude)

You
(Principle)

God
(Divine Intelligence)

I'm
(Individualizing)

Moving
(Rhythm)

In
(Unity)

Your
(Realization)

Divine
(Total)

Flow
(Consideration)